Negotiating the Sacred II

Blasphemy and Sacrilege in the Arts

Negotiating the Sacred II

Blasphemy and Sacrilege in the Arts

ELIZABETH BURNS COLEMAN AND
MARIA SUZETTE FERNANDES-DIAS (EDITORS)

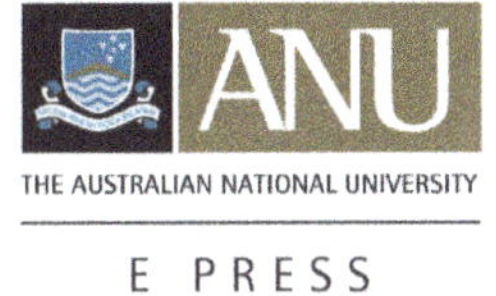

THE AUSTRALIAN NATIONAL UNIVERSITY

E PRESS

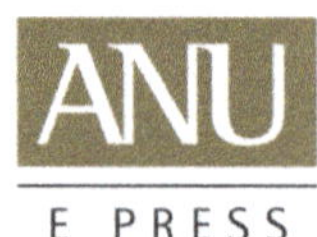

Published by ANU E Press
The Australian National University
Canberra ACT 0200, Australia
Email: anuepress@anu.edu.au
This title is also available online at: http://epress.anu.edu.au/nts02 _citation.html

National Library of Australia
Cataloguing-in-Publication entry

Title:	Negotiating the sacred 2 : blasphemy and sacrilege in the arts / editors, Elizabeth Burns Coleman ; Maria Suzette Fernandes-Dias.
ISBN:	9781921536267 (pbk.) 9781921536274 (pdf)
Subjects:	Arts and religion. Offenses against religion. Blasphemy. Sacrilege. Religion and sociology.
Other Authors/Contributors:	Coleman, Elizabeth Burns, 1961- Fernandes-Dias, Maria Suzette.
Dewey Number:	306.108

Cover design by ANU E Press
Cover photo by Lynne Broughton

Table of Contents

Section IV: Self-expression and Restriction   **145**

Contributors

Professor Peter Arnds
Peter Arnds teaches comparative literature and literary translation, as well as German and Italian at Trinity College Dublin. He is the author of two books, one on Wilhelm Raabe and Charles Dickens, and *Representation, Subversion, and Eugenics in Günter Grass's The Tin Drum*. He has published numerous articles on comparative literature from the eighteenth to the twenty-first century as well as on German and migrant literature.

Dr Christopher Braddock
Chris Braddock is an artist and academic. He is Associate Professor of Visual Arts in the School of Art and Design at Auckland University of Technology and Chair of the University's St Paul St Gallery. His research interests span the disciplines of art history, anthropology, and performance studies. He specialises in different aspects of modern and contemporary art including the part object in sculpture, performance, body art, and art and spirituality. In 2007 he was the International Artist-in-Residence at Melbourne's RMIT University and in 2004 he was the Arts Council of New Zealand toi Aotearoa Visual Arts Resident in New York City on the International Studio and Curatorial Program.

Dr Elizabeth Burns Coleman
Elizabeth Burns Coleman is a postdoctoral fellow in the Schools of English, Communications and Performance Studies and Philosophy and Bioethics at Monash University. She holds a PhD in philosophy from The Australian National University and has held a postdoctoral fellowship at the ANU's Centre for Cross Cultural Research. She has taught philosophy of art at the ANU, moral and political philosophy at La Trobe University, and philosophy of law at Wollongong University. She is the author of *Aboriginal Art, Identity and Appropriation* (2005), editor (with Kevin White) of *Negotiating the Sacred: Blasphemy and Sacrilege in a Multicultural Society* (2006) and has published numerous articles on indigenous art and cross cultural aesthetics. Her articles have appeared in the *Journal of Aesthetics and Art Criticism*, the *International Year Book of Aesthetics*, and the *Journal of Political Philosophy*.

Dr Glenn D'Cruz
Glenn D'Cruz is Senior Lecturer in drama, media and communication at Deakin University. He is the author of *Midnight's Orphans: Anglo-Indians in Post/Colonial Literature* (Peter Lang, 2006) and *Class Act: Melbourne Workers Theatre 1987-2007* (Vulgar Press, 2007).

Dr Carolyn D'Cruz

Carolyn D'Cruz is a lecturer in Gender Sexuality and Diversity Studies at La Trobe University. She is the author of *Identity Politics in Deconstruction: Calculating with the Incalculable* (Ashgate, 2008) and has published in *Contretemps: An Online Journal of Philosophy, Life Writing and Social Semiotics.*

Dr Maria Suzette Fernandez-Dias

Dr Maria Suzette Fernandes-Dias is Assistant Director of UN, International and Regional Organisations Section of the Commonwealth Department of Immigration and Citizenship. Previously she coordinated scholarly and Research activities at the Centre for Cross-Cultural Research, ANU. She holds a PhD in French (postcolonial literature) from the University of Goa, India. She has taught comparative literature, linguistics and francophone literature at the University of Goa, and has worked as the educational and cultural coordinator of Alliance Française de Goa, where she managed the AF Art Gallery. She has an edited collection, *Legacies of Slavery: Comparative Perspectives,* (Cambridge Scholars Publishing, 2007). Her literary awards include the Victor-Hugo Bicentenary Award (2002), Ford Foundation Campus Diversity Award (1996), OHeraldo Award for Children's literature (1989), and the Vidya Award (1995 and 1996).

Dr Caroline Josephs

Caroline Josephs is a free-lance educator, researcher, storyteller, writer, and artist. Her doctoral thesis was on sacred oral storytelling from four cultures (*Yolngu* Indigenous Australian, Zen Buddhist, Judaic, and Inuit).

Dr Michelle Langford

Michelle Langford is a lecturer in Film Studies in the School of English, Media and Performing Arts at the University of New South Wales. She is the author of *Allegorical Images: Tableau, Time and Gesture in the Cinema of Werner Schroeter* (Intellect, 2006) and has published on Iranian cinema in the journal *Camera Obscura*. Her current research focuses on the allegorical dimensions of Iranian cinema.

David Manning

David Manning is in the final stages of his PhD in History at Clare College, Cambridge. In a departure from the current historiography of blasphemy, his dissertation, 'Blasphemy in England, c.1660-1730', develops a cultural history of blasphemy as representation, exploring the nexus between conceptions and perceived manifestations of blasphemy in a theological context. In 2007 he was awarded second prize in the annual Pollard Prize of the Institute of Historical Research, University of London.

Dianne McGowan

Dianne McGowan is currently completing a PhD at the ANU. She holds two undergraduate degrees from the ANU: a BSc (psychology major) and a BA (anthropology major). Between graduating and her PhD research, she established and managed an Asian art gallery in Sydney, Beowulf Galleries. She is published in *Negotiating the Sacred: Blasphemy and Sacrilege in a Multicultural Society* (Coleman and White (eds.) ANU E Press, 2006).

Dr David Nash

David Nash is Reader in History, Oxford Brookes University, UK. He is the author of *Secularism, Art and Freedom* (1992), *Blasphemy in Modern Britain 1789-present* (1999) and senior editor for the *Journal for the Critical Study of Religion*. In addition to his historical expertise, he has had to draw upon legal studies, criminology, literary and film studies, area studies and philosophy for frameworks to explain blasphemy's history and how and why the phenomenon persists. His most recent book, *Blasphemy in the Christian World* (Oxford University, Press 2007), surveys the history of the subject throughout the West and speculates upon its future development. He has given verbal and written evidence to the House of Lords Select Committee on Religious Offences and has been in considerable demand by the British media to talk upon the subject (notably BBC Radio Four, TV Channel Four). He is an Executive Officer of the Social History Society of Great Britain and a Fellow of the Royal Historical Society.

Dr Jasdev Singh Rai

Jasdev Singh Rai is a medical doctor and spokesperson for the UK-based Sikh Human Rights Group. The organisation is based on the humanitarian aspects of Sikh philosophy: pluralism, non-discrimination, human dignity and bio-ecology. The group has branches in India, Canada, and the USA. The Sikh Human Rights Group is engaged in community cohesion and diversity issues in the UK. It conducts projects on transnationalism and human rights among other issues.

Dr Jeremy Shearmur

Jeremy Shearmur is Reader in Philosophy, ANU, and lectures in political, moral and social philosophy. He worked for eight years as assistant to Professor Sir Karl Popper, and is author of *The Political Thought of Karl Popper*, and *Hayek and After*, both 1996, and was co-editor, with Piers Turner, of Karl Popper's *After the Open Society*, 2008. He has taught at the University of Edinburgh, the University of Manchester, and at George Mason University, where he was a Research Associate Professor. He was also Director of Studies of the Centre for Policy Studies, in London.

Acknowledgements

This collection evolved out a two-day conference called 'Negotiating the Sacred: Blasphemy and Sacrilege in the Arts' held at the Centre for Cross Cultural Research at The Australian National University in November 2005. We would like to thank the ANU E Press board and the collection's reviewers for their suggestions and feedback which have helped shape and polish the collection. Adam Art Gallery, Éditions Typo and Denise Boucher, kindly gave us for permission for extensive quotations, and Cathy de Monchaux and the estate of Ian Breakwell gave permission to reproduce images of their artwork. We would also like to thank the staff of the Centre for Cross Cultural Research, Dr Kevin White, and the many volunteers from around the ANU, for their contribution to the success of the conference.

This is the second volume from a series of five conferences and edited collections on the theme 'Negotiating the Sacred'. The first conference, *Negotiating the Sacred: Blasphemy and Sacrilege in a Multicultural Society*, was held at the ANU's Centre for Cross-Cultural Research in 2004, and published as an edited collection by ANU E Press in 2006. Other conferences in the series have included 'Religion, Medicine and the Body' (ANU, 2006), 'Tolerance, Education and the Curriculum' (ANU, 2007), and 'Governing the Family' (Monash University, 2008).

Introduction

Lines in the Sand

Elizabeth Burns Coleman and Maria Suzette Fernandes-Dias

The sacrosanctity of religious dogmas and beliefs, stringent laws of repression and codes of moral and ethical propriety have compelled artists to live and create with occupational hazards like uncertain audience response, and accusations of deliberate misinterpretation of cultural production looming over their heads. In extreme cases, the battle between artistic iconoclasm and societal repression has forced creators to put their life on the line in defence of liberal self-expression.

Perhaps we should not write in the past tense. On 2 November 2004, Dutch film maker Theo van Gogh paid with his life for his supposedly offensive depiction of Islam in his film, *Submission* which denounced violence against women in Islamic societies. In February 2005, the 'Världskulturmuséet' ('Museum of World Culture') in Göteborg, Sweden decided to remove the painting *Scène d'Amour* by Louzla Darabi that was part of a temporary exhibition about HIV/AIDS, and depicted a man and a woman having sexual intercourse. The artist and the curator had received numerous death threats, some with the postscript 'learn from the Netherlands', from Muslims enraged over the Koran quotations that were featured in a corner of the painting. In September 2005, Europe suffered the violent outbreak of public outrage from the Muslim world (several dead, embassies burnt and international tension) when the Danish newspaper *Jyllands-Posten* printed 12 cartoons of Mohammed.

These are dramatic cases in contemporary culture wars, yet the issue is not merely about the relationship between Western artists and Islam. Banal use of religious symbols continues to spark controversy as some of us believe that excessively liberalised and interpretative use of religious symbols/icons/figures in art, divests these representations of faith, of their sanctity, and, at times, offends conventional piety. 1998 saw an unsuccessful private prosecution in New Zealand after the Te Papa museum displayed *Virgin in a Condom*. Protesters besieged the museum, and attacked the sculpture. In 2000, the *Sensation* exhibition at the Museum of Modern Art in New York was picketed because of its inclusion of a painting by Chris Ofili, *The Holy Virgin Mary*, which incorporated carefully placed elephant dung. The Australian National Gallery cancelled its display of the exhibition. In 2004, Oliver Stone's movie, *Alexander*, based on the life of the fourth century BC Macedonian king, evoked protests from the Zoroastrian diaspora for the use of a Zoroastrian holy symbol, the

Farohar. *Behzti,* a play by the British Sikh playwright Gurpreet Kaur Bhatti became the centre of a major controversy in the United Kingdom in December 2004 when the opening night was disrupted by a riot at the Birmingham Repertory theatre.

In *A Short History of Blasphemy,* Richard Webster suggested that Western liberals and artists deploy the rhetoric of a holy war in defence of freedom of expression just as readily as Muslims do in relation to their defence of Mohamed and the Koran, and indeed, hold the doctrine of freedom of expression nearly as sacred.[1] Lines in the sand have thus been drawn between those wishing to protect freedom of expression in the arts, and those who think blasphemy is wrong, and should be suppressed. What is consistent in the liberal position is that the 'opponent' is a 'zealot' or an intolerant moralising bigot seeking to impose his or her particular version of the good upon us all.

In his discussion of the British debates over the place of blasphemy law in Britain, Clive Unsworth sees a polarisation between those who see blasphemy law as supporting the role of religion and religious values in society, and liberals who object to blasphemy laws on the basis that the law's object is to protect some members of society from being offended, not merely by exposure to the blasphemy, but through the knowledge that other people may be viewing the material and not finding it offensive.[2]

The three events in Britain in the late twentieth century that re-ignited debates over blasphemy involved 'the insertion of elements of sexuality and sexual deviancy into the religious narratives'.[3] These events included the *Gay News* case, *Satanic Verses*, and the refusal to license the video *Visions of Ecstasy*.

In the 1977 *Gay News* case, Mary Whitehouse successfully invoked British blasphemy law against the editor of the paper, Denis Lemon, for the publication of the poem 'The Love that Dares to Speak its Name' by James Kirkup. Lemon was sentenced to nine months' jail, suspended for 18 months, and *Gay News* was fined £1000, with prosecution costs awarded against them. The decision and the interpretation of the crime were upheld by a majority of the House of Lords. Unsworth acknowledges that 'it was not the case that the blasphemous quality of Kirkup's poem was dependent upon its homosexual content, and indeed, supporters of the prosecution were anxious to maintain that the trial was not about homosexuality but about the vilification of Christ'. Yet, for Unsworth, the stated objection does not undermine their obvious bigotry: 'in the context of the wider belief system, the homosexual content of the poem cannot have done other than to aggravate the blasphemy and render it exorbitant in the eyes of those who so judged it'.[4]

This case started a vigorous campaign by artists and liberals to have the blasphemy laws abolished, a campaign that resurfaced almost 12 years later in the wake of the Rushdie affair. *The Satanic Verses*, a bitter satire on Islam, understandably gave serious offence in depicting Muhammad as 'Mahound', a calculating opportunist and debauched sensualist, and giving the names of Muhammad's wives to prostitutes in a brothel.[5]

The last case, *Visions of Ecstasy*, a 1989 short film directed by Nigel Wingrove, was refused certification by the British Board of Film Classification (BBFC) because of scenes featuring a sexualised representation of Saint Teresa of Ávila caressing the body of Jesus on the cross—scenes which could potentially make the film liable to prosecution for blasphemy. As cutting the scenes would remove approximately half of the film's content, the board decided to refuse certification altogether. In 1996, the distributor of *Visions of Ecstasy* took his case to the European Court of Human Rights where the BBFC's decision to reject certification was upheld. The Court concluded that: 'Freedom of expression constitutes one of the essential foundations of a democratic society. As paragraph 2 of Article 10 expressly recognises, however, the exercise of that freedom carries with it duties and responsibilities. Amongst them, in the context of religious beliefs, may legitimately be included a duty to avoid as far as possible an expression that is, in regard to objects of veneration, gratuitously offensive to others and profanatory.'[6] It is this that liberals are unable to accept.

One thing we may agree about is that the protection of religious sentiments appears to be the legally accepted purpose of blasphemy law. Unsworth writes:

> The crime of blasphemy is directed to the objective of protecting religious believers from outrage to their feelings from relevantly offensive material being in circulation, in the interests of a social value of maintaining respect for a sense of reverence of the sacred, so that it has to do with the social status of religion. It is the tenuous and intangible nature of the harm against which the offence protects that causes especial outrage to liberal exponents of the pre-eminent value of freedom of expression.[7]

We might be wary of Unsworth's portrayal of the issue in terms of the nature of the offence as a kind of prurient attitude towards sexuality. It may be the case that Mary Whitehouse was seeking to uphold moral sexual values. Yet, in *A Brief History of Blasphemy*, Webster reminds us that both Christian polemicists and Western orientalists for centuries 'sought to denigrate Islam by attributing to it a fantastic, disreputable or demonic sexuality'.[8] According to Webster, the Muslim objection to the use of sex within the *Satanic Verses* was not to sex itself, but to the use of obscenity as a form of vilification.

On the picture Unsworth presents, the conservative position on blasphemy is to uphold moral (sexual) values in society, and the liberal position is the standard position against legal moralism, that 'offence' is not a justified basis for the state to interfere with freedom of expression.

According to Caslon Analytics, an Australian research consultancy, voices decrying blasphemy against art have been inspired by 'overseas models, with local provocateurs, zealots and "concerned citizens" emulating excitement in London, New York or other cultural centres'.[9] The consultancy suggests that the protests have seldom sustained media attention or support of major religious groups or community leaders and have encountered a largely indifferent audience. This characterisation belittles those protesting against blasphemy in Australia as fringe groups, whose position is not worth considering, but it is true that, within Australia, the accusation of blasphemy does not immediately give rise to widespread public ire. Despite the very public claim made by Justice Harper, Supreme Court of Victoria, when refusing to grant an injunction to prevent the opening of Andres Serano's *Piss Christ* at the National Gallery of Victoria (*Pell v Council of Trustees of the National Gallery of Victoria*) that as a multicultural and tolerant society, Australia 'need not bother with blasphemous libel', the work was vandalised on two different occasions in two weeks, compelling the gallery to close the exhibition to prevent further assaults against its staff. The technicalities that quashed the injunction ('a civil court will not exercise criminal jurisdiction and will not restrain what may or may not be a legal act by using a civil remedy such as an injunction'[10]) and defences of the freedom of expression were not sufficiently potent to quell the passions that the image aroused in some members of the public and, in others, perceptions of an infringement of decency and good taste.

Webster suggests that blasphemy laws may have come to be considered obsolete because 'respect for the figure of Jesus and for Christianity in general has been inculcated so widely, even among non-believers, that the restraints of good taste have generally made the restraints of law all but redundant'.[11] He argues that it would be considered 'an unpardonable breach of good taste' for a sceptic or a non-believer to blaspheme in front of a believer, and that this amounts to an internalisation of the sacredness of Christian religion.[12] It is not the case, however, that the same respect would automatically be extended to other religious groups within our communities. He speculates that it is because of such internalised repression that 'the role of artists, poets, novelists and film-makers as 'agents' of blasphemy has become so important in the twentieth century'.[13]

Our aim in this book is to move beyond these portrayals of debates over blasphemy as a contest between fundamentalism or legal moralism and liberal freedoms and to re-examine the nature of the offence. To cut through the entrenched positions about blasphemy and freedom of expression, it is necessary to recognise that freedom of expression is a political right. The protection of this right does not mean that all acts of blasphemy are morally permissible or acceptable. Legal permissibility and moral acceptability are different, and one may have a political liberty to do something that is morally wrong. Moreover, the condemnation of repressive acts of violence in response to blasphemy is not incompatible with the condemnation of gratuitous disrespect of religious symbols and offence to others. There is a debate to be had, of course, about whether offence should be taken seriously morally, and whether offence is the correct characterisation of the wrong involved. The perspective of the religious persons may differ from that of those who do not share their belief. For legal philosopher Joel Feinberg's 'profound offence', the 'wrong' involved is not, or not merely, that someone has been offended; it is that they are offended because the act is wrong.[14] In such cases, mere knowledge of the act is sufficient to cause offence. The reason why religious beliefs are particularly susceptible to this form of offence is that they contain a sacral element that is missing from other strongly held beliefs.[15] (It does not follow from this that religious beliefs are the only form of belief that might be considered important in this regard, as the issue concerns the centrality of a belief to a person's life.)

Focusing on 'fundamentalism', or 'zealots' or 'legal moralism' blinds us to the broader social context. This debate is not merely about the role of Christianity in our society, but the place of religion in a multicultural society with numerous religious groups. Issues surrounding the rights of minority cultures, in particular indigenous cultures, to recognition and respect have raised new questions about the contemporariness of the construct of blasphemy and sacrilege. Controversies over the aesthetic representation of the sacred, the exhibition of the sacred as art, and the public display of sacrilegious or blasphemous works, have ignited heated debates and have invited us to reflect on binaries like 'artistic and religious sensibilities', 'tolerance and philistinism', 'the sacred and the profane', 'deification and vilification', and to reconsider what actually amounts to blasphemy and sacrilege in the present day context of multicultural cosmopolitanism and political secularism.

Although blasphemy is traditionally defined as 'a contemptuous or profane act, utterance, or writing concerning God or a sacred entity', 'the act of claiming for oneself the attributes and rights of God' or 'an irreverent or impious act, attitude, or utterance in regard to something considered inviolable or sacrosanct', the construct has extended itself to the domain of the secular, to include concepts like the desecration or flagrant disrespect of 'civil religion' and mythologies of nationalism and identity. Sacrilege is conventionally defined as the transgression against the virtue of religion in terms of 'violation of a sacred place', 'irreverent treatment of sacred things', 'defilement of honour of a "sacred" person', and it is not always clear where the line between blasphemy and sacrilege lies.

While the writers in this collection have approached the question of blasphemy and sacrilege very differently, the usages reflect many of the issues in negotiating the sacred in the arts, and, indeed, highlight how varied these issues may be. In our first chapter, Nash observes that in ancient and early Christian periods, blasphemy involved physical attacks on religious artefacts with the intent to damage the religious 'currency' of the religion so attacked. In contrast, medieval and early modern accounts of blasphemers see them as wilful heretics indulging their own pride, an 'active commission whereby doubts or errant opinions were actively vocalised'. David Manning, like Nash, sees blasphemy as primarily a crime within the Christian tradition, and contrasts the contemporary interpretation of blasphemy as an offence of people's sensibilities with an older interpretation of blasphemy as an offence to God. Coleman develops a broad interpretation of blasphemy as a failure to display the homage appropriate to what is represented by an image or symbol in order to extend the concept into cross-cultural settings, and to understand what is objectionable about aesthetically appreciating some indigenous religious objects. McGowan, in contrast, understands the placement of sacred objects in a gallery context not as blasphemy, but as a form of re-sacralisation. Both Coleman's and McGowan's cross-cultural interpretations would be rejected by Rai, who argues that Western academics fail to appreciate that there is no clear distinction between the sacred and the profane in Indic thought. As editors, we have not attempted to impose a concept of blasphemy or sacrilege; in contemporary debates such words count as markers of dispute over meanings, contexts, and uses. Our purpose is to highlight and explore these different uses, and to try to find a way to understand and negotiate differences between values. The sacred may be presented as an absolute, but may also be negotiated. Negotiation may mean discussion leading to some kind of agreement or settlement, but it may also mean to clear or pass an obstacle.

The justifications for artistic freedom in relation to blasphemy include the claim that art can, or should, be considered an autonomous practice that should be judged in terms of aesthetic merit; that the artists' intention, for instance to make a political comment or to break down barriers, justifies blasphemy, and that complete freedom of expression is necessary for the creation of art. The first argument involves the idea that literary genres, galleries, theatres and other forms of secular, public 'space' provide a context that allows us to recognise that what is occurring is 'a representation', and enable a specifically aesthetic form of interpretation. Many artists assume that such 'spaces' establish the framework for an interpretation and appreciation that is autonomous, and distinct from moral and religious evaluation.

As we grapple with the task of articulating how artists strive against ideological and religious sanctions to affirm the 'dissenting voice' and affirm its ability to 'enable people to question and assess the validity of dominant social norms and their institutionalisation',[16] we are also conscious of the means by which some achieve this without raising the ire of religious authorities, and alienating others within our societies.

The book is divided into four sections. The first provides four different accounts of blasphemy and sacrilege in the arts and in relation to religious artefacts that we may find displayed as arts. The second section is concerned with the motivations that artists may have in deploying blasphemous images. The third looks at two very different interpretations of freedom of expression, and the fourth is concerned with how artists express themselves from within religious traditions and despite restrictions.

In an age where politicians still use the oldest gimmick of justifying their oppressive acts as answers to a divine calling and align their motives to religiously sanctioned agendas, art continues to provide the transgressive space for subverting dominant ideological discourses. However, despite their emancipatory power, artists and their art occupy a liminal space wherein the contemporary socio-political climate of hegemonically-induced extremism and increased communal and religious sensitivity and intolerance, limit individual freedom of expression. Artistic articulation of individual conviction without the intention to offend can still potentially cause unrest. In a world that is becoming increasingly pluralistic and multicultural, it is necessary to step beyond the simplistic assertion that free speech should override religious sensitivities and to facilitate a discourse that will encourage a negotiation of definitions of blasphemy or sacrilege and a sensitisation of religious sensibilities, and limit the abusive deployment of freedom of expression. Artistic sophistication and layering of meaning with its 'virtues' of ambiguity, openness, and indeterminacy that prevent a single, blatant and overt interpretation of a creation as sacrilegious or blasphemous, presents one such means of reconciling potential conflict. Enabling and creating an environment of tolerance that is conducive to intellectual debate and not offence, is yet another. Respect for the religious and cultural sentiments of others is of the utmost importance, for, it is only in a society that respects difference that a forum for negotiation can evolve and the lines in the sand can fade.

Endnotes

[1] Richard Webster, 1990, *A Brief History of Blasphemy: Liberalism, Censorship and 'The Satanic Verses'*, Southwold: The Orwell Press.

[2] Clive Unsworth, 1995, 'Blasphemy, Cultural Divergence and Legal Relativism', *Modern Law Review*, vol. 58, pp. 658-677, at p. 665.

[3] Ibid., p. 664.

[4] Ibid., p. 671.

[5] Shabbir Akhtar, 'Be Careful With Muhammad!', cited in Webster, 1990, p. 39.

[6] http://www.sbbfc.co.uk/case_study_visionsofe.asp

[7] *Freedom, the Individual and the Law* (1993), p. 254, cited in Unsworth, 1995, p. 667.

[8] Webster, op. cit. , p. 40.

[9] http://www.caslon.com.au/blasphemyprofile4.htm#brian

[10] http://www.artslaw.com.au/Publications/Articles/97Blasphemy.asp

[11] Webster, op. cit., p. 25.

[12] Ibid.

[13] Ibid.

[14] Joel Feinberg, 1985, *The Moral Limits of the Criminal Law: Volume 2, Offense to Others*, New York: Oxford University Press, p. 67.

[15] Peter Jones, 1990, 'Respecting Beliefs and Rebuking Rusdie', *British Journal of Political Science*, vol. 20, no. 4, pp. 415-437, at p. 424-5.

[16] H. Marcuse, 1978, *The Aesthetic Dimension*, Boston: Beacon Press, p. 9.

Section I

Understanding Blasphemy and Sacrilege

The first four essays in this collection express a sense of bewilderment about accusations of blasphemy and sacrilege, and seek to understand the motivations behind them. In our first essay, historian David Nash suggests that in contemporary Western societies, blasphemy 'is back with a vengeance' and 'offers to trail blaze a path for religion and religious responses to become the cornerstone of the new politics of cultural identity'. However, he argues, we have no adequate theoretical models for understanding the place of religion in our societies. The rise of accusations of blasphemy, he suggests, is proof of the falsity of the secularisation thesis that modernity would bring about a lessening of religious feeling and greater tolerance. Claims of blasphemy seem to be increasing in Western societies. Assumptions that the process of liberalisation and secularisation would lead to the disappearance or privatisation of religion, and the disappearance of blasphemy as a crime, have been misplaced. Accordingly, secularisation theory does not provide a theoretical framework through which we can understand the changes occurring in our society. Rather, he suggests, that blasphemy is more than a transgressive activity. It is a place, he writes, 'where identities were forged and communities debated issues about public order'.

David Manning explores the evolution of the charge of blasphemy in England. During the reign of the last two Stuart monarchs, the English society was a deeply religious society and vexed by a perceived rise in immorality and irreligion. To the pious majority, licentious behaviour was at best a scourge on the respectability of society and at worst a threat to the very salvation of the nation. In 1698, Jeremy Collier's *A short view of the immorality and profaneness of the English stage*, sparked a debate in which the most zealous tracts and sermons demonised the theatres and accused some plays and actors of blasphemy. The investigation touches upon the nexus between theology and morality, the perceived complicity of audiences, and the conception of malicious intention and interpretation, to present a view of blasphemy that was more than a one-dimensional notion of intolerability. According to Manning, would-be reformers such as Tillotson, Collier, and Bedford perceived the nature of the wrong as the language used in theatre: it was not good or edifying. The context of performance, within a play on a stage, which might be considered by contemporary audiences as the means by which we distinguish between art and life, did not change the nature of the language. Manning concludes that belief in a providential God, coupled with conventional theology, may render seemingly innocuous plays and facile passages blasphemous and as a tangible threat to the nation.

Order and purity are themes that arise in our third chapter. Elizabeth Burns Coleman explores the concept of blasphemy in terms of a metaphysical relationship between the symbol and what it represents, and as a form of cognitive response to an image that places us in a certain relationship to it. These theories suggest that very different assumptions are made about the nature of a symbol to those generally found in the arts. Coleman discusses a seemingly innocuous poster for the 1998 Adelaide Arts Festival depicting a Madonna with a piano accordion and the objections that many indigenous peoples have to the display of their sacred objects within a gallery context. Coleman argues that these innocuous cases, which display no intentional or explicit attack against religion, are similar in terms of the lack of honour or respect shown to a symbol. From this, she argues that the concept of honour or respect is central to developing a cross-cultural concept of blasphemy. She argues that our comprehension of the meaning of symbols is shown by our actions in response to them. Our physical responses to symbols are a form of labelling, or understanding, that show us to be in a certain kind of relationship with them. Concerns about the proper use of sacred images, and about the contexts in which they appear, are concerns that we show appropriate respect through our behaviour.

Former curator and gallery director, Dianne McGowan tries to encompass the shifting nature of the concept of sacredness in a secular market economy oriented society; what was once sacred is now housed in art museums or decorating private homes or reproduced or appropriated. She analyses two paintings, Da Vinci's *The Last Supper* and a Tibetan Buddhist *thangka,* titled *Buddha Sakyamuni,* painted between 1050-1100. Both paintings were conceived for religious spaces and depict religious scenes. However, the *thangka,* on being consecrated by a Lama, ceased to be an object and became a living deity. *The Last Supper* on the other hand was not consecrated, but its presence in a holy precinct verifies its sacredness. McGowan argues that the gallery context does not desecrate, but creates a sacred space for viewing religious and sacred art.

1

Blasphemy and sacrilege: A challenge to secularisation and theories of the modern?

David Nash

In the penultimate episode of the recent beloved BBC science fiction series *Dr Who* the massed ranks of the Daleks made a long awaited re-appearance. In doing so they demonstrated a developed conception of amoral violence and the justification for it in a conception of blasphemy. When confronted by the possibility that they might contain human DNA, the Daleks considered this to be a suggestion that was potentially blasphemous. This is arguably a quite significant cultural moment for the confidence that underpinned our modernist vision of civilisation. The Daleks after all were created in the early 1960s, arguably the highpoint of post-war confidence in humanity's capacity to sort out social and economic problems. At this time, the Dalek was literally a modernist dustbin into which all that was unsavoury in human interaction was consigned. Yet the Daleks have returned to a world that has (since they've been gone) seen the concepts of 'ethnic cleansing', 'collateral damage', 'hate crime' and 'The War on Terror' emerge. The violent and unsavoury material consigned to the bin is climbing out to recolonise a world once thought confidently civilised. Moreover, it is concepts like blasphemy and other species of violent attack upon identity that potentially provides for the emergence of a more confrontational and violent world.

Discourses of blasphemy that might lead to its detection and indeed committal are back with a vengeance and offer to trail blaze a path for religion and religious responses. They are also seeking to become the highway leading towards the new politics of cultural identity. Moreover, discourses of blasphemy are invading culture itself to become something of a catch-all term that allows individuals to display frustration and to place distance and difference between themselves and others. Most of us in the West have considered religious and cultural tolerance to be an intrinsic and cherished part of the modernist dream. The modern world's communications technology seems to present an inescapable power that should transcend hatred, anger and misunderstanding. These days we can share our innermost thoughts and feelings with other people without facing or interacting with them. The internet has made this possible, fostering the growth of our own personal world of interests and adding apparent authority and validity to ever divergent opinions. Today we have an information society that is potentially overloaded with both facts and opinion. But, strangely, this 'opinion rich' society has become a society that has never seen individuals and groups more in conflict.

Freedom of expression and its development

The reaction to alien views in contemporary worlds and the historic past has quite often been termed blasphemy. In some respects it is easy to say that the outpourings of others deserve consideration and recognition whether or not their discourses or statements are coherent. But history reminds us that we must confront the consequences of the freedom that the modern world has given us. While those who fought for the extension of forms of democracy in the post-war world would celebrate the downfall of spurious and enslaving authority, the gap that this loss of authority left was large and threatening. Indeed, we should remember that there are important reasons for describing this situation as a gap. This became plain in a significant range of cultural discourses that talked about the 'end' of such reassuring concepts as civilisation, history, and, of course, the modernist project. Such discourses looked back at supposed species of tyranny and constraint that had apparently been transcended but scarcely, if at all, looked forward to a world of potential liberation and open ended expression. For the optimistic, and those who never gave a second thought to the fact that they themselves were empowered by culture, the future represented a wealth of opportunities. Clearly, empowerment was precisely the key to this so-called liberation. Those who had benefited from the material consequences of the modernist project, for example, through education, or through access to the public sphere and the media had simultaneously the wish, the means, and the ability to express themselves and to influence others. Paradoxically, the breakdown of confidence in these same mechanisms left others without such forms of liberation or expression. Moreover, this also contributed to their long-term loss of confidence in their own empowerment through the opportunities offered by the West.

The breakdown of this confidence emphasises how far we have grown deeply accustomed to writing an especially Whig, socio-democratic progressivist style history of both religion and rights in the West. A pejorative attitude to religion was also often present in modernisation theory which considered superstition and forms of belief to belong to primitive epochs and that these represented a phase through which human development passed.[1] Traditionally, Whig religious history has told us that religious tolerance has developed in Western nation states as a consequence of these states conceding species of human rights. This concession of human rights often went hand in hand with these states surrendering stewardship and authority over the ideological makeup of their citizen's moral and mental lives. Generally speaking, this stewardship was considered to be of a religio-moral nature and its withering away within this historical model of progress was often linked to the sociological theory of secularisation. In one branch of this theory, offered substantially in the 1960s by the then influential work of Peter Berger, the supposed authority of religion in the areas of behavioural morality, education and welfare were deemed to have been broken by developments within the post-war world.[2] Such developments had arguably been at work since the Enlightenment. Teleological notions of society's development from Hegel, Marx, Weber, Elias and Foucault envisaged the marginalisation of religion into various components. Whether this was brought about by revolution (Hegel/Marx), greater specialisation (Weber), civility (Elias), or the growth of the subjectively empowered self (Foucault), all theories predicted its potential demise.

A brief reflection over the last paragraph will alert readers to how old fashioned the secularisation paradigm sketched actually looks — yet systematic discrediting of its assumptions and conclusions is still required. Interestingly, the modernisation and peaceful transition model of religious change has a stunning longevity and some commentators have noted the capacity for such accounts to overwrite conflict models.[3] In his examination of the archaeological evidence of religious violence from the classical world, Eberhard Saur examined how the archaeological processes of excavation and restoration are capable of denying the phenomenon of iconoclasm. In discussing the public display and portrayal of one statue (the statue of Mithras from Ostia), Saur notes that its archaeological value is too often considered through its carefully restored state. In this, the mutilation of the statue has been forgotten and similar evidence of destruction, so Saur argues, has been neglected or ignored. A factor that obscures the history of religious conflict still further is what Saur describes as a trend within archaeological explanations of change to adopt gradualist models of 'acculturation'. Acculturation models argue for a much more gradual interleaving of cultures based around peaceful contact, mutual sharing of technology and cultural achievements — all opposed to ideas of conquest and cultural imperialism. Interestingly, this bears a striking resemblance to modern perceptions of the functioning and purpose of religious/multicultural tolerance. Of still greater concern is Saur's suggestion that the advocates of 'acculturation' theses of change are apt to describe destructive conflict models of change as old fashioned and shaped by discredited nineteenth century paradigms.[4]

Similarly, the Reformation was regularly described as a linear unstoppable process which came fundamentally to alter the social and religious makeup of the West. In this we are persuaded that the building blocks of modernism (constructed by More and Erasmus) were firmly in place before Marx, Hegel, Weber, and even Nietzsche put pen to paper. Likewise, the triumph of the Newtonian rational universe noted in the history of science and even within the histories of gambling and probability portrays a modernisation motif which explains rationality as the triumphant explanatory framework around which the universe turns.[5] No longer did the turn of the dice or the shape of natural phenomena or laws display the divine will but instead could be explained through natural laws or the secular notion of probability.

Saur reminds us how archeological models that display destruction and iconcoclasm are worth taking with us in any study of secularisation as a consensual linear and modernising history. Attacks upon religious images represent a significant portion of blasphemy's early history. Blasphemy in the ancient and early Christian periods most frequently comes down to the historian as the written record of individual acts of outrage. Like many other crimes, there must also have been a dark figure of iconoclastic acts against religious material culture that have subsequently left no trace. The wilful and calculated destruction of religious artefacts or buildings displayed an intent to damage the religious 'currency' of the religion so attacked. Evidence from the ancient world strongly suggests that monotheistic religions took the lead in iconoclastic practices and the identification of other religions as anathema. Pre-Christian Rome had been indulgent to both empire-wide and local deities and archaeologists have seen the widespread existence of some cults as tangible evidence of this. Individual deities were chosen for their usefulness and augmented existing belief systems rather than displaced them. It was monotheistic religions that set themselves against this equilibrium.[6]

The creation of a single autonomous religious truth and route to salvation provides the obvious explanation as to why this was clearly the case. When Pharaoh Akhenaten adopted monotheism in ancient Egypt the destruction of rival deities was a logical and inevitable consequence of this choice. Judaism similarly had scriptural precedent for violent action against pagan deities, although some of these examples were aimed at religious usurpation or the Israelites 'straying' from the true God. After Christianity's arrival, the trend was continued further by Islam's adoption of iconoclastic practices. As Islam spread East its iconoclasm left its mark upon the Buddhist shrines and idols of India.

Later Christianity also regarded pagan relics and practices to be capable of routinely contaminating the lives of true believers. The systematic nature of Christian iconoclasm can be contrasted with the haphazard and inconclusive actions of Roman predecessors. Sauer suggests that the Emperor Aurelian's capture of Palmyra resulted in half-hearted and piecemeal destruction of local sacred places and, perhaps, even represented a tolerance or respect for the deities of the defeated city.[7]

In sum, the linear models of secularisation producing and being sustained by tolerance and rationality from the Enlightenment to the dawn of modernisation deserve to be qualified if not wholly questioned. Models of acculturation, of which secularisation is surely one, can be shown to have overshadowed models of conflict and episodic reaction. Similarly the post-Enlightenment 'invention' of religious tolerance ignores the relative tolerance that existed within some early civilisations.

Blasphemy and the framing of secularisation

One relic of modernisation and Whig history that still has lingered longer than most is the theory of secularisation, although the secularisation theory which strove to have a dominant place in the history and sociology of religion has now retreated somewhat in the face of a number of intellectual and theoretical challenges, particularly from historians. If the theory of secularisiation no longer claims to offer an overarching explanation of the last millennium of Christianity's history, it can at least point to its description of general trends in belief and outlook as maintaining its validity. Secularisation theory, in various forms, suggests that the modern world is more secular than the pre-modern, and this in turn more secular than the medieval. It points to a whole host of indicators that have altered mankind's perception of the world and how it functions. These include the arrival of scientific beliefs to replace belief in providence, the transfer of education, welfare and medicine into the secular sphere and, lastly, the end of mass religious attendance accompanied by the retreat of religion from public life.[8] Moreover, secularisation's theoretical account of the historical past suggests that episodes such as the Reformation, the rise of Protestantism and the Enlightenment constitute milestones towards the creation of this secular society. The high watermark of confidence in the theory of secularisation occurred a generation ago, but it remains arguable that modern society is overall more secular than previous epochs.

However, blasphemy's history significantly contests the certainty and inevitability of this view of historical progress and offers a significantly different chronology for religious history. Certainly, it may be possible to argue that blasphemy itself represents a 'secularisation' of the concept of heresy. Heretics were quite regularly cast as victims of their errors that entered their minds unwittingly. Most medieval and early modern accounts of blasphemers see them as wilful individuals indulging their own pride. The investigations of early modern Germany, France and Switzerland would lend credibility to this view.[9] The offence of blasphemy became one of active commission whereby doubts or errant opinions were actively vocalised within the earshot of others. In contrast to heresy, blasphemy was increasingly considered to be a lapse of discipline rather than sincere religious error. Many medieval European cases display individuals as drunk or angry at some slight providence had wrought upon them. Others attacked the honour of God in anger against the ill fortune he had bestowed upon them, frequently at the gambling table.[10]

Nonetheless, other assumptions of the secularisation account of religion's supposedly waning importance do not fit with blasphemy's very different history. The Reformation, far from diluting the sacred, shifted the focus to scripture and the Bible. New light is also shed on this through noting how mediaeval conceptions of sin and shame equally had their later Protestant counterparts.[11] The Enlightenment, it might be argued, brought philosophical and later artistic questioning of the sacred and its place in society. This would fit with the history of the offence in England where French Revolution ideals were later replaced by arguments about free speech, individualism, and the removal of religion to the private sphere. Nonetheless, such a triumph was not linear, nor was it remotely complete since the link between church and state in England was never overthrown.

Secularisation theory itself has also never been comfortable in measuring Christianity's vibrancy within the realm of the private sphere. While it prefers to see privatisation as the story's conclusion, recent history has shown the sacred as capable of being mobilised from this area with a rapidity that would astonish the previous generation. In Britain at the end of the twentieth century and into the new millennium, isolationist agendas have sought to protect both Britain and its component nations from the European super state arguing for 'opt outs' in issues around obscenity and morality. In 1996, for example, a case reached the European Court in which the film maker Nigel Wingrove appealed against the refusal of the British Board of Film Classification to award an exhibition certificate on the grounds it breached his freedom of expression. The court eventually found in favour of the British government allowing it the margin of appreciation, a means by which important cultural areas that might be covered by overarching European Union Law would be allowed to opt out from this. Britain thus was allowed to keep a working legal concept of blasphemy alive. More damning evidence still comes from America, where an institutionalised cleavage between Church and State did not remove the concept of blasphemy from this society. Nor did the Constitution actively secularise American society, forcing religion into the private sphere. Religion has become a central part of American politics and has developed a rhetoric which increasingly attempts to define the state as secular rather than neutral, and is therefore able to describe secular stances and world views as unconstitutional if practiced by the government.[12] Even where it might be claimed that religion was successfully privatised, the conclusions we might draw from the evidence do not support components of the secularisation thesis. Religion becoming a matter for the private conscience occurred at precisely the same time as knowledge of the law and access to it became a real possibility for more individuals in the West.

Secularisation theorists argued that tolerance would be bred by greater contact between individuals, and that globalisation would homogenise religious outlooks and lessen differences between faiths and groups. In some respects the ecumenical agendas of Western churches in the 1960s and 1970s represents a good example of this, as does the modernisation agenda of Vatican II. Similarly, the arrival of scientific beliefs to replace beliefs in providence, and the aforementioned secularisation of education, welfare and medicine, accompanied the retreat of religion from public life.[13] This confidence has not been borne out by the evidence of the late twentieth century that has seen individuals reach for blasphemy as a tool capable of preventing the erosion of the sacred. For some individuals and groups, defending religion has rejuvenated nationalism in the face of the twin agendas of globalisation and, in particular, pan-European systems of morals and justice.

In England, blasphemy cases as far apart as the 1880s, the 1930s, the 1970s and the 1990s, all contained a fear of continental influences contaminating 'sacred' English morals. The case against Nigel Wingrove's film *Visions of Ecstasy* allowed the United Kingdom to maintain the Common Law of blasphemous libel as an element of its culturally distinct identity, similarly Mary Whitehouse had invoked the sacred nature of British morality in her campaign to exclude Jens Jurgen Thorsen's *Sex Life of Christ* from being shot in England in 1977. In accepting these as legal and policy decisions, English fears of the dangerous and foreign were enshrined in and influenced legal decisions.[14] Elements of these fears were evident in the cases against G.W. Foote in 1883, where the relevant newspaper's blasphemy could be shown to be directly influenced by French prototypes. In the 1930s Britain also witnessed an attempt to extend the blasphemy law as a means of excluding 'foreign' Jewish freethinkers and their ability to undermine the morals of the British Empire. Although this Bill passed a first reading in Parliament, the government moved swiftly to prevent it becoming law. The early 1990s saw the Salman Rushdie affair persuade some to see blasphemy as a multicultural issue. One of the arguments used was the suggestion that Britain's tolerance of other religions and cultures was a sham unless the law could be mobilised to protect the religious sensibilities of all. Early twentieth century America also witnessed a number of panics associated with the dangerous spirituality and anti-religious views of recent immigrants. In the immediate First World War period, a Lithuanian, Michael Mockus, stood trial for blasphemy and, upon conviction, the judge made clear reference to the potentially dangerous views held by immigrants. Mockus linked Christianity with class and economic oppression and argued that religion was essentially a conspiracy against the workers of the world.[15] Seventeenth century America had seen individual states operate their own penal codes, but latter day America also witnessed the use of blasphemy as a tool for the defence of local communities and their morals. The early twentieth century in particular saw American States pursuing blasphemers within their local and state jurisdictions (recognisably similar to early modern Geneva, Zurich or Venice) only to see these attempts to prosecute and convict quashed by federal law.[16] Nonetheless, individual communities have for some years now been able to operate their own local standards of decency in defiance of Federal law's long standing desire for equality of practice.[17] Thus, secularisation theory clearly does not offer any valuable framework to explain blasphemy's history and in particular its persistence. Moreover, it is possible to go further and argue that blasphemy's own history itself provided important material for a wider history of the sacred. Its persistence and its current relevance supply vital evidence of the survival of the sacred — not simply as a spiritual legacy but as a vital component of beliefs about nationalism and wider religious identity.

Many of our models (especially theoretical ones) concerning long term continuity and change offer inadequate explanations of blasphemy. The phenomenon itself does not readily fit with theories associated with modernisation and change. Following such models and their cultural intentions leads us to ask why blasphemy was not eradicated through the Enlightenment's search for freedom of belief and expression. If theories about the inevitable demise of religion were true, it could be expected that the crime of blasphemy would have been swept away by the eighteenth and nineteenth century revolutions in America and Europe, or fallen into desuetude in the more organic constitutions of Britain and its former English-speaking empire. In the non-English speaking world, the imposition of supposedly enlightened laws from the mother country ironed out local differences to provide what some have seen as an enduring solution.[18] The survival of blasphemy as a crime, and as an accusation, also offers a temptation to suggest that blasphemy as a cultural phenomenon may suit a more dystopian view of the West in crisis. Those Western critics who were (and are) suspicious of the Enlightenment, and its supposed empowerment of the individual, are the important figures here. Foucault, Derrida and the postmodernists not only regard this empowerment to be a sham but also are likely see the supposed authority of Enlightenment truth as a collection of controls whose ultimate explanatory cohesion disintegrates before them.

Blasphemy, identity and exploration

Blasphemy was, and is, more than a transgressionary activity. Its long history suggests that controversies about blasphemy are places where definitions of the universe and its working are debated; places where identities are forged and where communities debate issues about public order. All these lead us to a history away from the certainties offered by secularisation narratives. Blasphemy always reminded us that the relationship between individuals and the sacred were very often problematic. Secularisation theorists always spoke about ideas of collective, normal, and everyday belief, thereby homogenising both the experience of belief and the definitions that historians and sociologists would give to it. Blasphemy's illumination of conflict models and incidents showed that belief was capable of ebbing and flowing and appearing at pressure points in the interactions of individuals and societies. In this, the inevitable triumph of the secular over the sacred looks a far-fetched suggestion. Even if secularisation theorists did have some justification in arguing that religion would become less important, it remains a teleological theory of progress and continual enlightenment. But the religion supposedly supplanted by reason was not by any means destroyed or damaged beyond repair, and secularisation theorists failed to pay much attention to the residues and legacies that Christianity left in the West.

Artists who explore and contemplate the West's myths, stories and cultural legacy became the people who rescued religion from its appointed status on the periphery of experience. What motivates artistic consideration of the sacred, and why artists as diverse as Andres Serrano, Bettina Rheims, Tracey Emin and Tania Kovats have quarried the sacred for inspiration, are important questions. While these artists themselves may have lucid, exciting and informative answers, the wider 'influence' of the sacred needs to form exploration of the fuller context in this area.[19] In this respect, it is valuable to ask how far this art reflects a re-discovery or re-orientation around the sacred imagery of the past, or a simple acknowledgement of religion's enthralling nature as one of the West's strongest and most compelling 'stories'. In this, it has not been for many of these artists a re-evangelisation of life, or necessarily a quest for spiritual longing, but has equally sometimes been spawned by the simple curiosity of those brought up with secular outlooks.

This interest means that investigations of popular culture and media studies will inevitably be drawn to the sporadic appearance of the sacred in popular culture. In a sense, each particular media can be said to have its fifteen minutes in the spotlight. Irving Welsh showed the power of disreputable images of the almighty to shock in the context of the modern novel. His *Granton Star Cause* depicted a profane and drunken deity and was the last controversy Mary Whitehouse, Britain's premier twentieth-century critic of media morality, was involved in before her death. Madonna's sense of melodrama almost inevitably took her in the direction of the sacred long before she thought of actually being crucified on stage. In 2006, her 'Confessions' tour played with Catholic motifs and extended her belief that suffering and crucifixes could be 'made sexy'. Even culturally conservative British comedy, which always wishes it was more subversive than it ever manages to be, produced a publication with religious offensiveness as a keynote feature. The British comedian Rik Mayal's recent autobiography contained a picture of himself beatified and described as 'better than God'. All these are in danger of demonstrating a *de facto* cheapening and ubiquitousness of the sacred while noting the rediscovery of religion's powers to shock. Yet equating these with outright blasphemy brings problems of intention when, for example, Maddona had embarked on a quest to entertain as much as to problematise or inform her audience about religion and the sacred.

In particular, we might note how images and portrayals of Christ on film have caused especial problems of interpretation sometimes leading to accusations of blasphemy. Of greater concern have been the attempts to humanise Christ which, in some eyes, appeared to be an assault upon the idea of his divinity — a constant struggle in such depictions. Dennis Potter's *Son of Man* portrayed a Christ at war with himself and sceptical of the divine nature of his own destiny. Similarly, Scorsese's *Last Temptation* gave critics, both hostile and sympathetic, an opportunity to air the sheer variety of interpretation to which the gospel story, and its depiction, could be subjected. Yet, conclusions from this area were not readily transferable to other blasphemous instances. Films, and their subsequent greater availability on video, are capable of multiple consumption and re-consumption in the quest for favourable or unfavourable meanings.[20] But the engagement of artists and writers with the religious has provided the opportunity for religious world views to challenge ownership of these cultural ideas and have asked the searching question of whether the ideas of the religious belong to society as a whole. The protests against everything from *Last Temptation of Christ* to *Jerry Springer the Opera* have given religious individuals the opportunity to bring arguments about the sacred and its inviolability back to the public sphere. In this they are aided by agendas which promote social inclusiveness and the urge to marginalise differences of opinion and viewpoints in the more consensually driven societies of the new millennium.

These are all conundrums and challenges to artists and thinkers. In such a climate, it is scarcely surprising that a cultural phenomenon so capable of controversy should excite and fascinate the artistic mind used to sifting and redefining the problem areas of civilisation. In the end, we should protect such rights and imperatives since they offer a blueprint for possible change against regimes of abject quietism and stasis. This is necessary because all culture — religious or secular — is capable of development and change. Whether we really can provide an equality of public space for the religious and those who would denounce it to re-enter the public sphere is a difficult question for us to answer. Ironically, societies faced by these dilemmas will have to decide how far they can tolerate a conflict model between the religious and the free speech advocate in the name of so-called consensus.

Endnotes

[1] A classic example of this paradigm in use is Keith Thomas's 1971 *Religion and the Decline of Magic*, London: Weidenfeld and Nicholson.

[2] Peter Berger, 1967, *The Sacred Canopy: The Social Reality of Religion*, Garden City, N.Y.: Doubleday.

[3] We might contrast the Berger version of secularisation with that offered by Bryan Wilson, in his later *Religion in Sociological Perspective* (Oxford: Oxford University Press 1982). This envisaged religion ceasing to be important in the working of the social system but instead becoming personalised or privatised. Again we may wish to note how Western and Christocentric this analysis is, even for its time. Bryan Wilson also suggested that the process could be measured through churches becoming, among other things, mosques!

[4] Eberhard Sauer, 2003, *The Archaeology of Religious Hatred in the Roman and Early Medieval World*, Stroud: Tempus Books, pp. 15-18.

[5] See Gerda Reith, 1999, *The Age of Chance: Gambling in Western Culture*, London: Routledge.

[6] See Sauer, op. cit.

[7] Sauer, ibid., pp. 162-164, 30, 159, 46 and 162.

[8] Secularisation theory and its own history can be approached through D.S. Nash, 2004, 'Secularization's failure as a master narrative; Reconnecting Religion with Social and Cultural History', *Cultural and Social History*, vol. 1, no. 2, pp. 302-325.

[9] See Gerd Schwerhoff, 1998, 'Starke Worte: Blasphemie als theatralische Inszenierung von Männlichkeit an der Wende vom Mittelalter zur Frühen Neuzeit' in Martin Dinges (ed.), *Hausväter, Priest, Kastraten: Zur Konstruktion von Männlichkeit in Spätmittelalter und Früher Neuzeit, Göttingen*, pp. 238-263; Alain Cabantous, 2002, *Blasphemy: Impious speech in the West from the seventeenth to the nineteenth century*, Eric Rauth (trans.), New York: Columbia University Press; and Francisca Loetz, 2002, *Mit Gott handeln: von den Zürcher Gotteslästerern der Frühen Neuzeit zu einer Kulturgeschichte des Religiösen*, Vandenhoeck and Ruprecht Göttingen.

[10] For examples of this, see Maureen Flynn, 1995, 'Blasphemy and the Play of Anger in sixteenth century Spain', *Past and Present*, vol. 149, pp. 29-56, p.35-36.; Maureen Flynn, 1998, 'Taming Anger's daughters: New treatment for emotional problems in Renaissance Spain,' *Renaissance Quarterly*, vol. 51, no. 3, pp. 864-886, and Javier Villa-Flores, 2007, 'On Divine Persecution: Blasphemy and Gambling in New Spain' in Susan Schroeder and Stafford Poole (eds.), *Religion and Society in Colonial Mexico*, New Mexico University Press: New Mexico.

[11] It is worth comparing Delumeu's thesis about late medieval Christendom's own obsession with guilt alongside Max Weber's version for post-Reformation Protestant Europe. See Jean Delumeau, 1990 edition, *Sin and Fear: The Emergence of a Western Guilt Culture, 13th-18th Centuries*, Eric Nicholson (trans.), New York: St. Martin's Press.

[12] Marjorie Heins, 1993, *Sex, Sin, and Blasphemy: A guide to America's censorship wars*, New York: The New Press.

[13] Secularisation theory and its own history can be approached through D. S. Nash, 2004, 'Secularization's failure as a master narrative; Reconnecting Religion with Social and Cultural History', *Cultural and Social History*, vol. 1, no. 2, pp. 302-325.

Interights and Article Nineteen 1995, *Blasphemy and Film Censorship*, submission to the European Court of Human Rights in respect of *Nigel Wingrove v. the United Kingdom*. Article 19/Interights, London.

[15] See L. Levy, 1993, *Blasphemy, Verbal offense against the sacred, from Moses to Salman Rushdie*, New York: Knopf, pp. 513-515. See also Theodore Schroeder, 1970, [1919], *Constitutional Free Speech Defined and Defended in an Unfinished argument in a case of Blasphemy*, New York: De Capo Press, re-print of 1919 edition published by the Free Speech League.

[16] Such prosecutions became impossible after *Burstyn v Wilson*, 343, U.S. 495 (1952).

[17] See Heins, op. cit.

[18] See the Indian Criminal Code 'imposed' in 1860 which equalised the legal situation between all religious groups in India by outlawing all attacks upon religious artefacts and buildings. Indian Penal Code (1860), sections 295, 295a and 298.

[19] A recent contribution in this area is S. Brent Plate, 2006, *Blasphemy: Art that Offends*, London: Black Dog Publishing.

[20] It is worth noting also that individual films are probably just as likely to be viewed in the wider canon of their director than as a manifestation of a particular genre. For an example pertinent to this area, see Lawrence S. Friedman, 1997, *The Cinema of Martin Scorsese*, Oxford: Roundhouse, and Ian Christie and David Thompson, 2003, *Scorsese on Scorsese*, London: Faber.

2

'The devil's centres of operation':[1] English theatre and the charge of blasphemy, 1698-1708

David Manning

The dominant notion of blasphemy in Britain today is built upon a perception of what is offensive to the Christian religion. Derived from common law and fashioned by the dynamics of public opinion, this view has been employed to powerful effect in the *Gay News* trial of 1977 and, most recently, in charges against the BBC broadcast of *Jerry Springer the Opera* in 2005.[2] It would appear that the exclusively religious conception of blasphemy as a sin against God, punishable by God or His intermediaries, has been displaced by a more secular, politicised view which focuses on the relationship between human agents. The paradigm created by a broadly secular western democracy invariably places artistic representations of the sacred within a polarised debate between religious sensibilities and freedom of expression. In such a context, the need to negotiate the sacred becomes imperative to maintaining a *modus vivendi*. Practically, a model of upholding individual rights without risking a breach of the peace is one to be defended. However, if our intellectual discussions of the sacred become limited by such a framework, then we restrict our understanding of beliefs that are not similar to our own. It should be clarified that there are other, more profoundly religious, perceptions of blasphemy, and to conflate them with the notion dominant in Britain threatens the potential for us to negotiate the sacred successfully. By using an historical case study, this chapter will explore an exclusively religious context to blasphemy and, in so doing, reveal what might cause a devotedly religious individual to make the charge of blasphemy. Here, the application of history becomes particularly useful, because we can escape immediate bias that the charge of blasphemy is only made by cranks or fanatics, as well as preconceptions concerning the right of freedom of expression.[3] Let us, then, consider the reaction of pious Christians to the activities of the theatre, within the context of a devoutly Christian society.

Blasphemous theatres and plays

The only legislation ever passed with Royal Assent against blasphemy in England was the *Blasphemy Act* of 1698.[4] Political wrangling had limited the scope of the Act to a denunciation of anti-trinitarian conceptions of God; however, it was sold to the public as a realisation of King William III's personal commitment to 'discourage profaneness and immorality'.[5] The necessity of this presentation was borne out of a belief among growing numbers of Protestants that England was plagued by immorality and vice on a scale that risked divine punishment. At this time, England was a devoutly Christian society, and a belief in God's providence was virtually universal. Indeed, all major events were interpreted providentially and nationwide fasts were often instigated by the regime to appease the Almighty in times of perceived crisis. Furthermore, the most pious individuals believed that God shaped the very nature of human happiness and misery.[6] Those seized by the belief that vice plagued the nation had to look no further than the earthquake of 1692 for confirmation: God was angry. For zealous reformers, one of the most public and institutionalised centres of vice was the playhouse; for it had a 'natural and unavoidable tendency to that which [was] sinful and unlawful'.[7] Unlike the tavern or the whore-house, the theatre stimulated the mind as well as the body. It could promote many different vices to a diverse audience, who shared the experience together in place and time.[8] The playhouse was not simply a venue where vice was represented and then imitated by vulnerable members of the audience;[9] it was a place where playwright, player and audience met to collude in sin. Given that the state had seemingly failed to provide adequate direction on the matter, it was therefore timely that the pious clergyman Jeremy Collier published *A short view of the immorality and profaneness of the English stage* in 1698.[10]

Collier's work proved popular as most upstanding Christians would have probably acknowledged that some stages, particularly those at the annual Bartholomew Fair, attracted disreputable characters and promoted vices such as profane swearing, mocking of religion, lewdness and drunkenness.[11] As well as attacking these vices, however, Collier posited a much more unpalatable argument that the theatre as an institution was fundamentally evil. Within the pages of his substantial book he exposed specific plays as immoral, profane, and blasphemous; furthermore, he lambasted audience appreciation of these plays as tantamount to worshipping the Devil.[12] The ensuing controversy, which has become known to literary scholars as 'the stage debate', questioned the very existence of the playhouse in a godly society, and served as a searing indictment of past and contemporary regimes for their failure to define and condemn blasphemy in all its forms.

In 1698, there were two professional, permanent theatres in London, one in Drury Lane and the other in Lincoln's Inn Fields, and they were attended by a wide cross-section of society.[13] The Drury Lane theatre was known as the 'Royal', being patronised by the monarch, and its actors assumed the title of 'His Majesties Servants'. The idea that these playhouses could harbour evil was seen by many contemporaries as preposterous. While there was general support for Collier's call to reform the stage, few reformers endorsed his specific charges of profanity and blasphemy. By 1699 it became clear that parliament would not sanction any reform of the theatre, and support for the cause gradually waned. Indeed, most contemporaries would have probably forgotten all about Collier's charges of blasphemy had it not been for another providential act of God, and an astonishing historical accident.

On the evening of 26 November 1703, a great storm hit England which caused widespread damage and thousands of deaths.[14] The event was universally acknowledged by the nation's Protestants as a sign of God's wrath. To mark the severity of the situation, Queen Anne declared that a general fast be observed as public penance on 19 January 1704. Amidst the national distress, it was reported that a group of actors had only days after the storm performed a version of Shakespeare's *The Tempest*.[15] The failure of the playhouse to cancel this production in the aftermath of the storm caused pious campaigners once again to take up the pen and attack the stage, this time with a clear mandate from the Almighty. Collier quickly published a short, cheap summation of *A short view* which, along with a number of other zealous anti-stage publications, were bought and distributed in significant numbers as part of a massive propaganda campaign by the newly formed Society for the Promotion of Christian Knowledge (SPCK). In the following months, two prominent journalists, John Tutchin and Daniel Defoe, joined the fray by attacking the stage in their respective publications: *The Observator* and *A Review*. Two years later, the zealous clergyman Arthur Bedford capitalised on the momentum of the renewed campaign and published *The evil and danger of stage-plays* which claimed to list approximately 1400 examples of 'swearing, cursing and blasphemy' in plays of the previous two years alone.[16] Despite the ideological differences that would have existed between them, Collier, Bedford, Tutchin, and Defoe shared a common bond by stressing the profanity and blasphemy of the theatres, re-igniting the belief that playhouses were the 'Devil's centres of operation'.[17] The rest of this chapter will investigate why these men considered certain plays to be blasphemous. It will be shown that, far from a one-dimensional notion of offensiveness, the charge of blasphemy articulated complex and deeply held theological anxieties.

A religious critique of dramatic language

The interpretations that our anti-stage writers placed on dramatic texts might well appear facile or even absurd to modern readers and so, before turning to the evidence, we need to understand the way in which they would have approached play scripts. In proving specific plays guilty of blasphemy, it would appear that to men such as Collier, textual and/or dramatic context was a complete irrelevance. To explain why intelligent men could neglect the fundamental significance of context, most literary scholars have concurred with Aubrey

Williams that the clash between Collier and the playwrights was principally the result of opposing philosophical theories concerning the separation between life and art. This explanation cast Collier as a staunch defender of the Platonic notion that representation is a copy of reality, while placing the playwrights in an opposing Aristotelian camp which stressed that representation is merely a symbol of mental states that has no direct connection with reality. A number of playwrights did construct replies to Collier from an Aristotelian perspective;[18] however, I would argue that this evidence has guided scholars to make certain assumptions about Collier's position without considering the fact that he was a devout clergyman. Indeed, it would be almost inconceivable that Collier's method was not religiously inspired.

Before *A short view* was published, John Tillotson, the then Archbishop of Canterbury, delivered a sermon against the stage based upon Ephesians 4:29: 'Let no corrupt communication proceed out of your mouth, but that which is good to the use of edifying, that it may minister grace unto the hearers'.[19] In preaching that 'corrupt communication was evidence of a corrupt and impure heart',[20] Tillotson affirmed the decree of scripture to be absolute and he seemingly drew upon Augustinian theology to connect evil deeds to an evil will.[21] The implications for the stage were clear: in discerning between good and evil acts, context was an irrelevance. The significance of this judgment was fully acknowledged by Collier in the pages of *A short view* and in similar fashion Bedford stated that, 'whatever is a sin when spoken in another place is as much a sin when spoken in the play-house'.[22] Thus, any word or words could be legitimately censured, no matter what the context, if the accuser could convincingly argue that they were wicked. It seems evident, therefore, that it was an acute religious sensitivity to the word of God, rather than crude literalism or Platonic theory that formed the central component of our anti-stage writers' concerns. To appreciate their position fully, all intellectual preconceptions regarding the legitimacy of context and the separation between life and art need to be set aside. With this interpretative framework established we can now consider what caused our anti-stage writers to charge plays with blasphemy.

Both Collier and Bedford were often explicit about identifying certain words in play scripts as blasphemous; but the words were also understood within the wider category of profanity. For example, in *A short view*, Collier devoted a chapter to 'the profaneness of the stage', which was subdivided into two sections: 'cursing and swearing' and 'abuse of religion'. The former was acknowledged as being the most prevalent, while the latter, though less common, was perceived as the more dangerous, principally because sometimes it did not 'stop short of blasphemy'.[23] Profane swearing, such as 'e Gad' or 'Lard',[24] was quickly covered to give prominence to offences that were deemed blasphemous. It should, therefore, be stressed that swearing against God or any form of general irreverence towards God or Christianity, while contemptible and profane, was not actually viewed as blasphemy. Upon reading the anti-stage writings of the period, it can be shown that evidence used to prove plays guilty of blasphemy clustered around two central themes: corrupting the idea of God's providence and the use of demonic language.

The perceived attack upon God's providence

Shortly after the storm, Collier wrote that during the notorious production of *The Tempest* the 'audience were pleased to clap at an unusual length of pleasure and approbation' at the mention of chimneys being blown down.[25] The accuracy of this claim is suspect,[26] yet it demonstrates how the providential judgement of the storm had increased religious sensitivity to matters of timing and position vis-à-vis both action and reaction. In this instance, the subject matter of the play was broadly irrelevant, for it was completely superseded by the failure of the playhouse, the actors and the audience to act appropriately in the wake of God's divine judgement. The production of the play in question would most likely have been unrecognisable to audiences today. The play was probably one of two radical adaptations of Shakespeare's original work, which included significant alterations to the script and a good dose of devilish foolery and bawdyness.[27] Nevertheless, it would appear that it was the mere fact that a 'mock tempest'[28] had been played soon after the real, divinely sanctioned tempest that caused charges of profanity and blasphemy. Indeed, when the day of national penance arrived, the Bishop of Oxford told the Lords gathered at Westminster Abbey that the playing of *The Tempest* shortly after the storm was an 'unprecedented piece of Profaneness' that was an 'affront to God, unparalleled by any civilized nation'.[29] The reaction to the playing of *The Tempest* was certainly exceptional but for our anti-stage writers it was just one example among many that demonstrated not just a disregard for God's providence, but a fundamental corruption of it. As Collier put it, the players and playwrights had 'attempted as it were to scale the sky, and attack the seat of omnipotence: they have blasphemed the attributes of God, ridiculed his providence'.[30] To ignore the providential acts of the Almighty was represented by anti-stage critics as a terrible attack upon God, mocking His powers as if He did not exist.

In Sir John Vanbrugh's play, *The Relapse*, the character Young Fashion schemes to seduce his brother's fiancée in order to secure her substantial dowry. Upon devising a workable ploy with his accomplice, Fashion declares, 'providence thou see'st at last, takes care of men of merit'.[31] Collier was so incensed by these words that he singled them out as 'plain blasphemy' and 'an eruption of hell with a witness'.[32] The charge of blasphemy was acknowledged and taken seriously, for it was one that playwrights did much to discredit. In defending his work, Vanbrugh stated: 'every body knows the word providence in common discourse goes for fortune and yet no one ever thought it blasphemy to say, fortune's blind, or fortune favours fools'.[33] Michael Cordner has suggested that Collier's allegation of blasphemy was predominantly levelled in reaction to a playwright's failure to construct pious sentences from a common religious vocabulary.[34] This interpretation of literary literalism seems rather one-dimensional. It should be noted that acts of providence were believed to be instances of God's omnipresent governance, which were designed to protect the good and give warning and punishment to the wicked.[35] The slightest suggestion that God could smile upon wicked men would have been seen by Collier as impossible, and not only an affront to the providential workings of God, but a sign of devilish pride.

In another example, Collier denounced the following words from Thomas D'Urfey's version of *Don Quixote* as 'directly blaspheming the Creation, and a Satyr upon God Almighty':[36]

> Providence that form'd the Fair
> In such a charm Skin,
> Their Outside made his only Care,
> And never look'd within.[37]

In this passage, the last two lines communicate the blasphemy because they were seen as giving rise to the suggestion that God's providence was only concerned with the outward and superficial. The idea that God did not care for a person's soul would clearly render much of the Christian faith meaningless. The seemingly innocuous passage from *Don Quixote*, to the hyper-sensitive reader, was tantamount to an open denial of the truth of God's working in the world. It would appear that the charge of blasphemy allowed Collier to bypass lengthy explanation and communicate the true wickedness of the passage to less astute persons or those believing the words to be harmless. Blasphemy was a highly evocative term; contemporary readers would have been well aware of God's terrible punishment of blasphemies related in the Bible.[38] While it seemed unbelievable that such a passage could be wicked, the fact that a clergyman labelled them as blasphemous would have meant that they could not be assumed harmless with a clear conscience.

In his newspaper, *The Observator*, Tutchin attacked an adaptation of Shakespeare's *Macbeth* which had also been performed shortly after the Storm.[39] Contrary to the reaction against *The Tempest*, Tutchin's grievance lay squarely on the content of the play. He believed that the occult, evil forces prevalent in the text of the play were presented as indistinguishable from God's providential powers, perverting the unique and infinitely good character of God.[40] As it has been shown, the fictional status of the characters was no excuse; real people were still saying the words in the script and those words existed in print. God alone was providential and so, according to Tutchin, the play was proof that the actors were 'impious and blasphemous wretches' who had 'ridiculed God's

Amazing and Stupendous Judgment' of the Great Storm. The severity with which Tutchin viewed this transgression against God's providence was made clear when he concluded that, 'this is a sad omen of our [the nation's] hasty destruction'.[41] It is, therefore, evident that the charge of blasphemy communicated a very grave sin indeed.

Invoking devils

Many anti-stage writers expressed a belief that the playhouse was the Devil's domain. The origin of this belief dated back to the writings of the influential second-century Christian Tertullian, who reported on an instance where a woman attended a Roman theatre and became possessed by a devil.[42] I have yet to come across any reports of early eighteenth-century audiences being overcome by such forces and even actors who directly invoked the Devil were not explicitly described as being possessed, though their words were often denounced as blasphemous. Indeed, the evidence used to censure plays as blasphemous appears to have relied heavily on quotations that explicitly referred to devils and damnation. Such language was not uncommon in plays of the period, being used metaphorically and more readily as alternative modes of expression to taking God's name in vain. The plays in question, however, rarely contained anti-religious themes, and most contemporaries would have deemed the language fairly innocuous once set in context. Nevertheless, phrases which, for example, appeared to represent acts of swearing by 'death and the Devil'[43] were plucked out of scripts by men such as Bedford and denounced with vitriol as instances of 'unparalleled blasphemy'.[44] For anti-stage critics, to mention demons in swearing, cursing, or just an exclamation was evidence of actually calling upon the forces of darkness. Before turning to the evidence, it would be useful to establish the conceptual relationship between words that invoked devils, the charge of blasphemy, and the notion that the theatre was demonic.

In *The evil and danger of stage-plays*, Bedford stated in no uncertain terms that blasphemy was 'a sin of that heinous nature, which the damned in Hell are guilty of, and which makes them incapable of recovery'.[45] At first glance, this belief seems to be forged from an inaccurate reading of Matthew 12:31: 'All manner of sin and blasphemy shall be forgiven unto me: but the blasphemy against the Holy Ghost shall not be forgiven unto men',[46] whereby Bedford gives no consideration to the scriptural differentiation between pardonable and unpardonable blasphemy. It transpires, however, that Bedford's perception of blasphemy shows remarkable similarities to the doctrine put forward by St. Thomas Aquinas: to speak any sort blasphemy was a mortal sin which rendered the utterer damned and those that were damned also blasphemed, to show their hatred of the punishments inflicted upon them.[47] Invoking devils was, therefore, an example of the latter case (for who but the damned could possibly utter such words). Put plainly, it was believed that only the damned could call upon devils and such an act was blasphemous because it demonstrated that the sinner, even in the grip of God's divinely sanctioned punishment, continued to defy the Almighty. Collier similarly concluded that the profanity of the stage was 'the language of the damned'[48] and that to pay to watch such sin was to 'make a contribution for blasphemy, and raise a tax for the government below?'[49] In demonological theory, the damned were understood to be controlled by devils.[50] Therefore, actors who revealed themselves to be damned by their blasphemies, could be construed as the devil's agents and consequently to attend the theatre was, as Tutchin put it, to 'buy vice at the Devil's shop'.[51]

In *A short view*, Collier attacked John Dryden's version of *Amphitryon*[52] for furnishing Jupiter with the omnipotence of God. To Collier, this was 'blasphemy on the top of the letter, without any trouble of inference, or construction'.[53] The representation of heathen gods on stage could have been seen as idolatrous and a violation of God's first commandment. Yet, in stating that the 'cover of an idol is too thin a pretence to screen the blasphemy',[54] Collier hinted that the sin of blasphemy was of an even greater magnitude. In this case, it would appear that the notion of blasphemy went well beyond blurring the *mythos* of the ancient gods with the *ethos* of the one true (Christian) God. Early Christian Fathers such as Tertullian had claimed that Roman gods were in fact devils and for men such as Collier, who were knowledgeable of and believed in such early Christian writings, this view continued to hold credibility.[55] Implicit in Collier's treatment, Jupiter was neither simply a representation of a mythical figure nor a potential religious idol, but a devil. In light of Collier's belief in the conceptual relationship between blasphemy and the demonic, it would appear that the charge of blasphemy articulated a belief that Dryden had sought to award omnipotent powers to a devil, thus subverting the differentiation between good and evil and laying waste to God's truth.

In giving examples of the 'blasphemous' expressions of the stage, Tutchin turned to the words of Vanbrugh's *Provok'd Wife*: 'Satan and his equipage; woman tempted me, lust weakened me, and so the Devil overcame me, as fell Adam, so fell I'.[56] It would appear that the words that evoked the charge of blasphemy were 'the Devil overcame me', as they could have been construed as an open admission of a compact with the Devil. Such a view is confirmed when Tutchin later went on to censure the phrase 'hail powers beneath!' from John Corny's version of *Metamorphosis*.[57] Bedford denounced similar passages from other plays that displayed a relationship between human and devil, such as the invocation 'to the Devil, so she bring no children', from the anonymous play *The roving husband reclaim'd*.[58] On occasion, Bedford perused this interpretation with a zeal that seems positively ludicrous to the modern reader. For example, he condemned the phrase as 'a devil a wit' from the play *The northern lass*, which he annotated 'i.e. no wit'.[59] For Bedford, these words constituted praise to the devil, which he believed was the 'highest blasphemy that mortals can invent'.[60] It seems clear that the meticulousness and fervour of Bedford's interpretation was but a genuine reflection of his fear of God's wrath and an attempt to implement what he believed to be God's wishes as directed by Scripture, earlier Christian writings and above all else God's unmitigated providential warning.

It has been shown that our anti-stage writers genuinely believed that the blasphemies of the theatre denigrated the truth of God's workings in the world and advanced the position of devils. In both method and substance, this view was supported by a combination of Scripture, early Christian writings and the work of eminent Christian theologians. Significantly, Tutchin, Bedford and Collier were not considered cranks and their views held significant credibility in the period of heightened theological anxiety after the storm of 1703. To these men, the godly reformation required to stave off further divine punishment simply could not be completed unless the theatre was drastically reformed. In the final section of this chapter I want to return to the issue of negotiating the sacred and reflect upon how our anti-stage writers sought to apply their examples of blasphemy to affect actual reform.

The plight of God-fearing Christians

First of all, it must be stressed that, for pious English Protestants, the notion of the sacred extended well beyond a collection of discrete beliefs, words, actions or objects.[61] In general terms the sanctity of God's truth was universally accepted and so playwrights, audiences and anti-stage writers all worked within, and agreed upon, the same religious paradigm. This chapter has shown that the act of negotiating the sacred in the stage debate was not complicated by questions concerning the nature of the sacred or how it should be accommodated, but rather how sensitively providence should be interpreted and how vigorously God's truth should be maintained and protected. It has already been noted that our anti-stage campaigners sought more forceful and comprehensive reform than did the governing regime, and yet God's providential intervention of 1703 made it impossible for the administration wholly to dismiss the claims of our writers. Consequently, it would appear that in a state that held the sanctity of God's truth as its governing paradigm, the correct interpretation of God's will rested exclusively on His perceived intermediaries (i.e. the Monarch and her Bishops). Yet, in times of crisis, the paradigm also allowed for a circumvention of the authority of the Church and the law because God was ultimately the arbiter.[62]

The main strategy employed by reformers against immorality and lower-level profanity was to appeal to magistrates to be more effective in the punishment of the wicked.[63] Yet, it is notable that this approach was not adopted by Collier, Tutchin and Bedford. The main reason for this was probably pragmatic: it would have been futile to appeal for state intervention against words that the state did not recognise as sinful.[64]   However, I would suggest that the unique way in which our anti-stage writers conceived of the theatre as the devil's domain also significantly influenced their approach. Their consistent reference to the theatre as the 'Devil's chapel', or the 'Devil's engine', or the 'Devil's shop'[65] took the literal observations of the early Christian Fathers and re-interpreted them afresh for the eighteenth century by playing upon contemporary fears about the prevalence of evil and socio-religious concerns among reformers that the theatre had become anti-church. Importantly, the labels of theatre as the Devil's 'chapel', 'engine' or 'shop' also indicate how our anti-stage writers believed that the sins of the theatre were perpetuated. When the writings of our anti-stage writers are taken in the round, it becomes clear that the main target of the campaign was not the sinful playwrights and actors, but rather potential theatre goers and people of influence. It was believed that the effectual reform of the playhouse lay with the source of the problem — the audience. Collier's view that the audience were complicit has already been noted above, and Defoe was under no illusion that the 'Errors of the Stage, lie all in the Auditory' for the actors were but their 'Humble Servants'.[66] Indeed, it was the audience's attendance, money and applause that supplied the Devil with his congregation and ensured that God's truth continued to be denied. The outrage created by such evil 'competition' and the extent to which the charge of blasphemy exposed fundamental and dangerous untruths is evident in a satirical poem by Daniel Defoe, which was published on occasion of a new theatre being built at the Haymarket in 1705. An extract of the poem reads as follows:

> View but our Stately Pile, the columns stand,
> Like some Great Council Chamber of the Land:
> When Strangers view the Beauty and the State,
> As they pass by, they ask what Church is that?
> Thinking a Nation, so Devout as we,
> Ne'r build such Domes, but to some Deity;
> But when the Salt Assembly once they View,
> What Gods they Worship, how Blaspheme the True;
> How Vice's Champions, Uncontrol'd within,
> Roul in the very Excrements of Sin:
> The Horrid Emblems so Exact appear,
> That Hell's an Ass, to what's Transacted here.[67]

The primary approach of our anti-stage writers was, therefore, to appeal to the Christian conscience of the potential theatre goer, thus bypassing the worldly restrictions of politics and law and asking each individual to scrutinise their actions more closely.

The polemical claims of Collier, Tutchin and Bedford formed a desperate attempt to expose the wickedness of the stage. Citing play passages as blasphemous was crucial to the argument that the words in particular were indeed fundamentally evil. Inflammatory passages attacking God's providence and invoking Devils were of little significance in isolation; but if they were proved blasphemous, then anti-stage writers hoped that audiences would be forced to accept that plays were evil and risked provoking God's wrath. With no earthly, objective judge, such issues were intractable and, for the victimised playwrights and no doubt many humble audience members, it was actually men such as Collier who were guilty of blasphemy by seeing wickedness where there was none. As one eminent playwright put it: 'where the expression is unblameable in its own clear and genuine signification, he [Collier] enters into himself like the evil spirit, he possesses the innocent phrase, and makes it bellow forth his own blasphemies'.[68] After His intervention in 1703, God did not venture to give any further clarification on the matter and with His apparent acquiescence, the heat of the stage debate subsided. The SPCK propaganda campaign wound down in 1708 drawing to a close any serious chance of theatre reform on the basis of its profanity and blasphemy.

Acknowledging modern providentialism

In conclusion, it has been shown that for pious English Christians of but three centuries ago, the charge of blasphemy was a very grave one indeed. Conceptually, blasphemy was conceived as a form of profanity that ranged from cursing through to an inversion of God and the Devil. Extreme blasphemies sought to subvert some of the most fundamental Christian truths, and were denounced as irredeemable sins. Practically, it has been demonstrated how a belief in a providential God, coupled with relatively conventional theology, rendered seemingly innocuous plays and facile passages blasphemous and thus a tangible threat to the whole nation.

This chapter has shown how the meaning of art can be construed from an exclusively religious point of view. As a result, we should perhaps be more ready to acknowledge that for those who believe in a providential God and active devils, philosophical theories of representation and/or political rights of freedom of expression pale into insignificance. A strong belief in providentialism is certainly in evidence in many countries throughout the world and we need only look to the Evangelical Christian lobby in the USA or the Islamic regime under President Mahmoud Ahmadinejad in Iran to see the vitality and influence of such beliefs. To assume that all charges of blasphemy against art are limited to notions of offensiveness between human agents, even within the West, significantly limits our understanding of how profoundly religious individuals and societies conceive of the world they live in. To devout believers defending the sacred is a matter of life and death.

Endnotes

[1] T.C. Curtis and W.A. Speck, 1976, 'The Societies for the Reformation of Manners: a case study in the theory and practice of moral reform', *Literature and History*, vol. 3, no. 1, pp. 45-64, at p. 49. I would like to thank my supervisor, Mark Goldie, for his comments and advice throughout the writing of this paper. I am also grateful for the travel grants given to me by the Arts and Humanities Research Council and Clare College, University of Cambridge, which enabled me to attend the 'Blasphemy and Sacrilege in the Arts' conference.

[2] For a valuable introduction to the development of this form of blasphemy see: David Nash, 1999, *Blasphemy in Modern Britain 1789 to the Present*, Aldershot: Ashgate.

[3] I would suggest that the Salman Rushdie affair, for example, has introduced significant challenges to a constructive debate of blasphemy.

[4] 9 & 10 Guill. III. c. 32.

[5] *Journal of the House of Lords*, vol. XVI, p. 175: opening of the ninth session of Parliament, December 3, 1697.

[6] John Spurr, 'Virtue, Religion and Government': the Anglican Uses of Providence' in Tim Harris; Paul Seaward and Mark Goldie (eds) 1990, *The Politics of Religion in Restoration England*, Oxford: Blackwell, pp. 29-47.

[7] John Edwards, 1705, *The preacher discourse shewing what are the particular offices and employments of those of that character in the Church*, (part 1), London. p. 100.

[8] I would suggest that fundamental similarities between the mechanisms employed by the theatre and church provide a significant sub-plot to the whole controversy which has yet to be acknowledged by scholars. For an introduction to some of the main themes from another period, see Bryan Crockett, 1995, *The Play of Paradox: Stage and Sermon in Renaissance England* , Philadelphia, PA: University of Pennsylvania Press.

[9] This view is implicit in another contemporary argument that the theatre glorified vice and downplayed virtue. See John Dunton, *The Athenian Mercury*, vol. 6, no. 17 (22 March 1692); vol. 8, no. 25 (22 Nov. 1692); vol. 12, no. 7 (14 Nov. 1693).

[10] For an excellent and seemingly ignored study of Collier's life and work see E.A. Ewan, 1961, 'A Study of the Works of Jeremy Collier' (D.Phil thesis, Oxford University). A short view went through four editions in the first eighteen months and evoked about twenty replies in the same period, see Robert D. Hume, 1999, 'Jeremy Collier and the Future of the London Theatre in 1698', *Studies in Philology*, vol. 96, no. 4, pp. 480-511, p. 495.

[11] Sybil Rosenfeld, 1960, *The theatre of the London fairs in the 18th century*, Cambridge: Cambridge University Press.

[12] Jeremy Collier, *A short view* (London, 1698), unpaginated preface and contents pages.

[13] Richard Burridge, *A scourge for the play-houses: or the character of the English-stage* (London, 1702); Harold Love, 1980, 'Who were the Restoration Audience?', *The Yearbook of English Studies*, vol. 10, no. 1, pp. 21-44.

[14] Daniel Defoe, *The storm: or a collection of the most remarkable casualties and disasters which happen'd in the late dreadful tempest both by sea and land* (London, 1704).

[15] *The Tempest* was played on 1 December at the Lincoln's Inn Fields theatre, see: Emmett L. Avery (ed.) 1960, *The London Stage 1660-1800*, vol. 2, Carbondale, IL: Southern Illinois Press, pp. 49-50.

[16] Arthur Bedford, *The evil and danger of stage-plays* (Bristol, 1706), p. 81.

[17] Curtis and Speck, 'The Societies for the Reformation of Manners', p. 49.

[18] For example William Congreve, see Aubrey Williams, 1975, 'No Cloistered Virtue: Or, Playwright versus Priest in 1698', *Publications of the Modern Language Association*, vol. 90, no. 2, pp. 234-246.

[19] John Tillotson, *Fifteen sermons on several subjects*, (London, 1702), pp. 289-323.

[20] Tillotson, *Fifteen Sermons on several subjects*, p. 301.

[21] For Augustine, 'an evil will is the efficient cause of an evil deed', and so it may be suggested that an evil deed is evidence of an evil will. See Augustine, *The City of God*, XII, Ch. 6, translated by Philip Levine (London: Heinemann,1966), p. 25.

[22] Bedford, *The evil and danger of stage plays*, p. 188.

[23] Collier, *A short view*, p. 60.

24 The switching of vowels in words such as 'God' was a technique used by playwrights to avoid infringement of the 1605 Act 'for the preventing and avoiding of the great abuse of the holy name of God, in stage-plays' (3 Jac. I c. 21). It is curious to note that a similar technique is still employed today to circumvent censure, for example in the British television sitcom *Father Ted*, the word 'fuck' is replaced with 'feck' to allow for a pre-watershed broadcast.

25 [Jeremy Collier], Mr. Collier's dissuasive from the play-house; in a letter to a person of quality, occasion'd by the late calamity of the tempest (London, 1704), p. 16. For the offending passage in the play, see Sir William D'Avenant, *Macbeth a tragedy with all the alterations, amendments, additions and new songs* (London, 1695), p. 20.

26 Due to his religious convictions Collier never actually attended a theatre.

27 John Dryden and Sir William D'Avenant, *The Tempest, or the enchanted Island* (London, 1670); Thomas Duffett, *The Mock-Tempest: or the enchanted castle* (London, 1675). For further details on the content and significance of these adaptations see Montague Summers, 1922, *Shakespeare adaptations: the tempest, the mock tempest*, and *King Lear*, London: J. Cape, Introduction; Christine Dymkowski (ed.) 2000, *The Tempest*, Cambridge: Cambridge University Press; Sandra Clark (ed.) 1997, *Shakespeare made fit, London*: Dent, pp. xli-lxxviii;

28 William [Talbot], *A Sermon preach'd before the Lords spiritual and Temporal in Parliament assembled, in the Abbey-Church of Westminster, on Wednesday, Jan. 19. 1703/4.* (London, 1704), p. 17.

29 Ibid.

30 [Collier], Mr Collier's dissuasive, op. cit., p. 6.

31 John Vanbrugh, *The Relapse* (1697), p. 19; cited in Collier, *Short view*, op. cit., p. 84.

32 Collier, op. cit., p. 84.

33 [John Vanbrugh], A *short vindication of the relapse and the provok'd wife, from immorality and prophaneness* (London, 1698), p. 25.

34 Michael Cordner, 2000, 'Playwright versus priest: profanity and the wit of Restoration comedy', in Deborah Payne Fisk (ed.), *The Cambridge Companion to English Restoration Theatre*, Cambridge: Cambridge University Press, p. 215.

35 William Sherlock, *A practical discourse concerning a future judgement* (2nd edn. London, 1692), pp. 14-65.

36 Collier, op. cit., pp. 196-197.

37 Thomas D'Urfey, *The comical history of Don Quixote*, (London, 1694), part 1, p. 20; cited in, Collier, op. cit., pp. 196-197.

38 2 Samuel 12:14 and Ezekiel 35:12-15.

39 Sir William D'Avenant, *Macbeth, a tragedy. With alterations, additions, and new songs* (London, 1674).

40 G.R. Elliott, 1958, *Dramatic providence in Macbeth: a study of Shakespeare's tragic theme of humanity and grace*, Princeton, NJ: Princeton University Press.

41 Tutchin, *The Observator*, vol. 2, no. 77 (29 Dec/1 Jan 1704).

42 Tertullian, *De Spectaculis, XXVI*; T.R. Glover (trans.) 1966 , London: Heinemann, p. 291.

43 Vanbrugh, *The confederacy* (1706), p. 29; cited in, Bedford, *The evil and danger of stage-plays*, p. 40.

44 Bedford, *The evil and danger of stage-plays*, ibid., p. 40.

45 Ibid., p. 27.

46 Also see, Mark 3:28-30 & Luke 12:10.

47 Aquinas, *Summa Theologica* 2ae XIII.

48 Collier, *A short view* , op. cit., p. 96.

49 [Collier], *Mr Collier's dissuasive*, op. cit., p. 15.

50 Philip C. Almond, 1994, *Heaven and Hell in Enlightenment England*, Cambridge: Cambridge University Press, pp. 86-87.

51 Tutchin, *The Observator*, vol. 2, no. 31 (21-24 July 1703).

52 John Dryden, *Amphitryon: or the two Sosia's* (London, 1690). For details of the play and Dryden's adaptation in particular, see Örjan Lindberger, 1956, *The Transformations of Amphitryon*, Stockholm: Almqvist and Wiksell, pp. 90-120.

53 Collier, *A short view*, op. cit., p. 183.

54 Ibid.

55 Tertullian, *De Spectaculus*, X, cited in Collier, *A short view* (1698), p. 255. Also see William Bisset at St. Mary-le-Bow, 27 March 1704, p. 57.

56 Vanbrugh, *The Provok'd wife* (1697), p. 77; cited in, Tutchin, *The Observator*, vol. 2, no. 78 (1-5 January 1704).

57 John Corny, *The metamorphosis: or, the old lover out-witted* (London, 1704), p. 14; cited in, Tutchin, *The Observator*, vol. 4, no. 46 (5-8 September 1705).

58 [Anon.], *Roving husband reclaim'd* (London, 1706), p. 8; cited in, Bedford, *The evil and danger of stage-plays*, p. 41.

59 Richard Brome, *The northern lass* (1684), p. 5; cited in, Bedford, *The evil and danger of stage-plays*, p. 41.

60 Bedford, *The evil and danger of stage-plays*, p. 41.

61 Justin Champion, 1992, *The pillars of priestcraft shaken: the Church of England and its enemies, 1660-1730*, Cambridge: Cambridge University Press, pp. 6-7.

62 I have endeavoured to sketch only the most basic outline of the contemporary debate necessary to sustain my argument.

63 Tina Beth Isaacs, 1979, 'Moral crime, moral reform, and the state in early eighteenth century England: a study of piety and politics', PhD thesis, University of Rochester, NY.

64 There is no evidence to suggest that the theatres, playwrights or actors suffered legal censure for blasphemy. However, there were a few instances where actors were prosecuted for lower level profanity and licentious behaviour. For an authoritative account of these cases, see: Joseph Wood Krutch, 1924, *Comedy and Conscience after the Restoration*, New York: Columbia University Press, pp. 167-178.

65 For 'Devil's chapel' see: Tutchin, *The Observator*, vol. 2, no. 77 (December 29-January 1, 1704); for 'Devil's Engine' see, Defoe, *A Review*, vol. 3, no. 95 (8 Aug. 1706); for 'Devil's shop' see, endnote 53.

66 Daniel Defoe, *A Review*, vol. 2, no. 26 (May 3, 1705).

67 Ibid.

68 William Congreve, *Amendments of Mr. Collier's False and Imperfect Citations* (London, 1698), pp. 4-5.

3

Madonna and piano accordion: Disrupting the order of the world[1]

Elizabeth Burns Coleman

In 1997, a poster depicting an icon of the Madonna playing a piano accordion was produced to promote the Adelaide Arts Festival. The Madonna was depicted enthroned against a background that was recognisably of the park that extends from the Adelaide Arts Centre to the Torrens River, with one of the major cathedrals in the background. She was surrounded by outlines of gods from other religions, including Buddha, Ganesh, and an Aboriginal Wandjina. The style of presentation was recognisably Middle Eastern, a point emphasised by the gold mosaic frame, and the 'Greek' lettering of the announcement of the event and its main sponsor, Telstra. It appeared, by all publicity standards, to be a fantastic poster. It was beautiful, and it was rich with connotative association that made it appropriate for the festival. Adelaide is known as 'The city of churches', so the poster was very specifically appropriate to the Adelaide arts festival, as opposed to an arts festival in some other place. A third feature of the poster that made it so good was that the image of the Madonna with an accordion is inclusive of what may be considered a form of high art as well as popular culture. Moreover, the image was inclusive of different religious and community groups and the art of different cultures and, as such, reflected and celebrated a multicultural recognition of the value of the arts across different cultures. However, within weeks, the poster was withdrawn from circulation by the Festival organisation because the Greek Orthodox Church had complained it was an inappropriate and offensive use of one of their icons.

Since 1978, the Zuni people of Mexico have been demanding the repatriation of their war gods, or Ahauutas, from museums around the world, including the Smithsonian. Their case involves two issues: first, in Zuni eyes the Ahauutas are communal property and by definition, it is claimed, consider their ownership by museums not ownership but theft. The second issue is one that concerns us here. According to James Clifford, 'Zuni vehemently object to the display of these figures (terrifying and of great sacred force) as "art". They are the only traditional objects singled out for this objection'.[2] This same kind of issue may arise in relation to the display of replicas of sacred objects. In 1975, an ethnologist at the National Museum of Canada wrote to the director suggesting the removal of Iroquoian false face masks on the basis that 'The Iroquois consider the masks highly sacred and even "dangerous" objects that should be viewed only at the time of curing rituals'.[3] The masks were removed five years later, but a proposal to replace them with fibreglass casts of the original was objected to by the Grand Council of Hodenosaunee (or Iroquois Confederacy). The Council denied the existence of a distinction between ritually and commercially carved masks and forbade the exhibition of any masks. It also forbade all forms of reproduction, and the distribution of any information about them.[4]

Both the poster and the display of indigenous artefacts appear to be completely innocuous. The poster did not defile, ridicule or attack Mary or the Church, and the display of the Zuni war god, and the Iroquois false face masks, was simply that — their display. So the objections expressed by the Orthodox Church and the Zuni are mysterious. It is hard to understand why they are objecting, let alone why we might care about their objections. Both cases challenge important values we hold. One case confronts the value of freedom of expression. The second confronts the value of knowledge and the practice of collection for the purposes of study, public education and aesthetic appreciation.

I will argue these two cases are similar, and that this similarity shares features in common with blasphemy, despite the fact that it is not obvious that either of these cases are instances of blasphemy. The attempt to understand what is 'wrong', that is, to grasp what appears to be mysterious in both these cases, will provide us with a better understanding of blasphemy. The structure of this chapter will be as follows. In the first part, I address the idea that these cases are dissimilar, because they involve a symbol on the one hand, and an object on the other. I argue that there is no clear distinction between an object and a symbol. I will also address the concern that the intention to blaspheme, or to offend, is a necessary element of blasphemy. In the third part of the chapter I will draw out some of the important features of these icons and beliefs about their connection to the order of the universe in order to show how we might understand these cases to be connected to each other, and to blasphemy.

Definitions of blasphemy

In contrast to the delicacy with which the Adelaide Arts Festival treated Orthodox sensibilities in relation to the poster including an image of the Virgin Mary, the National Gallery of Victoria displayed no such misgivings about the display of Andres Serrano's controversial photograph, *Piss Christ,* which showed an image of a crucifix immersed in the artist's urine, as part of the Melbourne City Festival in 1998. This image might be considered paradigmatic as a case of blasphemy. Various Christian churches sought the removal of the image from public display, and after the negotiations with the gallery and government proved fruitless, the Catholic Archbishop sought a legal injunction against the gallery displaying the image, on the grounds that it was blasphemous, indecent and obscene at law.

According to Anthony Fisher and Hayden Ramsey, the Archbishop's action was supported by the leaders of other Christian churches, as well as the Jewish and Muslim communities.[5]

Justice Harper of the Supreme Court of Victoria commented in his refusal of the application for the injunction that the photograph 'of itself' might be seen as 'inoffensive',[6] on the grounds that it was beautiful, and showed the crucified Christ in a golden light; the knowledge that the image was created by immersing a crucifix in urine is clearly connected to sacrilege. Sacrilege is the violation of sacred things, and blasphemy, according to Fisher and Ramsey, may be defined as speaking against God or the sacred or ridiculing things consecrated to God or held sacred.[7] However, as Fisher and Ramsey point out: 'most sacrileges do imply blasphemy in the narrower sense of ridiculing the sacred'.[8] Yet, it might be argued, a plastic crucifix is not a sacred object, at least in any legalist theological sense. A plastic crucifix has not been dedicated or consecrated, or, as is done with church bells, baptised. But a plastic crucifix is a symbol; it represents the sacred. Hence, we should not think that there is a clear distinction between the use of an object, and the use of a symbol.

However, these 'innocuous' cases do not appear to be cases of blasphemy, because there does not seem to be any involvement of a deliberate offence. Deliberate offence, that is, intentional offence, is intrinsic to some definitions of blasphemy. For instance, Roy Perret defines blasphemy as 'an illocutionary act which is a function of the agent's complex intention. In the case of a blasphemous speech act, the speaker intends that the hearer should come to believe something through the recognition of the speaker's intention that the hearer do this'.[9] Perret supports this intentional interpretation of blasphemy as theologically correct with a quotation from Thomas Aquinas' *Summa Theologica:*

> ...a man failing to advert to the blasphemous nature of his words, and this may happen through his being moved suddenly by his passion so as to break out into words suggested by his imagination, without heeding to the meaning of the words: this is a venial sin, and is not blasphemy so called. (*Summa Theologica* II,ii,13)

This definition suggests that neither kind of case I mentioned, of the display of the Zuni war gods or of the use of the icon, could be considered cases of blasphemy. Neither obviously involves the intention to offend, or a propositional content that the speaker intended the hearer to come to believe.

The *Piss Christ* example is much more clearly a case of blasphemy than the cases I described in the introduction to my chapter because it appears to involve intention. It is also interesting that apologists for Serrano, and Serrano himself, appealed to the artist's intention in order to argue that it was not blasphemous. Fisher and Ramsay reported that, as the scandal progressed, the artist repudiated his earlier claim that his art is simply colourful and deliberately shocking, and asserted that, instead of intending to scandalise, 'his goal all along had been to increase the devotion of his fellow Christians by helping them identify better with Christ in his pain, suffering an humiliation'.[10]

In contrast to the definition of blasphemy in terms of intentional offence, Frank J. Hoffman understands blasphemy to be a family of concepts that may be explicated by determining what the religious points are in each case, and determining what social practices exist for homage and desecration in each case.[11] Hoffman's culturally relative account is consistent with Fisher and Ramsay's position that objects symbolising mysteries 'can only be understood in the context of the religious culture and history of practice from which they emerge'.[12] Hoffman argues, against Perret, that there is no single perspective from which to define blasphemy. He points out that blasphemy, like obscenity, is often dependent partly on the attitude of the hearer or recipient. He illustrates this point with an 'amusing' story:

> Suppose, for example, that there is a pet parrot who is capable of uttering a perverse litany impugning the religious focal points of the 'great religions' of the world. Now, just as the parrot has completed impugning the God of Christianity along with the rest, Aunt Millie, being a frightfully devout (and easily scandalised) Christian lady, indignantly rushes in from the kitchen with the carving knife, ready to lop off the poor parrot's head. Feathers fly, and in the wink of an eye, the badly mangled parrot has sung his (black) swan-song. Aunt Millie is unlikely to be repentant at the thought that the parrot did not *intend* to blaspheme.[13]

Despite this unpleasant picture of the people who make claims that something is blasphemous as the kind of people who would kill parrots, it does seem arbitrary to insist on a strictly intentional definition of blasphemy, supported by an appeal to religious authority. Given that we are dealing with a phenomenon of offence that has broad agreement across different religions, and is of concern in relation to political issues such as how we should relate to other people's religious beliefs in a multicultural society, we require a less culturally specific, and less religiously specific, definition than the intentional account given by Perret.

But even if intention should not appear as part of the definition of blasphemy, Aunt Millie's lack of appreciation of the parrot's lack of intent is also significant. If intention matters, it may not be the case that it defines *whether* something was blasphemous, but the level of culpability. We might appeal to the doctrine of double effect: it might be thought that the blasphemy might be permissible, or at least more acceptable, if the blasphemy is the 'unintended side effect' of a good intention, such as the liberation of mixed up human beings from the tyranny of apostles of purity, or the education of the general population of the suffering of Christ. In suggesting this use of the doctrine of double effect, I suggest that intention may play a different role from that argued by Perret. Rather than a definition of the act, intention may play a role in our understanding of the moral significance of the act. Similarly, while thinking killing someone is wrong *prima facie*, we distinguish between different acts on the basis of the killer's intention. For instance, we distinguish between calculated murder, crimes of passion, manslaughter, reckless disregard of other people's safety, killing in war, and justifiable self defence. These distinctions rely at least in part on the intentions of the killer. Similarly, in cases of blasphemy, we may refer to cases where we think it justified (such as the exposure of hypocrisy in the Church, or the exploration of sincere, but heretical, belief) and 'gratuitous' acts of offensive behaviour.[14]

Fisher and Ramsay appear to agree with Hoffman that the cultural context within which the objects are created provides conventional and appropriate responses for how artists may depict certain images, and for what may count as blasphemy. Their argument that Serrano's *Piss Christ* is unacceptable depends on a conventional account of what it means to immerse a crucifix in urine. It 'can only be a profanation according to the standards of the culture and religion of which it is an artefact, and photographing it and displaying such a deed can only be a blasphemy in that culture'.[15]

This may be made as a stronger, universal claim about defilement. In her classic text *Purity and Danger*, Mary Douglas makes some general, and widely accepted as important, observations about the nature of defilement and its relation to the manner in which we comprehend the world, and organise our societies.[16] However, the attempt to maintain purity and to avoid defilement should not be seen as a desire that is necessarily totalitarian or fundamentalist. It is something that is part of everyday consciousness. Dirt, she claims, is matter out of place. The coffee in my cup is clean, but if I spill it on clothes, I am dirty. According to Douglas, 'dirt is essentially disorder…Eliminating it is not a negative movement, but a positive effort to organise the environment'.[17] And she claims that this is not only true of Western secular societies:

> If this is so with our separating, tidying and purifying, we should interpret primitive purification and prophylaxis in the same light…rituals of purity and impurity create unity in experience. So far from being aberrations from the central project of religion, they are positive contributions to atonement. By their means, symbolic patterns are worked out and publicly displayed. Within these patterns disparate elements are related and disparate experience is given meaning.[18]

According to Douglas, the categorisation of purity and danger is a major structuring organisation of our society — representing social hierarchy, differentiating between groups within and between societies and cultures, but also of structuring our relationship with other people in our societies — and extends beyond human life to the order of the cosmos. We fit into a broader pattern of relationships. Keeping the purity rules therefore maintains a pattern or order to the world. If Douglas is correct, the concept of defilement and purity will be central to all societies, as well as all religions.

In summary, it appears that blasphemy is connected to sacrilege, as what we do with objects, and how we represent them may both involve defilement. The idea of defilement is cross-cultural, and not merely associated with fundamentalist or totalitarian religions. Our intentions do not define whether something is blasphemous, as what counts as the defilement of an object or symbol is dependent on socially agreed norms. It is still not clear, however, that the Madonna and piano accordion is an act of defilement, or that the display of a Zuni god is an example of such contempt. This is what makes them such interesting cases. There is nothing clearly offensive about them. In order to explore what is wrong with such acts, or at least what is perceived to be wrong about such acts, I explore the cognitive content involved in recognising certain kinds of symbols.

Rules of depiction and the order of the world

The connection between how we may represent a symbol, and how we should respond to one, are linked in Christian tradition. To explain this connection, let me first address the depiction of Mary, and how she may be depicted in icons. Then let me turn to how she is used within religious worship.

Mary holds a special place within Greek Orthodox worship. She was *Theotokos*. The title, *Theotokos,* does not simply mean 'Mother of God', but more precisely 'the one who gave birth to the One who is God'.[19] According to John of Damascus, 'The name [*Theotokos*] in truth signifies the one subsistence and the two natures and the modes of generation of our Lord Jesus Christ'.[20] As 'the one who gave birth to the One who is God', she is represented not only as human, but also as divine.[21] Within the Western Church, Mary was not considered divine, but as being conferred a special grace by God: she was free from original sin.[22]

As *Theotokos*, Mary, as well as her icon, was the legitimate subject of Orthodox veneration, but under challenge from iconoclasts, the nature of this veneration needed clarification. Because of her status, Mary has a special place in the distinction between the adoration, *latreia*, which was reserved for God, and reverence, *douleia*. Thomas Aquinas thought this distinction did not do full justice to the special position of the *Theotokos:* she was less than God, but more than an ordinary human being and more than any saint; therefore, she was not entitled to *lateria,* but she was entitled to more than *dulia.* She was entitled to *hyerdulia.* [23]

While many contemporary artists may consider the signifier as distinct from the signified, that is, the mental concept may be considered distinct from the material aspect in which it is represented, no similar distinction is made in relation to icons in the Orthodox tradition. Within the Orthodox tradition, the arbitrary nature of the relationship between icon as a symbol and what it represents is denied. In the icon, the image and the idea are inseparable.[24] George Galavaris writes,

> Based on Neo-Platonic theories, the icon is thought basically a mystery, a vehicle for divine power and grace, a means of God's knowledge. It is not merely a symbol of the archetype, but the represented becomes present through the icon. The Council of Nicea of 787 declared that at the adoration of the icon of Christ the faithful should say, 'this is Christ the Son of God'...The icon participates in the holiness of the represented.[25]

Accordingly, the honour displayed to the icon is not directed toward the material object, but to what it represents. It seems that by exploring Platonic ideas we might understand one way in which an image may be understood as a means of spiritual knowledge, and how an image may be considered to participate in a supernatural world.

Plato's understanding of art rests on idealistic assumptions that are first outlined by the Pythagoreans. According to Liberato Santoro-Brienza, for the Pythagoreans, art is a 'therapy of the soul and the body, as a path to attunement with the secret harmony of the universe, and as a key to decode the order of reality'.[26] The Pythagoreans believed that the entire universe is ruled by mathematical laws and the connection between the cosmic order, numerical proportions and musical harmony provided a conception of beauty in terms of order, measure, proportion and harmony.[27] Similarly, for Plato, the ground of reality is presupposed by any human activity, and guides artistic activity. Empirical reality is a copy of the true reality that is constituted by perfect forms, and the artist imitates empirical reality.[28] It follows from this that the arts are inevitably deceptive, as they are twice removed from reality, yet the artist may also be elevated, by inspiration, into the realms of divine harmony.[29]

Philosophers of the Middle Ages developed and elaborated on Greek philosophy, but abandoned the Platonic assumption that art is fundamentally mimetic of empirical reality. Plotinus wrote: 'The arts do not simply copy visible objects, but reach out to principles of nature; the arts provide much themselves, for they can add where there is deficiency; they can do so since in themselves they possess beauty'.[30] Art, on this understanding, is superior to nature. God was thought of as the supreme artist: the whole cosmos is a work of art, and the artist was conceived of as a kind of creator, emulating God's activity. The artist's task was to transform matter into form, and nature into spirit: it was the spiritualisation of matter.[31] The arts, therefore, have a cognitive, rather than expressive, character; they involve the recognition and recreation of divine order, and art works also enable others to understand the world, as artists produce tokens and symbols of divine perfection.[32]

From this discussion of Medieval conceptions of beauty, Santoro-Brienza reconstructs a picture of what is involved in the experience of beautiful things:

> In the presence of beauty, our senses perceive sensory properties that stimulate and gratify the sensory functions. Furthermore, in their immediate apprehension of physical properties, the sensory experiences lead to an intellectual insight into the structure, order, and form of the object, so that the intellect is, in turn, stimulated and gratified by an intuitive grasp of the form... In the harmonious correspondence of the object to all our faculties and, in turn, all our faculties to the object, our senses, intellect, our will are satisfied and result in a condition of delight...The aesthetic experience is, in other words, a harmonious and unifying experience of immediate and intuitive fusion in which subject and object cannot be separated and distinguished. That experience is akin to the experience of love, both physical and spiritual, and of deep reflection, prayer, and the anticipated beatific vision.[33]

In the experience of an image, therefore, we may participate in the nature of the universe and experience unity with it.

In Medieval thought, everything participates, in various degrees, with the perfection of being and, because of this, the different entities share a fundamental trait or a kind of unity. Santoro-Brienza states: 'It is in the light of this principle that we fully understand the Medieval preoccupation with symbolism in general and the conviction that everything is linked to everything else...being in general is one, true good.'[34] However, the Platonic idea that the arts could be deceptive, and fail in this task of spiritualising matter, remained important. Augustine argued that works of art must be partially false insofar as they are the result of imaginative fiction.[35] There is a dual moral aspect to artistic production. Beauty may align the will and the intellect in desire for and recognition of the form, but it may also mislead. Symbols, therefore, must be reproduced correctly, as they have a devotional purpose.

Within the Greek Orthodox tradition, the liturgical arts are one of the ways in which man becomes divine by grace, and the icon is one of these arts. The prototype of the image belongs to the corrupt world, but its transcendental quality can be expressed by the fixation of the type from all that is ephemeral. 'This', Galavaris states,

> is why icons cannot be painted according to the imagination of the artists or a living model. The relationship between the prototype and the image would have been lost. For this reason the icon-painter uses manuals…which describe the iconographic scenes and colours to be used. But the use of manuals alone does not guarantee the painting of the sacred image. The painter must himself be "illuminated".[36]

In the *Painter's Manual*, Dionysius of Fourna tells his pupils that they must not 'carry out this work haphazardly, but with the fear of God and with the veneration due to a sacred task'.[37] The technical skill is only part of this task, as the icon painter is engaged in a work that externalises spiritual reality. The true iconographer is engaged in a work of prayer, so that what he creates stems both from holy tradition and the artist's own experience of the work of grace.[38]

The painting of an icon, therefore, may be seen as a form of meditation, and the manifestation of 'the other' that that subject 'participates in', or makes manifest. Its contemplation is a means of revelation, and provides a means for an audience to engage with this other. The icon used for the poster of the Adelaide Arts Festival is obviously of Mary. I believe that one may safely assume that the painter of the Madonna with a piano accordion was not using a manual. Moreover, I assume that the painter of the Madonna with a piano accordion was not illuminated, let alone offering each stroke of the brush in prayer. The Madonna is out of context — the syntax of the painting is wrong. She is generalised, a symbol of a religious art form among other symbols of religious art. She does not require veneration; she is one among many religious figures. Given this context, we may understand why this image may be considered to be connected to blasphemy, as blasphemy is connected to honour due to the divine or sacred, and the poster subverts or misrepresents what the Greek Orthodox Church takes to be the nature of the icon, and of Mary.

But can we, through this discussion, also understand a religious tradition that is alien to us, such as the Zuni reaction to the display of their war god? There are obvious, and serious, difficulties. One is that the entire Platonic tradition of associating beauty and art is dissimilar to many indigenous conceptions of beauty, and the role of beauty in the production of indigenous artefacts. The anthropological evidence from other cultures, and common sense, should stop us from generalising across cultures on the role of aesthetic experience here.

Yet there are some aspects of many indigenous claims and Platonic thought about the metaphysical nature of representations that appear to be similar. One is the association of the object with what it represents in such a way that it makes little sense to say that something is 'a representation'. For instance, I have heard it said that when Maori see images of the ancestors, they do not view or respond to the image as a representation, but respond to the image by greeting the ancestors. The idea that the image and what is represented, or the concept and image, cannot be separated appears to be common to many indigenous concepts of religious objects and to Orthodox understandings of icons. I do not mean to imply that Greek Orthodox metaphysics of symbols are the same as indigenous ones (the Eastern metaphysics of icons is not even the same as the metaphysics of the Western Christian church); rather, my point is that the Orthodox and some indigenous metaphysics of symbols may be *contrasted* to an understanding of a symbol as a 'mere' symbol. Another aspect of this similarity that appears highly significant in the current discussion is the normative aspects of behaviour that follow from the metaphysical aspects of the symbol, as religious traditions involve norms about how an object may be treated, as well as how it may be produced.

There are norms of behaviour for relating to religious objects, and these norms express the relationship we have with them. For instance, the icon does not merely represent Mary; the image and the idea are considered inseparable. Because of this metaphysical relationship, the honour that is due to the icon is *hyerdulia*. The acknowledgment within a ritual or religious context is physical. A priest may kiss the icon in recognition. People light candles to the Virgin, cross themselves and genuflect. Similarly, there are norms of remorse in response to blasphemy: the tearing and rending of garments.[39] Again we find there are norms of responses to indigenous religious objects. The Maori may greet certain objects. Other objects, such as the false face masks of the Iroquios, should not be viewed except within certain contexts.

The norms of acknowledgment are not empty gestures, but are elements of cognition and classification. Nelson Goodman calls these gestures labels. He writes: 'Nods of agreement or dissent, salutes, bows, pointings, serve as labels… The same is true of such activities in response to music as foot- and finger-tappings, head-boppings, and various other motions. That these are called forth by the music, while the conductor's gestures call it forth, does not affect their status as labels; for labels may be used to record or to prescribe — "strawberry", "raspberry", "lemon", and "lime" may tell us what *is* in or what *to put* in the several containers.'[40] The significance of our responses to music, Goodman thinks, is their role in analysing, organising and registering what we hear.[41]

This relationship between action and concept formation is also held by philosophers who are opposed to a rationalistic understanding of language. D. Z. Phillips draws this point out in his discussion of Wittgenstein and religious observance. I will come back to a discussion of religious observance shortly; for the present I wish to focus on the connection between action and categorisation. According to Wittgenstein, religion is a language game, and its basis is not in conceptual understanding but in our responses to certain symbols and sensory experiences. For Wittgenstein, 'primitive reactions', that is, our reactions to pain, colours or sounds, are fundamental to language development. The reactions of jumping with fright, calling colours light or dark or sounds loud or soft, crying out in pain or expressing shock at the pain of others are fundamental to the development of concepts. Wittgenstein wrote: 'The origin and the primitive form of the language-game is a reaction; only from this can the more complicated forms grow. Language…is a refinement; "in the beginning was the deed".[42]

Douglas's account of dirt avoidance similarly links sensory impression and the recognition of categories that are expressed in labelling gestures, and explains the process by which those categories are developed and are involved in the recognition of value. Douglas states: 'perceiving is not a matter of passively allowing an organ — say of sight or hearing — to receive a ready-made impression from without…As perceivers we select from all the stimuli falling on our senses only those which interest us, and our interests are governed by a pattern-making tendency, sometimes called *schema*…'.[43] These schemas are learned, first as response, and then named. These names act as labels. Douglas writes: 'Their names then affect the way [sensory impressions] are perceived next time: once labelled they are more speedily slotted into pigeon-holes in future.'[44] Dirt provides an example of how these categories are ordered into a normative pattern of schema. Dirt is a residual category, that which is rejected from our pattern or scheme of classifications — it is out of place.

There is a broader generalisation that may be drawn from these observations that actions are cognitive labels. If actions are cognitive labels, then in making certain physical responses to religious images we are classifying or categorising them. But in failing to respond, we may be failing to categorise or to acknowledge the honour that is due to something as well. Let me give you an example of a non-religious, conventional response to emphasise this point about the withholding of a gesture as a display of a lack of respect. After a musical performance, it is conventionally accepted that clapping hands is an appropriate form of acknowledgment of the performers' skill. Withholding this gesture, or clapping weakly, is a way of expressing dislike. For the performer, a lack of applause must be devastating.

The difference between this kind of labelling of music and the conventional ways in which we pay respect to something and the form of ritualistic response that can be seen in acts of devotion, is that in acts of devotion we also recognise a hierarchy of value and the relationship between the object and observer. Ritualistic or normative responses are not merely the recognition and classification of icons and other religious subjects; they acknowledge a relationship between ourselves and what we have classified or recognised through the gesture, and to withhold the gesture may be considered a form of disrespect, or a failure to apprehend its meaning. The Zuni demand their war gods returned because they should not be looked at. Clifford tells us that they are considered terrifying images of great power; as is appropriate to an image of war. Moreover, we can imagine that the properties used to present these gods exemplify the terror of war. It is not surprising to find people averting their gaze at certain horrors, or thinking it would be inappropriate to look upon certain things, such as the horror of war, with the same disinterested appreciation with which they gaze at art.

Even if gazing upon objects such as sacred masks was 'an appropriate' response, indigenous groups might well resent their display. The Grand Council of Hodenosaunee for instance, has a policy of forbidding the display of medicine masks that makes a connection between respect for the masks, and the well-being of the community. The policy states:

> The exhibition of masks by museums does not serve to enlighten the public regarding the culture of Hodenesaunee, as such an exhibition violates the intended purpose of the mask and contributes to the desecration of the sacred image.[45]

A claim about the relationship between the 'order' of communities and the treatment of the objects is made explicit. Ruth Phillips reports: 'The statement requests the return of masks to the 'proper caretakers among the Hodenosaunee' because 'it is only through these actions that the traditional culture will remain strong and peace be restored to our communities'.[46]

This involves a further element of these rules about how we represent, and acknowledge images or objects that is important in respect to how we comprehend what might be wrong with the failure to show respect, at least from the believer's perspective. This may concern the role of such acts in upholding or maintaining the order of the universe. Douglas refers to this as a primitive world view, but it might also be thought of in terms of God's providence. This perspective seems alien to contemporary, secular scholars, and is thought to be based on mistaken beliefs about the metaphysical relationship between humans and the world in which they live, and the nature of causation. However, as I will argue in the next section, we need not accept either belief, and yet still behave in certain ways that acknowledge respect for certain kinds of representations.

The order of the universe

Douglas characterises what she calls 'the primitive world view' as a man-centred universe: 'A primitive world view looks out on a universe which is personal in several different senses. Physical forces are thought of as interwoven with the lives of persons. Things are not completely distinguished from persons and persons are not completely distinguished from their physical environment. The universe...discerns the social order and intervenes to uphold it'.[47] This is because the transforming energy of the universe is 'threaded onto the lives of individuals so that nothing happens in the way of storms, sickness, blights or droughts except in virtue of these personal links'.[48] The universe is capable of discerning disorder in social relations and social codes, such as whether partners in sexual relationships are related within prohibited degrees, or whether a person has murdered a fellow tribesman or a stranger, and an individual's hidden emotions.[49] There is a connection between the individual and the world in terms of an order in the world, but this order needs to be maintained. It requires maintenance through the maintenance of purity rules, but also in terms of the structure of relationships.

Such ideas are also found in the history of Western religious thought. We find a similar pattern of thought expressed in the speech Shakespeare gives Ulysses in *Troilus and Cressida*. The order of the universe includes the orbits of the planets to the season to the offices and custom of societies. When this becomes unbalanced, and when things are not in their order, chaos and calamity follow. What maintains the cosmic order for the Elizabethan is the recognition of degree or value, and the maintenance of social order. Each person and thing has its place, and its place must be recognised and acknowledged.[50]

It would be tempting for a non-believer to interpret the need to maintain order as simply a false understanding of the nature of the universe and of the causal relations in it. In particular, it might be thought, the causal understanding of the relationship between failing to show respect to a symbol and social or natural calamity is false. But, we need not think that a belief in a simple causal relationship is at work here, and this may be the wrong way to understand the nature of religious beliefs and gestures of acknowledgment.

Phillips thinks that we do not need to believe in the order of reality as a chain of being, or to hold a particular metaphysical idea about pictures, to think we would be concerned about doing certain things to images. He agrees with Searle that one of the most powerful aspect's of Wittgenstein's *On Certainty* is its attack on the philosophical tradition 'according to which all our meaningful activities must be the product of some inner theory...Wittgenstein points out that for a great deal of our behaviour, we just do it'.[51] The explanations should be considered not to be theories explicitly held, but as means of explicating what is believed after the act has taken place.

He supports this with an empirical experiment, inspired by the idea of 'acting out' a wish suggested by H. O. Mounce.[52] Mounce supposed that it would be hard for almost anyone to comply with a request that they stick pins into the eyes of a drawing of their mother; but supposing one did do it, and shortly after one's mother developed an affliction in the eye and was in danger of going blind, then it would be difficult to resist the feeling, if only momentarily, that there was some connection between the two events. Phillips tested this by asking a group of 40 students whether they would be prepared to stick pins in the eyes of a drawing of their mother, and whether, if their mother developed an affliction in the eye, they would feel guilt. Fifteen of the students said that they would have no difficulty sticking a pin in the eye of the drawing, and if their mother subsequently became ill, they would not feel guilt. Their explanation was that 'it was only a picture', and that there could be no causal connection between the two events. The remaining students said that they would not stick pins in the picture, but that if they did, they would feel guilt if their mother subsequently developed an affliction of the eye. But, Phillips suggests, the students who said this were not positing a causal connection when they said they would feel there was a connection between the two events: '[What] they meant was something like this: they felt that sticking pins in the picture reduces serious possibilities to a game; it plays around with things. When the affliction occurs, an internal relation between "playing around" and the event makes the guilt understandable.'[53] Phillips concludes from this that it is not the case that the students would refuse to stick pins in a drawing of their mother as a consequence of beliefs about the causal connections between the drawing and the outcome, but that a primitive moral response occurs and that people, if asked to reflect on their response, may reply this way.[54]

There must be some explanation of why most people would not stick pins into an image of their mother. Douglas's explanation of 'the primitive world view' in terms of explicit beliefs about an order of the world that needs to be maintained if chaos and misfortune are to be avoided is one way of understanding this connection. But the explanation does not address why Phillips's students would not stick pins in the eyes of a picture of their mother. Moreover, if Douglas's account of this world view could cover all responses to blasphemy, we would expect the primary response to blasphemy to be fear, rather than offence or distress.

Yet the fact that most people, and it seems even people without religious beliefs, would not stick pins into a drawing of their mother can be accounted for in terms of what people hold dear to them, and the respect in which they hold their mothers. This is consistent with Douglas's broader claim about the association between sensory impressions, schema, and values, and Goodman's general claims about our responses being a part of the process of cognition. In recognising something to be an image of 'our mother', we classify such images under a general concept that determines our relationship to it.

An icon of the Virgin Mary may similarly be treated with respect, simply because she is held dear. Non-religious people should not consider such sentiments to be alien to them. When a non-religious person tears up a photograph of a person they once loved, their act is one of anger and disrespect; when they refuse to stick pins in the eyes of an image of their mother, or would feel momentary guilt if something later happened to their mother, they also are refusing to treat images as 'mere pictures'. Similarly, we may turn away from representations of war in horror, even if we know they are fictional. Our responses to the image may be understood as recognition of the meaning or content of the image, its value, and an expression of our relationship with it.

Blasphemy and homage

My interest in this chapter has been to attempt to gain some kind of insight into what is 'wrong' with the seemingly innocent acts of depicting images without following the rules of their depiction, as in the image of a Madonna with a piano accordion, and of viewing depictions of gods and indigenous sacred objects within a museum context. I have attempted to provide as sympathetic account of these claims and of the religious symbols involved as possible. Because I am an atheist, I have not been concerned with an assessment of the truth or adequacy of these ideas, but with their explication, in an attempt to understand a different perspective. Nor has my objective been to provide a moral argument in support of or against claims that these acts are actually wrong. My objective has been to explore whether there is, as my initial intuition suggested, some similarity between seemingly very different acts, and blasphemy.

My conclusion is that the claims that objects should not be displayed in museums and that certain images are inappropriate are connected through the idea that neither act displays an appropriate act of homage or respect to what is represented by the object or symbol. This feature of homage is also central to the concept of blasphemy, if blasphemy is defined as showing contempt for God and religious matters through one's words, thoughts and actions. There is, of course, a difference between the acts of showing contempt of other people's beliefs or of particular beliefs and values, as may occur in intentional blasphemy, withholding acknowledgment (for example, refusing to applaud a performance), and failing to acknowledge because you do not 'understand' what something is. In this third case, absolutely 'nothing goes on' in our heads when we do not genuflect or acknowledge a religious meaning. There is no cognitive process. Just as a parrot may blaspheme without intent, a person may blaspheme without any recognition of value. Just as there are people who would kill a parrot for blaspheming, there are people who would stick pins into the image of their mother, and who cannot understand the perspective of people who would refuse to do this to an image of their mother. Their mistake is to treat images as 'mere' symbols.

Endnotes

[1] To Robert and John, with my thanks for their conversation, their warmth, and for sharing their ceremonies with me.

[2] James Clifford, 1988, *The Predicament of Culture: Twentieth-Century Ethnography, Literature and Art*, Cambridge (MA): Harvard University Press, p. 209.

[3] Memo from Michael K. Foster to Dr Barrie Reynolds, Chief Ethnologist, Canadian Ethnology Service, 10 March 1975, File E7-6R, Canadian Ethnology Service, Canadian Museum of Ethnography. Cited in Ruth B. Phillips, 2004, 'Disappearing Acts: Exposure, Enclosure, and Iroquois Masks', in M.S. Phillips and G. Schochet (eds.) *Questions of Tradition,* Toronto: University of Toronto Press, p. 74.

[4] Ibid., pp. 74-5.

[5] Anthony Fisher and Hayden Ramsey, 2000, 'Of Art and Blasphemy', *Ethical Theory and Moral Practice*, vol. 3, pp. 137-167, p. 138.

[6] Ibid., p. 155.

[7] Ibid., p. 139.

[8] Ibid., p. 139, note 3.

[9] Roy W. Perret, 1987, 'Blasphemy', *Sophia,* vol 26, no. 2, pp. 4-14, at p. 5.

[10] Fisher and Ramsay, op. cit., p. 156. One might question the veracity of this account of Serrano's on the basis that Fisher and Ramsay are at points quite sardonic about Serrano's artistic intentions.

[11] F. Hoffman, 1989, 'More on Blasphemy', *Sophia*, vol. 28, no. 2, pp. 26-35, at p. 30.

[12] Fisher and Ramsay, op. cit., p. 157.

[13] Ibid., p. 28.

[14] People may accept the doctrine as a factor in determining moral culpability, but, like Fisher and Ramsay, remain dubious of the artist's claims about his or her intention or, like Webster, remain dubious that the artist's intention is relevant to the interpretation of the work.

[15] Fisher and Ramsay, ibid., pp. 157-8.

[16] Mary Douglas, 1966, *Purity and Danger*, London: Routledge and Kegan Paul.

[17] Ibid., p. 2

[18] Ibid., pp. 3-4.

[19] Jaroslav Pelikan, 1990, *Igmago Dei: The Byzantine Apologia for Icons*, The A.W. Mellon Lectures in the Fine Arts, 1987, The National Gallery of Art, Washington, D.C.: Princeton University Press, p. 134.

[20] Ibid., p. 135.

[21] Ibid., p. 142.

[22] Ibid., p. 140.

[23] Ibid., p. 139.

[24] Ibid., p. 3.

[25] George Galavaris, 1981, *The Icon in the Life of the Church*, Leiden: E. J. Brill, pp. 3-4.

[26] Liberato Santoro-Brienza, 2003, 'Art and Beauty in Antiquity and the Middle Ages', in Stephen Davies and Ananta Ch. Sukla (eds.), *Art and Essence*, Westport, Conneticut: Praeger, p. 56.

[27] Ibid., p. 57.

[28] Ibid., p. 58.

[29] Ibid., pp. 58-9.

[30] Plotinus 1966-88, Enneades, v 8, 1, translated by Liberato Santoro-Brienza, ibid., p. 63.

[31] Ibid.

[32] Aquinas, In De Dev. Nom., IV, lectio 5, translated by Liberato Santoro-Brienza, ibid., p. 70.

[33] Ibid., p. 70.

[34] Ibid., p. 69.

[35] Ibid., p. 63.

[36] Galavaris, op. cit., p. 4.

[37] Cited in John Baggley, 1987, *Doors of Perception: icons and their spiritual significance*, London: Mowbray, p. 55.

[38] Ibid.

[39] Helen Pringle, 2006, 'Are we capable of offending God? Taking blasphemy seriously', in Elizabeth Burns Coleman and Kevin White (eds.), *Negotiating the Sacred: Blasphemy and Sacrilege in a Multicultural Society,* Canberra: ANU E Press, pp. 31-43, at p. 32.

[40] Nelson Goodman, 1968, *Languages of Art,* Indianapolis: The Bobbs-Merrill Co. Inc., p. 61.

[41] Ibid., p. 62.

[42] Ludwig Wittgenstein, *Culture and Value,* (translated by Peter Winch, 1980, Basil Blackwell, 1980, p. 31) cited in D.Z. Phillips,1993, "Primitive reactions and the reactions of primitives", in D.Z. Phillips, *Wittgenstein and Religion,* New York: St Martin's Press, p. 114.

[43] Douglas, op. cit., p. 36.

[44] Ibid. p. 36.

[45] Cited in Ruth Phillips, op. cit., p. 75.

[46] Ibid..

[47] Douglas, op. cit., p. 88.

[48] Ibid., p. 85.

[49] Ibid., p. 87.

[50] E.M.W. Tillyard, 1974 (1943), *The Elizabethan World Picture,* Harmondsworth: Penguin, pp. 17-8.

[51] John Searle, 1987, 'Wittgenstein: Dialogue with John Searle', (in The Great Philosophers, Bryan McGee, BBC Books, p. 346,) cited in D.Z. Phillips, 'Searle on Language-Games and Religion', op. cit., p. 28.

[52] D. Z. Phillips, 'Primitive reactions and the reactions of primitives' op. cit., p. 115-6.

[53] Ibid., p. 116.

[54] Ibid.

4

Materialising the sacred

Dianne McGowan

This chapter illustrates the shifting meanings of sacred/religious objects, in particular the recent phenomenon of sacred/religious into fine art commodities. This process, however, may lead to concerns about the new ways in which religious objects are valued. It is often suggested that this process of secularisation and commodification is a failure to respect the people who created it, and in some way presents a harm to the object itself.

According to the Oxford definition, the sacred belongs to the consecrated and the religious; to dedicated objects or purpose; and, objects or persons affiliated with a deity/god or venerated as holy.[1] The aim of this chapter is to reflect on what has made an object sacred in the past, and perhaps discover a basis to explain what makes an object sacred in today's predominantly secular world. I have selected two religious paintings. Both mark crucial transformative events. One is drawn from Christianity, the *Last Supper* by Leonardo da Vinci. The other is a Tibetan Buddhist *thangka* (painting) of *Buddha Shakyamuni*.[2] I have chosen these two images to juxtapose their sacredness and how they have changed, been re-written or appropriated over time. They are also well-known representations, requiring no introduction.[3] Numerous copies and similar illustrations are on exhibit in art museums and decorate private homes.

I argue that the meaning and value of religious objects is not rigid, but is fluid and open to modification or re-writing, irrespective of governing norms. Both the *Last Supper* and *Buddha Shakyamuni* paintings originated within a religious context but have since been appropriated into the Western fine art scene.[4] At the same time as the meaning and value of objects is re-written, however, I argue that the museum context provides a reverential context for their appreciation. These objects have been formed and shaped from physical materials, yet appear to be invested with another 'meta'-materiality. This something is beyond the tactility of pigment, cloth, wood or bronze. It reaches across corporeal boundaries, beyond the written word and, for many people, resonates a sacredness.

The paintings

Leonardo da Vinci began the *Last Supper* in 1495, on the refectory wall of the Sta Maria della Grazie, a Dominican convent in Milan. Leonardo's innovation was capturing the moment when *Jesus* announces that someone at the table will betray him this night.[5] The revelatory moment is realistically portrayed by Leonardo, capturing a wave of emotions — such as surprise, angst, anger, sorrow, and denial. It took Leonardo twelve years to complete this masterpiece, which has since been continuously restored and reproduced. The *Buddha Shakyamuni thangka* is estimated to have been painted between 1050 and 1100. In this painting, the Buddha's right hand is touching the earth, calling the earth to bear witness to his enlightenment.[6] *Shakyamuni* is attended by two standing bodhisattvas, the bodhisattva of compassion, Avalokitesvara, and the future Buddha, Maitreya.[7] There are two seated monks above the bodhisattvas. On the top row stand seven past-Buddhas and another version of Maitreya. The five dhyana or directional Buddhas sit along the bottom.[8] This was a significant painting when it was executed and today is a highly prized item within a private Western collection.

Both paintings were commissioned. Ludovico il Moro, Duke of Milan, employed Leonardo to paint, sculpt and design various works, the *Last Supper* among them. We know the *thangka* was commissioned because these details are written in red Tibetan dbu med script on the back.[9] The name of the donor is not recorded. The *Last Supper* is large, 460 by 880 cm, and was painted directly onto a wall. The *thangka* is 47 by 32 centimetres and was painted on cloth, with supporting textile mountings and dowel rods at both ends. This construction permitted it to be rolled up and transported or stored.

The themes in the two paintings were not unusual. The *Last Supper* was created as a fresco in the dining room of a convent. The painting depicts a supper in progress — breaking bread, sharing olives and wine — an everyday practice. On a religious level, it is at this supper that Jesus initiates his disciples into the Christian ritual practice of the Holy Eucharist — the consecration of bread and wine into body and blood.[10] The *thangka*, on the other hand, was a *stupa* furnishing for the eleventh century Tibetan lama and translator Gos Lotsava.[11] A *stupa* is an architectural hollow bell-shaped vessel in which are placed highly valued items considered worthy to be remembrance offerings.[12] These offerings are not travelling companions on an afterlife journey such as is the Egyptian practice, but sacred objects offered in appreciation of the person now departed. Even though both these were conceived for religious spaces and depict religious scenes, only the Tibetan painting was consecrated. A lama ritually opens-the-eyes of a *thangka* by painting them in, thereby transforming it from a representation into a potent living deity.[13] I have not found a reference to the *Last Supper* being consecrated.

Sacred meaning

Research on the sacred is hampered by the 'injudicious' use of the term 'sacred', which is too often conflated with the term 'religious'. Peter Fingesten states categorically that 'religious' and 'sacred' art are 'neither synonymous nor interchangeable…[and] these terms should be applied henceforth with greatest discrimination in order to avoid confusion'.[14] Fingesten defined 'sacred' art as objects and symbols, which conformed to religious law and were consecrated by prayers, rites or rituals. This would include altars, vessels, vestments, architecture, sculpture and paintings, whereas, 'religious' art is produced outside of religious restrictions.[15] Such a definition would mean that the *thangka* would be categorised as sacred art, because it was not only consecrated but executed according to religious conventions. The *Last Supper*, however, would be designated religious art, because it was Leonardo's expression, he constructed the scene and the actors' reactions. It was not a reproduction of an officially sanctioned painting, rather, Leonardo used everyday practice as his inspiration.

The *thangka* is not simply an idol but enjoys a status equivalent to Greek or Russian Orthodox icons.[16] They are sacred manifestations. According to Jackson and Jackson, *thangkas* were a crucial medium by which the 'ideals of Buddhism were evoked and brought alive. A sacred painting was for the Tibetan a physical support — in other words an embodiment — of enlightenment'. They also note that the simple *Buddha Shakyamuni* image was commonly commissioned for accumulating merit towards spiritual advancement.[17]

Wandering Buddhist teachers made use of the portability of *thangkas* to illustrate and inculcate religious messages for the nomadic illiterate population.[18] The pictures told familiar stories, in the same manner as the stained glass windows, paintings and sculptures of the Christian church. The wrath of God unleashed upon the fallen sinner or the innocence of a lamb protected by the shepherd was silently impressed upon a significantly illiterate population. They were visual reminders of how to conduct their lives properly, under the omnipresence of an all-seeing God. The angelic forms of heaven and the horrors of purgatory were all pictured — graphic reminders that life's actions were judged at death.

Both paintings, therefore, had a specific religious purpose, and it might be argued that this purpose 'fixes' the meaning or significance of the object, in contrast to the meaning or significance it has as fine art, in which it is considered primarily as an object with aesthetic and historical value, but also, problematically, a commodity to be bought and sold. Yet, we find such objects have always had financial and aesthetic values that displayed the status of the possessor.

'Materialising' the sacred

While the depth of understanding of the spiritual world represented by a *thangka* or the church windows may have differed between the illiterate and the aristocracy, the elite also used their access to resources to highlight their higher spiritual position and access to the sacred. For example, in Florence during the 1400s it was common practice for churches to sell altar naming rights. Prominent families would engage prestigious artists to create new altars or altar pieces. Nor was it necessary for a client to commission an artist. Open market stalls sold sculptures, paintings and elaborate wooden altars. Contemporary sources of the day describe these objects as fine art — beautiful but expensive. This ready-made market also catered for bulk purchases, evidenced by the payment of import duties for 30 statues of Madonna entering Rome in 1450.[19]

At the time the *Last Supper* was being painted there were Christian authorities who were condemning painterly extravagance because they claimed the worshipper was being distracted by the skills of the artist.[20] In 1494 Girolamo Savonarola decries the contemporary painterly figures in churches. In his words, they 'are with such artifice, adornment and virtuosity that they block the light of God and true contemplation; people do not consider God, but only the artifice of the figures'.[21] The unpretentious images spelt out their message by repeating familiar iconography, symbols and colour systems, which the uneducated understood. In contrast, many popular artists of the Renaissance wanted to display their skills and their patrons wanted to sponsor art as a display of their power, wealth and prestige.[22] For example, Leonardo painted the *il Moro* family crest above the *Last Supper*, to remind the religious fraternity of the wealth and beneficence of the *il Moro* family. Likewise, as already noted, a common purpose for commissioning a *thangka* was to gain merit. Quite often the donor was represented as a small figure sitting respectfully in the lower right hand corner.[23] The needs of the wealthy and supplicants created a demand for images of Jesus and Shakyamuni respectively.

Arthur Danto notes that art is constantly validated and revaluated by its activity in the marketplace, either as an original or as a copy.[24] Public presentation and discourse, whether exhibitions, catalogues, advertisements or tourist souvenirs, such as posters and postcards, negotiates a consensual view of an objects' fitness to be recognised and appreciated as art. This process of reproduction fuels the desire for art as a collector's item and commodity. Put crudely, the greater the recognition/reputation, the greater the desire to own.[25] The reproduction of images also contributes to a process in which the object is considered of value in itself, and the image becomes recognised and adapted in other images.

While access to the *Last Supper* remains restricted, Andre Malraux notes that its readily available reproductions has ensured that it is entered into our own personal lexicon, even though we may never visit Milan to see the original.[26] Any member of today's general public would be able to recall many images that they have never set eyes on. The profusion of printed material, television, computers and other technological advances has expanded public access to visual images. With sufficient fame, the image becomes 'iconic'.

In the same fashion as the image of *Sakyamuni* has become essentialised as *the* historic Buddha, the depiction of the *Last Supper* by Leonardo is accepted as the authoritative depiction of that Biblical event. However, the recent clean and repair by restoration artist Pinin Brambilla Barcilon highlights questions about the authenticity of the *Last Supper* as we know it today. Just two generations after the *Last Supper* was completed, it was declared that the painting was already ruined and in need of repainting.[27] In 1652 a doorway had been cut into the centre of the *Last Supper* wall, destroying part of the lower portion, which included Jesus' feet. Thankfully, the early popularity of the painting had spawned copies and they were used as models for later restorations.

There has been a constant reproduction over centuries. Today's artists have used the *Last Supper* to incorporate new socio-political configurations, such as race and gender. Such uses may be controversial. Recently, the *Last Supper* was used as a template for a fashion advertisement. It caused an outcry in France and Italy, where it was first released and was subsequently banned. A French judge ruled that the display was a 'gratuitous and aggressive act of intrusion in people's innermost belief'. The posters were ordered down. The prosecuting lawyer stated 'when you touch on sacred things you create an unbearable moral violence which is a danger to our children'. In response, the defence argued that 'the work is a photograph based on a painting, not the bible...It is a way of showing the place of women in society today, which is a reflection of our changing values'.[28]

Christina Toren, reports on the appropriation of Leonardo's *Last Supper* by the Fijians.[29] She notes that Jesus and his twelve apostles, as illustrated in the *Last Supper*, represent the same traditional social spacing as the Fijian chiefs. Both parties sit above the general public. Both parties share a ritual repast.[30] With the introduction of Christianity, the *Last Supper* has opened a space by which the sacredness and authority of the ancestors through the hereditary chiefs remains potent. Many carpet reproductions of the *Last Supper* hang in Fijian churches. They were brought back from Lebanon by young Fijian servicemen serving under the United Nations Interim Forces in Lebanon. The fact that the carpet is contemporary and is a product from the Holy Lands transmutes and while re-writing traditional Fijian sacredness, it also reinforces these sacred values.[31]

The sacralisation of the aesthetic gaze

The availability of reproductions of the *Last Supper* has made it 'portable' and, as such, it has crossed cultural borders. The portability of *thangka*s guaranteed that they could be easily stored rather than destroyed. Further, because *thangka*s were consecrated, their disposal could only be by ritualised burning.[32] Plainly, the *thangka* of *Buddha Shakyamuni* has suffered sacrilege in the sense that it must have been looted from the *stupa* in which it was originally deposited. The looting may have been by rival monastery centuries ago, or a fortune seeker yesterday. Since then, the *thangka* has crossed national boundaries and has become a possession in a Western art collection.

Unlike the familiar sacredness of Christian imagery it has taken the West some time to become familiar with Tibetan art and to understand its sacred nature. Tibetan images reflected Catholic missionary thought and were considered the Devil's idols. In 1676, the first Western traveller to Lhasa, Jesuit Father Grueber wrote 'that our Religion had been here to fore profeffed in this place'. But the Devil 'hath had the malice to transfer and usurp all the other mysteries of our faith to his own worship'.[33] Missionaries were still promoting this concept into the early twentieth century. The 1903-04 British expedition into Tibet, led by Major Younghusband witnessed over 400 official mule loads of objects leaving Tibet (not including personal souvenirs).[34] Many of the Tibetan objects were settled behind glass vitrines in museums or in curio cabinets in private homes, occasionally appearing in the market place or auction house. During the early 1900s, few Westerners would have thought of the *thangka*s as sacred.

The contemporary world market is preoccupied with age and worth, whether it is the church, museum or collector valuing their material assets. Museums and collectors show little interest in collecting modern *thangka*s by Tibetan Masters no matter how traditional they may appear.[35] Further, contemporary Tibetan painters are not encouraged within their own communities to be innovative or employ contemporary Western styles. This is not a case of potential sacrilege but a political attempt by the diasporic Tibetan community to appear as the authentic agents of the sacred wisdom of Tibet's lost traditions.[36] Jean-Hubert Martin writes: 'Religious art is valued when it is ancient, and there is general recognition that it engendered humanity's greatest masterpieces.' He adds that contemporary works are not thought of as authentic because 'of the nostalgia for a time before'.[37] There is a sense in the Tibetan aesthetic art world that age reflects the quality of sacredness.

However, the rarefying of Tibetan material culture by Western collecting and exhibiting negotiates another performance space. The very nature of a museum implies that objects have been detached from their original contexts.[38] The *thangka* is re-imagined and re-written, not as an object of sacred worship but as a fine art object precious to Western art tastes.[39] According to Stephen

Greenblatt, museum objects can be thought of not so much as material artifacts but as visual memory, or memorial.[40] The objects are then reduced to tokens of immortality, the relics of a lost past or monuments to the frailty of cultures.[41]

In museums, fine art historians, expressing values concerning 'art-for-art's sake' set about coding the 'real' value of the object. In an interview, the veteran Tibetan art curator, Pratapaditya Pal, speaks of the connection between economic value and its aesthetic qualities. He states that 'my primary goal is to establish a yardstick for beauty in Himalayan art. After all, the price of an object is generally determined by its aesthetic quality'.[42] Ivan Gaskell comments that the collecting emphasis on aesthetics and art history discourse has decontextualised the objects, reducing them to collectibles. He states that such discourse is a 'very effective means of expunging the sacred qualities of objects'.[43] However, I contend that museums have not necessarily expunged but add a new exterior gloss by relating to the object with Western values. The cynic might consider this the addition of a purely economic value. The Tibetan art on view in museums are curated as aesthetic masterpieces. Many of these items are borrowed from private lenders and therefore are still in the marketplace. As such, it could be said that Western collecting aesthetics has forged a new Holy Trinity of 'authenticated masterpiece' equals 'good investment' equals 'sacredness'.

We need not be this cynical. Museum 'aesthetic' values and the nature of something as 'sacred' may not be incompatible. Ivan Gaskell also notes that aesthetic qualities are often allied with the sacred. John Huntington is of the same opinion when he writes: 'The exceptional artworks gathered here reflect the religious practices that lead to this compassionate, illuminated state of being, as well as the myriad aesthetic expressions of its attainment.'[44] Present day museums exhibit to the general public a more acceptable version of the sacred — non-threatening and non-religious.[45] Yet, museums have continued the church tradition of lighting the pilgrim's path. Along the way, intensified pin-spots of light in a subdued space announce the next masterpiece. By presenting their artworks in an outer silence and under intensified light, the museum removes sensory distractions, thereby intensifying sensorial experiences, the precursor of sacred experiences.[46] Art philosopher Karsten Harris writes: 'Stepping into a museum or a concert hall we enter an aesthetic church, a sublime and rather chilly necropolis, stretching back across time…What needs preserving does so precisely because it has lost its place in our world and must therefore be given a special place.'[47]

Prolific publishing of affordable books has opened the world of art to the general public. The art historian can describe and interpret a painting for the uninitiated, however, they cannot experience the painting for the viewer. All artwork needs spectators to decipher and interpret meaning.[48] Images need the human gaze to give them voice and pre-eminence over other artworks. The power of the object is created and deployed by the gaze. As such, the image is appropriated by the social operation of seeing.[49] David Freedberg writes that the power of images 'cannot be thought of apart from the desires, needs, projections, and learned expectations of their viewers'.[50] David Morgan calls this 'the sacred gaze'. He stresses that the sacred gaze 'designates the particular configuration of ideas and attitudes, and customs that informs a religious act of seeing as it occurs within a given cultural and historical setting'.[51] He contends that the sacred gaze is ruled by protocols that demand a particular performance and response from the viewer. I would argue that it is only in the last 50 years that the general public has learned to fix the Western constructed sacred gaze onto Tibetan *thangkas*, whereas the *Last Supper* had long been fixed by the sacred gaze. It was an important stop on the 'Grand Tour' of Europe.[52]

Conclusion

It is commonplace within some disciplines to suggest that changes of value and meaning are ethically problematic. This is considered to be a particular problem for sacred objects.

By juxtaposing the two paintings, I believe that I have been able to isolate certain aspects of what makes manifest an object's sacredness to audiences at particular points in time and in specific contexts. Aspects such as religious subject, physical setting such as a church or museum, painted by a master, nostalgia, age, aesthetics and monetary values, all appear to have varying roles in constructing, maintaining or denying an object's sacredness. However, I still believe that the essential ingredient still resides in the paintings themselves. They appear to have the ability to bridge civilisations and mediate between history and mutable traditions. The paintings condense multiple messages and convey these to the senses in a way that language cannot.[53] They appear to be vehicles with the capacity to configure spiritual power.[54] The *Last Supper* and *Buddha Shakyamuni* reach out and materialise something greater than the physical materials that went into making them; a resonance that has outlived their makers and their original audiences; and a resonance that has overcome restorations, reproduction and relocation. Today's commodity-orientated world has enhanced the power of these paintings by exposing them to even greater audiences. *Buddha Shakyamuni* and the *Last Supper* rest in our museum-without-walls lexicon categorised and stored as both sacred and valuable.

Endnotes

[1] *The Oxford English Dictionary*, Oxford: Oxford University Press, 1970, vol. IX, pp. 16-7.

[2] I have maintained the title spelling of the catalogue. *Shakyamuni* can be equally spelt without an 'h'. Image and description of cat. No. 114 taken from Pratapaditya Pal, 2003, *Himalayas An Aesthetic Adventure*, Art Institute of Chicago, Chicago, pp. 174-5.

[3] It also means that for most readers there is no need for a visual prompt. An illustration of public familiarity is entering the names into 'image google'. In just 15 seconds over 2000 hits were recorded for *Last Supper* and 2500 hits for *Buddha Shakyamuni*.

[4] James Clifford, 1988, *The Predicament of Culture: Twentieth-Century Ethnography, Literature and Art*, Cambridge, Mass: Harvard University Press.

[5] The betrayal passage can be found in *New Testament*, Mark 14:20-1.

[6] Earth-witnessing mudra (*bhumisparsha*) is formed by the extended fingers of the hand touching the ground. It symbolises *Shakyamuni's* enlightenment under the bodhi tree. He summoned the earth goddess, Sthavara to bear witness to his attainment of enlightenment. Robert Beer, 1999, *The Encyclopedia of Tibetan Symbols and Motifs*, London: Serindia Publications, p.154.

[7] The Dalai Lama is said to be the earthly manifestation of Avalokitesvara.

[8] The Five Dhyani Buddhas are the heads of five Buddha families. They are Vairochana, Akshobhya, Ratnasambhava, Amitabha and Amoghasiddhi. Each represents a cardinal direction with one in the centre. They are not historical figures, like *Buddha Shakyamuni*, but transcendent beings. Each is associated with a colour, mudra, an animal that supports his throne, an attribute and *bija* (seed syllable). A good introduction is the website 'Tibetan Buddhist Teachings on The Mandala of the Five Dhyani Buddhas', http://www.tsl.org/Masters/buddhas/dhyani/frintroduction.html. (Viewed September 2006.)

[9] The script is in the form of *dbu med* (without head), which means it is less cursive than the commonly used *dbu can* (with head) script. The Tibetan language was adapted from Brahmi and written down at the time Buddhism was introduced into Tibet, seventh century. *Dbu med* first appears in the twelfth century. The *stupa* is bell shaped and represents the enlightened mind.

[10] In reference to taking the bread and the wine, Jesus told his twelve disciples: 'Do this in remembrance of me', 1 Cor 11:23-25.

[11] Gos Lotsava (c.992-1074), also known as Drogmi Lotsawa, traveled to India and, after many years of study, returned to Tibet bringing with him instructions of almost 80 major tantras, including the important Hevajra tantra. See 'HH the Sakya Trizin Visits North America', *The Snow Lion Newsletter*, http://www.snowlionpub.com/pages/N50_1.html. (Viewed September 2006,)

[12] His Holiness Dilgo Khyentse Rinpoche (1910-1991), the head of the Tibetan Nyingmapa school, noted: 'When a great teacher passes away, his body is no more, but to indicate that his mind is dwelling forever in an unchanging way in the dharmakaya, one will erect a *stupa* as a symbol of the mind of the buddhas.' See Stupa Information Page, http://www.*stupa*.org.nz/. (Viewed September 2006.)

[13] 'Ronald Knox, an Englishman who lived in Sri Lanka in the 1660s and 1670s, observed bronze foundry practices there. Before the eyes of a Buddha image are made, 'it is not accounted a God, but a lump of ordinary metal, and thrown about the shop with no more regard than anything else... The Eyes being formed, it is thence a God.' David Freedberg et. al., 1994, 'The Object of Art History', *The Art Bulletin*, vol. 76, no. 3, pp. 394-396 at p. 85. Furthermore, according to Robert Thurman, the Tibetans believe that the paintings and sculptures of deities are an extension of the deity. Marilyn Rhie and Robert Thurman, 1991, *Wisdom and Compassion: The Sacred Art of Tibet*, London: Thames and Hudson, pp. 36-37.

[14] Peter Fingesten, 1951, 'Toward a New Definition of Religious Art', *College Art Journal*, vol. 10 no. 2, pp. 131-146, at p.144.

[15] Ibid., p.133.

[16] However, unlike the Greek and Russian understanding that icons are (re)produced by the hand of the spirit, the Tibetans are 'ordinary' artisans, generally born into the profession. There is a repeated idea that strenuous yogi-like practices precede Tibetan painting. Jackson and Jackson, state that this is a myth perpetuated by the idealism of textual sources, although, there are historical exceptions and the ritual practice of the 'day-*thangka*'. David Jackson and Janice Jackson, 1988, *Tibetan Thangka Painting: Methods and materials*, Ithaca: Snow Lion Publications, p. 12. Oleg Tarasov, 2003, *Icon and Devotion: Sacred spaces in Imperial Russia*, London: Reaktion Books.

[17] Ibid., pp. 9, 11.

18 Ibid., p. 11. See also figure on p. 9 captioned 'People of Tarap (Dolpo) viewing *thangka*s during a religious gathering'.

19 Creighton Gilbert, 1998, 'What did the Renaissance patron buy?', *Renaissance Quarterly*, vol. 51, no. 2, pp. 392-450, at p. 407.

20 George Wolfe, 2002, 'Inner Space as Sacred Space: The temple as a metaphor for the mystical experience', *Cross Currents*, vol. 52, no. 3, pp. 400-411.

21 Savonarola (1452-1498) was an Italian Dominican priest and leader of Florence from 1494 until his execution in 1498. He was known for religious reformation, book burning, and the destruction of art he thought not suitable. In 1497 he set alight the 'Bonfire of the Vanities', here he burnt the excesses of moral permissiveness, such as mirrors, cosmetics, fine dresses and gaming tables. Artist Sandro Botticelli threw his own art onto these pyres. Savonarola is thought of as a precursor to Martin Luther (1483-1546). Gilbert, 1998, op. cit., p. 413.

22 Ibid., pp. 439, 444.

23 Western painters have often signed their paintings in this same corner.

24 Arthur Danto, 1989, 'Critical Reflections', *Artforum International*, vol. 28, (September), pp. 132-133, at p. 133.

25 Howard Becker, 1982, *Art worlds*, Berkeley: University of California Press, pp. 306-307.

26 Andre Malraux, 1974, *The Voices of Silence*, St Albans: Paladin, p.16.

27 Giorgio Vasari (1511-1574).

28 The defense lawyer also noted that the photograph was inspired by the popular Dan Brown's *Da Vinci Code*. Anon., 2005, 'French Court Bans Christ Advert', BBC NEWS (online), 11 March, http://news.bbc.co.uk/2/hi/europe/4337031.stm. (Viewed September 2006.) See 'Marithe & Francois Girbaud: Last Supper' for photograph. http://www.epica-wards.org/assets/epica/2005/finalists/print/images/27020%20%20%20MFGSPRIN.jpg. (Viewed September 2006.)

29 Christina Toren, 1988, 'Making the present, revealing the past: The mutability and continuity of tradition as process', *Man* (n.s.), vol. 23, no. 4, pp. 696-711.

30 The Christian bread and wine ritual to the traditional Fijian practice of kava drinking. Ibid.

31 The fact that the *Last Supper* is a textile is also relevant to Fijian tradition and the ritual importance of bark cloths. Ibid., p. 711.

32 Ann Shaftel notes that according to Mingyur Rinpoche the power/spirit of a Tibetan object is only destroyed when it is either burned or buried. This means that Tibetan objects held by public and private collections continue to be ritual objects irrespective of who owns them. Mingyur Rinpoche is a venerated teacher and master of the Karma Kagyu lineage of Tibetan Buddhism. Personal communication.

33 Jesuit Father Grueber travel diaries and letters were documented by Athanasius Kircher (ed.), 1677, *China Illustrata*, Amstelodami: apud Jacobum á Meurs, pp. 109, 118.

34 Michael Carrington, 2003, 'Officers, Gentlemen and Thieves: The looting of monasteries during the 1903/4 Younghusband Mission to Tibet', *Modern Asian Studies*, vol. 37, no. 1, pp. 81-109, at p. 104.

35 Contemporary *thangka*s of traditional style are actively commissioned by Western Tibetan Buddhists.

36 Clare Harris, 1999, *In the Image of Tibet: Tibetan painting after 1959*, London: Reaktion Books.

37 Jean-Hubert Martin, 2003, 'The World's Altars and the Contemporary Art Museum', *Museum International*, vol. 55, no. 2, pp. 38-45, at p. 39.

38 Ibid., p .41.

39 For the sake of this argument I have ignored Western Tibetan Buddhist practitioners.

40 Stephen Greenblatt, 1990, 'Resonance and Wonder', in Ivan Karp and Steven Lavine (eds) 1990, *Exhibiting Cultures: The poetics and politics of museum display*, Washington D.C.: Smithsonian Institute, pp. 42-56, at p. 46.

41 Bernard Faure, 1998, 'The Buddhist Icon and the Modern Gaze', *Critical Inquiry*, vol. 24, no. 3, pp. 768-813, at p. 774. Also, Greenblatt, 1990, op. cit., pp. 43-4.

42 Jane Casey Singer, 2000, 'Pratapaditya Pal: Champion of the Himalayas', *Cloudband Magazine*, July 21, http//:www.cloudband.com/magazine/. (Viewed December 2003.)

43 Ivan Gaskell, 2003, 'Being True to Artists', *Journal of Aesthetics and Criticism*, vol. 61, no. 1, pp. 53-60, at p.150.

44 John C. Huntington and Dina Bangdel, 2003, *The Circle of Bliss: Buddhist Meditation Art*. Chicago: Serindia, p.19.

45 Gaskell,,op. cit., p. 149.

46 Wolfe, op. cit., pp. 400-11.

47 Karsten Harris quoted in Donald Kuspit, 2004, *The End of Art*, New York: Cambridge University Press, p. xiv.

48 Karen Stone, 2003, *Image and Spirit: Finding meaning in visual art*, London: Darton, Longman and Todd, p12.

49 David Morgan, 2005, *The Sacred Gaze: Religious visual culture in theory and practice*, Berkeley: University of California Press, p. 232.

50 David Freedberg, 1994, 'The Object of Art History', *The Art Bulletin*, vol. 76, no. 3, pp. 394-396, at p. 395.

51 Morgan, op. cit., p. 3.

52 The Grand Tour was popular from the 1660s to the 1820s and was a tour of European cultural venues. It was an educational rite of passage for wealthy-born bachelors. A grand tour could last from several months to several years.

53 Stone, op. cit., p. 102.

54 Titus Burckhardt, 1967, *Sacred Art in East and West: Its principles and methods*, London: Perennial Books, p. 7.

Section II

Motivations for Artistic Blasphemy

The second section explores uses of 'blasphemy' against secular and religious sacred symbols as forms of political protest, or as a force of liberation. 'The sacred' may be understood as a hierarchical structure of symbols that constrain thought through maintaining stereotypes and social systems of values. In this sense, what is sacred may be understood in both secular or religious terms, and its transgression as a means of undermining this hierarchy. This liberating force is widely accepted by theorists. Herbert Marcuse hails art as a liberating experience of 'aesthetic sublimation' that 'removes the audience from immediate engagement with reality' and 'subverts the institutionalization of instrumental reason'.[1] In his 1993 book, *Blasphemy*, David Lawton opines that blasphemy in the arts is healthy because it 'often registers the irruption of a new reading community'[2] and marks such a community's rite of passage. The issue of blasphemy normally arises in a community that is divided, and it generally arises because the community is divided. The arts provide a transgressive context in which artists can challenge established social structures and ideological agendas. Even moderate voices, those less inclined to celebrate or condone all forms of blasphemy seem prepared to accept this role.

Peter Arnds, a literary critic, examines some of the most influential books of the twentieth century and their subversive use of blasphemy and sacrilege in order to attack the serious official discourse of totalitarian governments and preserve the spirit of democracy at times when it is threatened or even disappears. His project hinges on the philosophical dichotomy between rationalism and irrationalism, that pivotal conflict within modernity and its *enfants terribles* — Nazism, Stalinism, and Colonialism. Grass's *The Tin Drum* is an allegorical critique of the Nazi ideology of race and eugenics. Grass's most blasphemous scenes are levied against the Church in Germany, specifically its silence during the Nazi period. Bulgakov's *The Master and Margarita* is a grotesque retelling of Christ's ascent to Golgotha and his execution, written during the dark era of the Stalinist purges. To Arnds, it is a 'novel about the evils of Stalin's Russia and as such a monument to the indestructibility of art' which 'revives what the Nazis had tried to eradicate as degenerate'. Both novels parody God and install Satan as the central figure. Rushdie's *Midnight's Children* is secular blasphemy — it subverts the official view of Indian history as a success story, reinstalls 'low' culture over 'high' culture, and elevates the marginalised over those at the centres of power. As in Grass's novel, the subversion of an official discourse is achieved specifically through the sacrilegious conflation of important historical events with the banality of the protagonist's private life and through a revival of myth and irrationalism suppressed by the new state, under Nehru's politics of secularisation. In *Satanic Verses*, Rushdie indulges in what Arnds calls 'the blasphemous mixing of religious icons'. The mixing of Islamic elements with Hinduism earned Rushdie the ire of both communities, including a fatwa from the former.

In the next chapter in this section, Fernandes-Dias explores the controversy surrounding *Les fees ont soif* (1978), a play which is considered in the literary and in the cultural paradigm as a prominent marker of the post Quiet Revolution assertion of the feminine identity and the social rupture from religious dogmatism in Québec. *Les fees ont soif* roused controversy and was banned because of its polemical attacks on the Québécoise society, the Church, marriage as an institution, the judiciary and its blasphemous depiction of the Holy Virgin. In Fernandes-Dias's essay, the theatrical stage becomes a transgressive space where the Holy Virgin, the Housewife and the Whore can explore the oppressive analogies in their exalted or banalised or denigrated roles and voice their profane polemical attacks on the existing social hierarchy that has subjugated and stifled them from being more than just their socially accorded functions.

The third chapter in this section reminds us that blasphemy need not be considered an attack on religion, but can occur within a religious tradition with the emergence of new interpretations. Carolyn D'Cruz and Glen D'Cruz argue that the film *The Temptation of Christ* is not so much a critique of religion, as an exploration of what it meant for God to give the world his son as a human. Instead of emphasising the divine element of Christ, this film emphasises his humanity. Here, blasphemy is devotional rather than antagonistic. The chapter shows that a religion cannot be defined by its orthodoxy, and that orthodoxy must always be partial. Blasphemy is the means by which religions evolve.

Endnotes

[1] H. Marcuse, 1978, *The Aesthetic Dimension*, Boston: Beacon Press, p. 7.

[2] David Lawton, 1993, *Blasphemy*, Philadelphia: University of Pennsylvania Press, p. 139.

5

Blasphemy and sacrilege in the novel of magic realism: Grass, Bulgakov, and Rushdie

Peter Arnds

Fortunately, at times in which the right to freedom of speech is threatened, there are artists who remind us of that right. In the face of those telling us that we ought to stand united behind our political leaders and who want to blacklist unpatriotic academics, in the face of these, we ought to brandish certain books. Books full of blasphemy and sacrilege reminding us that at times of political and religious monologism, we need to hear conflicting voices in order to preserve the spirit of liberalism. Mikhail Bakhtin's theory of heteroglossia still enforces this message. According to the Russian critic, in the comic modern novel, heteroglossia is 'parodic and aimed sharply and polemically at the official languages of its given time'.[1] Bakhtin challenges the tyranny of unitary languages of regimes founded on religious, national, cultural, racial, or even linguistic monologues. What are some of these liberal, liberating books that make the principle of heteroglossia their own in order to subvert political and religious monologism? To demonstrate how blasphemy and sacrilege are used to attack secular and religious ideologies, this article will take a closer look at three world-renowned authors and their texts: Grass's *The Tin Drum*, Bulgakov's *The Master and Margarita*, and Salman Rushdie's *Midnight's Children*.

Grass

John Irving once called Grass's *The Tin Drum* the greatest novel by a living author. To this day, Grass's book remains one of the most important works of literature for the construction of postwar German identity. As a writer, Grass traditionally sides with the oppressed, with society's marginalised figures. His novel is, among other things, a literary treatment of the Nazi ideology of race and eugenics, resulting in the persecution of asocials as 'life unworthy of life', their extermination in psychiatric institutions in the Third Reich, and their marginalisation in the Adenauer period. Grass's *Tin Drum* is the story of Oskar Matzerath who refuses to grow up during the Nazi regime. Oskar literally stops growing at the age of three and through his child-like actions of drumming and screaming glass to pieces, protests against the adult world that surrounds him.

After the war, he transforms from a child who does not want to grow into a grotesquely deformed dwarf, whose hump is symbolic of Germany's ugliness, of the burden of history that Germany carries upon its shoulders. *The Tin Drum* reflects all those paradigms of the carnival with its potential of blasphemy and sacrilege that Bakhtin outlines in his monumental study *Rabelais and his World*. All three authors, Grass, Rabelais, and Bakhtin, react through their works to the oppressive regimes of their times, the rule of Charles V in Rabelais, Stalinist Russia in Bakhtin, and the Third Reich in Grass. For Rabelais, Bakhtin, and Grass, the spirit of carnival with its emphasis on the grotesque signifies the symbolic destruction of authority and official culture and the assertion of popular renewal. A fascinating parallel between Bakhtin and Grass, one that makes it impossible to read *The Tin Drum* without thinking of the Russian critic, is that both writers critique the official discourse of a regime that appropriates folk culture for its oppressive politics and for rejecting and killing undesirable individuals. While Bakhtin uses theory, the theory of blasphemy to attack Stalinism, Grass attacks German conservatism more directly through fiction. While for obvious reasons, the more muted criticism of Stalinism by people like Bakhtin and the Russian novelist Mikhail Bulgakov was levelled entirely at the State, Grass's most blasphemous scenes are levelled against the Church in Germany, specifically against its silence during the Nazi period.

The difference between aboriginal peoples and pagan societies, which manage to wed the forces of chaos with the forces of order, and Christianity, which started separating these two principles by distinguishing between Jesus and Satan, becomes interesting within the context of Grass's novel, which reflects this pagan union of the Apollonian and Dionysian sphere. It does this by merging in Oskar Matzerath the figures of Jesus and Satan, of victim and fascist. Oskar can never be just one: the dividing line of any dialectic is blurred in this book and, like all archetypal tricksters, Oskar finds himself on the threshold between two domains. The trickster's typical location in European culture is the marketplace, and as Bakhtin tells us in the Middle Ages and the Renaissance, this was the place in which curses, profanities, and oaths reigned.[2] While the sacred was reserved for the church, the profane reigned outside of church, primarily in the marketplace. *Pro-fanum* translates into 'before the temple'. In early modern European culture, the grotesque became most visible in the marketplace, a place not only of multicultural interaction but also a venue for all sorts of groups that later became increasingly segregated from society: gypsies, transient musicians, exotics of doubtful origin, freed slaves, midgets and giants.[3] Yet with the formation of the bourgeois class, socially inferior classes in marketplaces and fairs increasingly became the 'object of the respectable gaze'[4] by which the bourgeois class was able to confirm its own superiority. Particularly, the slave from the colonies, the dwarf, and the pig were displayed and celebrated at the fair because of their low status. Alongside with their segregation within the forming nation-state, slaves and dwarves then became increasingly banished from church.[5] Oskar's presence in church is in itself a violation of the sacred realm through the profanity of his grotesque body and all his body stands for, as opposed to one of his counter images, the classical body of the athlete on the cross, who is flexing his muscles and expanding his chest over the main altar of the Danzig Sacred Heart Church. In addition, Oskar repeatedly violates this physical division between the sacred and the profane by taking profane language and actions into church. As a culture of shame and guilt, Germany in the 1950s had its areas of silence — the Nazi crimes, the Holocaust and euthanasia. A central moment of breaking this silence about the Holocaust, in which Oskar accuses the church, that sacred domain opposed to the grotesque, of its passivity in the face of Nazi atrocities, occurs when he gives the Jesus figure his drum and tells him to use it, as a way of protesting against what is happening on the political stage at the same time. This is a double disruption of the sacred, both in the sense that Germans in the 1950s did not want to hear about the Holocaust and the war, and in locality, the desecration of the sacred ground.

The Catholic Church in particular is the target of Grass's satire. As Günter Lewy has shown, the Catholic Church silently supported the Final Solution, while it followed the general public in its outcry against the practice of euthanasia.[6] The main reason for the Catholic Church's protest against euthanasia was that here Germans were killed while the Final Solution targeted the Jews, who had killed Jesus Christ.[7] In 1939, Archbishop Gröber argued that because the Jews had killed God, Christianity was not to be regarded as a product of the Jews but was 'in the most intimate union with the Germanic spirit'.[8] This appropriation by the German church of Jesus into its own ranks is reflected in Grass's Aryanisation of the Jesus figure *à la* Leni Riefenstahl. Grass's church scenes exhibit some of the most offensive passages in the book by conflating sacred images with what Bakhtin calls the material bodily lower stratum, as Catholicism never ceases to inspire Oskar with blasphemy. In picaresque fashion, Oskar mutters commentaries on the Mass while moving his bowels, he equates Jesus with his philandering father Jan Bronski, he touches the little Jesus figure's penis, his watering can, as he calls it, thus giving himself a massive erection, and he sits on the Virgin Mary's thigh. In the marketplace, Bakhtin argues, 'the most improper and sinful oaths were those invoking the body of the Lord and its various parts, and these were precisely the oaths most frequently used'.[9] Oskar's drumming, and especially the drumsticks, belong to a series of phallic symbols. Being dactyls like the Tom Thumb figure himself that Oskar is partly modelled on, these are grotesque images of potency that contrast starkly with Jesus's own flaccid penis as a symbol of the church's political impotence. These carnivalesque images subvert the authority of the church, conflating the theme of the Holocaust with folk humour.

Oskar's blasphemies turn into crime when he steals nativity figures from numerous churches. In these later church scenes, Oskar uncrowns the church Jesus by adopting his name as the leader of a street gang and by sawing him off along with the other two figures, John the Baptist and the Virgin Mary. He has his 'disciples', the gangsters named the Dusters, perform Catholic rituals such as genuflections by the holy-water font or enact an impromptu Mass and invoke the *ite missa sunt*, a line that was also the object of derision in the medieval Feast of Fools, where it was converted into the threefold braying of an ass performed by the priest.[10] We can see to what extent Grass's book from 1959 is steeped in these early cultural traditions of Europe. In synchrony with other tricksters who muddy high gods and 'are made in and for a world of imperfections', in which they 'do not wish away or deny what seems low, dirty, and imperfect',[11] Oskar's blasphemies in church challenge religious idealism and indict the church's silence towards the Nazis' practice of euthanasia, of the killing of the physically and mentally degenerate, of doing away with what seemed to them low, dirty, and imperfect. This union between the church and the totalitarian state is explicitly addressed in Grass's equation of the classical body of Jesus and the perfect Aryan body, the athletes of the 1936 Olympics and Jesus's blue eyes, and the equation of the holy cross and the swastika. Oskar questions Jesus as a culture-hero and concludes that he, Oskar, is a more genuine Jesus than the other, for at least Oskar drums resistance to the Nazis with his tin drum. His actions seem to imply the question: Where was God during the Holocaust? Where were Jesus's miracles then? Moreover, Oskar's second form of protest, his desire to scream glass to pieces in church, could be read as a form of protest against the broken glass during Reich Crystal Night and the church's silence.

Bulgakov

Grass's book is part of a tightly woven fabric of texts that are steeped in the tradition of the Menippean satire. The revival of this genre in the twentieth century, whether in Russia or Germany, has the function of social criticism. It is subversive, blasphemous and sacrilegious literature that forms a carnivalesque counter-culture to the seriousness of any officialdom. Bakhtin wrote his book on Rabelais with this intention and he did for literary theory what Mikhail Bulgakov's *The Master and Margarita* did in fiction. The publication of both books was delayed for many years due to the censorship under Stalinism. Bakhtin's dissertation on which his book is based was not completed until 1940, he did not receive his degree until 1951, and the book was not published until 1965. Bulgakov's novel experienced a similar publication history: it was started in 1928 but was not published until 1966, 26 years after his death, as a censored version in a Moscow journal. Mikhail Bulgakov's *The Master and Margarita* is a novel of grotesque, fantastic realism written during the dark era of the Stalinist purges, a novel about the evils of Stalin's Russia and, as such, a monument to the indestructibility of art much like Grass's novel, which also revives what the Nazis had tried to eradicate as degenerate. Bulgakov's satire, too, lends itself to a Bakhtinian interpretation with its concept of the carnival as a temporary liberation from the prevailing truth and from the established order. Like Grass's novel, *The Master and Margarita* was itself influenced by Rabelais. Bulgakov's novel is about the fate of a novel about Pontius Pilate and Jesus Christ, written by the protagonist, the Master. It blends a retelling of Christ's ascent to Golgotha and his execution with the incredible events surrounding a visit by Woland, Satan, the central trickster figure in this text, and his minions, to the Moscow of Stalinism. The presence of Jesus, Ieshua, as a character of a novel was unthinkable for the atheist Stalinist era. This is very different from Grass's kind of blasphemy, a blasphemy within and directed against the Church. Bulgakov's novel abounds if not in blasphemy then in a sort of secular sacrilege targeted at the state and the absence of any church. In the two central figures, the Master and Pontius Pilate, we obtain the two positions of the persecuted artist and the tyrant. The Master is to an extent a self-portrait of Bulgakov and his difficulties as a writer under Stalin. Stalin can be discerned both in the figure of Pontius Pilate, who condemns innocent people to death, and Woland, the Devil. The novel shares with Grass's *The Tin Drum* the installation of a vagrant Jesus figure, who in both cases has to carry the burden imposed upon him by the crimes of a totalitarian regime, its cowardice, betrayals, and murders. That Oskar Matzerath increasingly identifies with Jesus at the end of Grass's novel indicates that he is the victim of the crimes of humanity *par excellence* and, like Bulgakov, Grass intends to remind us that the story of Jesus continues to have metaphorical relevance for our own day, that there will always be a Pontius Pilate who ends up crucifying a Jesus.

Bulgakov's novel can quite literally be characterised as a work of magic realism. It engages in mock uncrownings of officially respected figures from the world of literature and theatre and makes fun of the mysterious disappearance of Moscow inhabitants, a common phenomenon under Stalinism. The unreality of the totalitarian regime, which Hannah Arendt has described as a 'superior realism' surrounding these regimes, may be the reason why some artists respond to these times with works of magic realism.[12] Mikhail Bulgakov, for fear of retribution, never talks openly about Stalinism but refers to it as witchcraft: 'And it was two years ago that inexplicable things began happening…people started disappearing without a trace. Once, on a day off, a policeman appeared, summoned the second lodger (whose name has been lost) into the front hall, and said that he had been asked to come down to the police station for a minute in order to sign something. The lodger told Anfisa…he would be back in ten minutes…Not only did he not return in ten minutes, he never returned at all…it was witchcraft pure and simple, and …as everyone knows, once witchcraft gets started, there is no stopping it'.[13] One of the most famous lines from this novel

— 'once witchcraft is started, there is no stopping it' — expresses totalitarianism's self-consuming racism, the never-ending process of having to find enemies. It is passages like this one that mark moments in the text where, due to the conflation of reality with surrealism, the term 'magic realism' becomes justified in the highest degree. Evidently, at times of extreme censorship only metaphorical language can save the artist from persecution; hence the magic realist novel can be a tool to express and attack the politics of totalitarian regimes. What this novel describes as witchcraft and fantasy, was, however, a grim reality that had nothing to do with magic. The novel displays a rediscovery of the iconography of Hell, which had gone missing in the bourgeois age, that joyful hell, of which Bakhtin speaks, to be found in medieval carnival and in Rabelais. Griboedov House, for example, the primary hangout for the Muscovite literary world and for Woland and his devils is such a hell. Particularly its famous restaurant, in which Woland gives his satanic ball, with its incredibly loud jazz band and the laughter that roars through its vaults is the main carnival locus which parades beauty and ugliness, life and death, and is reminiscent of Grass's restaurant, the Onion Cellar and its own jazz band. In Grass's Onion Cellar, Germans are taught to mourn by crying over onions. In both novels jazz has a liberating function from oppression. In *The Tin Drum*, Oskar disperses a Nazi party rally from inside a rostrum by drumming to the rhythm of a Charleston, 'Jimmy the Tiger', which has the power to dissolve the uniformity of the saluting *Volkskörper*, the folk body. In accordance with Cornel West's thoughts in his recent book *Democracy Matters* on the potential of jazz and blues to resist the stifling of democracy and to give tragicomic hope in the face of racism, Oskar's music temporarily dissolves the rigidity of the *Sieg-Heil* salute, a central symbol of the Nazi race ideology. Similarly, the jazz in Bulgakov's Griboedov House can be read as a carnivalesque form of resistance to the Puritanism of Stalinism.

Like *The Tin Drum*, *The Master and Margarita* parodies God, installs Satan as a central figure, is intertextual with Goethe (Faust in Bulgakov, the Goethean Bildungsroman in Grass), conflates the rational with the irrational, pits irrational elements against the rationalist party monologue, cosmopolitanism with nationalism. Bulgakov's devil Woland, for example, is described as a polyglot foreigner. In both novels, the idea of cosmopolitanism clashes with the politics of rootedness. Primarily, however, Bulgakov's novel fulfils what Bakhtin saw in Dostoevsky's novels, their polyphony, heteroglossia, a never-ending dialogue in opposition to the monologism of Stalinism, a novel that is open-ended, unfinalised. In a key moment, in the Master's novel within the novel, he has Yeshua save Pilate from eternal damnation, thus guaranteeing the persistence of a dialogue between irrationalism in the form of faith (Jesus) and reason (Pilate, Stalin). This union between rationalism and irrationalism also comes about in *The Tin Drum*, where Oskar advocates a union between the Apollonian and the Dionysian principles borrowed from Nietzsche's *Birth of Tragedy*. It seems that these two European novels finally attempt to achieve to mend the central split that goes through the cultural history of modernity, that split between reason and unreason that emerges from the Enlightenment.

Rushdie

While Grass writes against the political abuse of folk culture in Nazi Germany, Bulgakov writes against the suppression of the Christian myth following the Communist revolution. In both books, myth is disentangled from the grasp of ideological abuse. This also happens in Rushdie's books, both in *Midnight's Children* and *Satanic Verses*. As Grass's *The Tin Drum* draws on previous texts, it becomes the palimpsest for later texts. Salman Rushdie openly admitted to having been influenced by Grass.[14] The parallels between these two authors are legion. While Grass juxtaposes Germans and Poles, one of Rushdie's central themes is the relationship between Muslims and Hindus. The works of both writers display a high degree of intertextuality and heterogeneity and both have provoked strong reactions from the people who do not agree with their use of blasphemy and sacrilege, although arguably conservative reactions to Grass's *The Tin Drum* in places like Bavaria in the early 1960s and Oklahoma in the mid-1990s fade in comparison with the *fatwa* which Khomeini placed on Rushdie after the publication of *The Satanic Verses* in 1989. One of the most interesting connections between *The Tin Drum* and *Midnight's Children* is their fantastic realism, their revival of the picaresque tradition. Most of Rushdie's characters display the kind of homelessness of which Bakhtin speaks, the dubious origin of the picaro, that great blasphemer in world literature. We realise to what extent the picaro himself stems from an intercultural archetype that transcends Europe, the mythological trickster, whose central function is to criticise society from its margins. As tricksters, Oskar Matzerath and Saleem Sinai, the hero of *Midnight's Children*, have in common that they are equipped with magic weapons allowing them to commit deeds of blasphemy and sacrilege. What is Oskar's scream, by which he destroys the glass in churches, is Saleem's extremely sensitive nose that allows him to smell the thoughts of people. As tricksters, they are marginalised, figures on the threshold, and find themselves in what the anthropologist Victor Turner has called a zone of liminality.[15] It is precisely from their liminal position that they are able to levy acts of blasphemy criticising official ideologies, the times in which they live. Both stand on the threshold between two historical ages, Nazism and post-war Germany on the one hand, India as a British colony and postcolonial India on the other. Both texts revolve around the *Stunde Null*, the zero hour of the nation state, 1945 in Germany and 1947, the day of Indian Independence. 1945 marks the date when Oskar is transformed into a grotesquely misshapen dwarf, while precisely at the stroke of midnight preceding Indian independence, Rushdie's protagonist Saleem Sinai is born together with the other thousand midnight children. What moves these two novels into close proximity is the grotesque body of the protagonist and their grotesque, sacrilegious representation of history. While Oskar's hump is a symbol of German guilt that he carries on his shoulders and while his deformity also reflects the ugliness of Germany after 1945, Saleem Sinai, whose physiognomy resembles that of the Hindu Elephant God Ganesha, carries the very shape of the Indian subcontinent in his face, as his teacher Zagallo points out with his Peruvian accent:

> 'Sons of baboons! Thees object here' — a tug on my nose — '*thees* is human geography!' 'How sir where sir what sir?' Zagallo is laughing now. 'You don't see?'he guffaws. 'In the face of thees ugly ape you don't see the whole map of *India*?' 'Yes sir no sir you show us sir!' 'See here — the Decan peninsula hanging down!' Again ouchmynose. 'Sir sir if that's the map of India what are the stains sir?' It is Glandy Keith Colaco feeling bold. Sniggers, titters from my fellows. And Zagallo, taking the question in his stride: 'These stains,' he cries, 'are Pakistan! Thees birthmark on the right ear is the East Wing; and thees horrible stained left cheek, the West! Remember, stupid boys: Pakistan ees a stain on the face of India!' 'Ho ho,' the class laughs, 'Absolute master joke, sir!' But now my nose has had enough; staging its own, unprompted revolt against the grasping thumb-and-forefinger, it unleashes a weapon of its own…a large blob of shining goo emerges from the left nostril, to plop into Mr Zagallo's palm. Fat Perce Fishwala yells, 'Lookit that, sir! The drip from his nose, sir! Is that supposed to be *Ceylon*?'[16]

The text abounds in 'images of the grotesque body draining into the world' which serve 'a Menippean vision of renewal and progress' that is 'referentially directed towards the qualities of Indian society that Rushdie valorises: pluralism, democracy, hybridity, and change' and they satirically attack the 'forces in modern India and Pakistan that deny those principles: fundamentalism, despotism, purity, and stasis'.[17]

The representation of history in *Midnight's Children* is steeped as much in folk culture as that of *The Tin Drum*. In a conversation that Grass and Rushdie had in the mid-1980s, they both admitted to each other that their use of the fantastic and of the fairy-tale world stems from their cultures' individual literary heritage. While Rushdie emphasises the importance of the *Arabian Nights* for his novel, of the stories of *A Thousand and One Nights*, Grass's literature is deeply rooted in the German Baroque and Romantic tradition, the picaresque novel and the fairy tales. Like Grass, who destabilises the mendacity of post-fascist rationalism, Rushdie attempts to subvert the official view of Indian history as a success story, as what Nietzsche called 'monumental history', the history of India's great leaders.[18] Against this monumental vision of India's history, Rushdie offers his critical view of history. The story of Saleem Sinai is the story of India's common people. Like Grass, Rushdie thus reinstalls 'low' culture over 'high' culture, elevates the marginalised over those at the centres of power. The subversion of an official discourse is, in both cases, achieved specifically through the sacrilegious conflation of important historical events with the banality of the protagonist's private life and through a revival of myth and irrationalism suppressed by both new states, both under Adenauer's politics of rationalism and Nehru's secularisation. In order to show how ludicrous the concept of the *Stunde Null*, the zero hour, this sort of tabula rasa made of Nazism or colonialism, really is, Rushdie recycles a central scene from Grass, the Onion Cellar episode, which resurfaces as Mumbai's 'Midnite Confidential Club'. Both authors want to bring back the past and understand that nothing will disappear, everything will come back. What is catharsis through onions in Grass corresponds to Rushdie's chutney, the sweetsour 'chutney of memory'.

Preserving the past is a concern in all three books. Rushdie's image of the pickling factory that Saleem works in is a fitting motif for this *chutneyfication* of history and the narrator compares his thirty chapters with pickle jars in which the past is preserved. Grass, Bulgakov, and Rushdie engage in myth in order to preserve the past and a cultural heritage that the great rulers of their countries threaten either to manipulate or to suppress. Grass offers his vision of myth and folk culture in opposition to the Nazis' ideological manipulation of myth and folk culture and the spirit of rationalism under Adenauer. By way of parody, Bulgakov reinstalls central icons of the Christian myth in opposition to Stalin's imposed atheism. Rushdie writes in opposition to Jawaharlal Nehru and his daughter Indira Gandhi's suppression of Hindu and Muslim traditionalism for the sake of their monumental vision of history that focuses on the great leaders but not on the people. In *Midnight's Children*, he revives Hindu myth, for example, in the character of the Widow who drains all hope from the 1001 children born at the stroke of midnight of 15 August 1947, the day of Indian Independence from colonial rule. This figure can serve as a *pars pro toto* to demonstrate that this novel is a work of magic realism, for, at a realistic level, the Widow symbolises Indira Gandhi and her rule of terror during the Emergency period (1975–77), while at the level of myth, she is made to resemble the evil goddess Kali, who is often represented 'with protruding tongue, garland of skulls, and hands holding weapons and severed heads, stark naked upon the prostrate body of her beloved consort Shiva'.[19]

This revival of Hinduism becomes even more problematic in *The Satanic Verses* where, in truly satirical manner, elements are shamelessly mixed, in this case the blasphemous mixing of religious icons. When the Muslim Gibreel, one of the two central characters, enters the film world, one of his first roles is to play the Hindu god Ganesha, with elephant trunk and large ears. Later, he metamorphoses into Hanuman, the monkey king from the epic Ramayana. Rushdie's deconstruction of the dictatorial politics of the Indian film industry reminds us of Grass's and Bulgakov's parody of monological prose like the Bildungsroman of German Classicism and Socialist Realism, but among the greatest offences is Rushdie's mixing Islam with Hinduism.

In conclusion, one could argue that the literature of magic realism attacks primarily the official discourses of the church and the state. In this satirical literature, which is steeped in earlier European traditions such as the menippean satire or the picaresque novel, blasphemy and sacrilege, the rupturing of the sacred realm (church and state) through the profane (pro-fanum), are levelled against the Church's and the State's mechanisms of oppression. If we believe with Horkheimer and Adorno in the dialectic of Enlightenment, this implies that reason can become oppressive, that rationalism can reach a point at which it perverts into irrationalism, which no doubt it did under totalitarian rule. In the fiction of magic realism, Western rationalism becomes the target of satirical representations of irrationalism. What Deleuze and Guattari have, in their book *Mille Plateaux*, called the arborescence of Western societies, the deep roots of their teleologies and their territorialism, is being subverted through what they call the rhizome, the shallow roots associated with deterritorialisation, nomadism, and homelessness, for which tricksters, picaros, and other literary nomads are literary representations. In this body of literature, the official world is always being subverted through modes of the rhizome. We encounter these two realms, Deleuze's arborescence versus rhizomatics, in authors like Grass, Irving, Rushdie, Tournier, Garcia Marquez, but also in Bruce Chatwin's *Songlines*, to add an example from Australia, where the rhizomatic world of the indigenous peoples clashes with Western racism and its arborescence. As jazz and blues are part of the rhizomatic world giving tragicomic hope to African Americans so are the songlines, that intricate web of dreaming paths as the manifestation of an ancient nomadic culture. The trickster and the picaro are the great wanderers and blasphemers of the mythological and fictional world challenging the Gods, the rulers, and the sedentary bourgeois who hold still in the face of misrule. A question that remains is: Who will write the great heteroglot novel that parodies the Bush era and America's foreign policy? To date it has not yet been produced.

Endnotes

[1] Mikhail Bakhtin, 1981, *The Dialogic Imagination: Four Essays by M. M. Bakhtin*, Caryl Emerson, Michael Holquist (eds.), Austin: University of Texas Press, p. 668.

[2] Mockery, abuse, and embarrassment in the marketplace seem to be a European phenomena. By comparison, in Native American cultures like that of the Hopi, laughter itself is often sacred and lacks cynical undertones, a fact which is confirmed by their rituals in the plaza, the centre of the pueblo. Here rituals in which clowns allude to the sexual act and the process of defecation are performed without embarrassment and accompanied by laughter that contains no derision. See Richard Erdoes and Alfonso Ortiz 1998, *American Indian Trickster Tales*, London: Penguin, p. xxi.

[3] Peter Stallybrass and Allon White, 1986, *The Politics and Poetics of Transgression*, Ithaca: Cornell University Press, p. 36.

[4] Stallybrass and White, p. 42.

[5] Jack Zipes (ed.), 1987, *The Complete Fairy Tales of the Brothers Grimm*, New York: Bantam, p. 659.

[6] Günter Lewy, 2000, (1964), *Nazi Germany and the Catholic Church*, New York: Da Capo Press, p. 292.

[7] Ibid., p. 279, for example: 'the veteran National Socialist priest Father Senn…in 1934 hailed Hitler as the tool of God, called upon to overcome Judaism'.

[8] Ibid., p. 279.

[9] Mikhail Bakhtin, 1984, *Rabelais and his World*, Bloomington: Indiana University Press, pp. 192-93.

[10] Jung quoted in Paul Radin, 1972, *The Trickster: A Study in American Indian Mythology*, New York: Schocken Books, p. 198.

[11] Lewis Hyde, 1998, *Trickster Makes this World*, New York: North Point Press, p. 90.

[12] Hannah Arendt, 1973, *The Origins of Totalitarianism*, New York: Harcourt Brace & Company, p. 353.

[13] Mikhail Bulgakov, 1996, *The Master and Margarita*, New York: Random House, p. 63.

[14] For example, the work of Patricia Merivale, 1990, 'Saleem Fathered by Oskar: Intertextual Strategies in 'Midnight's Children' and 'The Tin Drum', *Ariel: A Review of International English Literature,* vol. 21, no. 3, pp. 5-21; Rudolf Bader, 1984, 'Indian Tin Drum', *The International Fiction Review*, vol. 11, no. 2, pp. 75-83; and E. W. Herd, 1989, 'Tin Drum and Snake-Charmer's Flute: Salman Rushdie's Debt to Günter Grass', *New Comparison*, vol. 6, pp. 205-18.

[15] K.M. Ashley, 1990, *Victor Turner and the Construction of Cultural Criticism*, Bloomington: Indiana University Press, p. xviii.

[16] Salman Rushdie, 1980, *Midnight's Children*, New York: Knopf, p. 294.

[17] John Clement Ball, 1998, 'Pessoptimism: Satire and the Menippean Grotesque in Rushdie's *Midnight's Children'*, *English Studies in Canada*, vol. 24, no. 1, pp. 61-81, at 73-4.

[18] David Price, 1994, 'Salman Rushdie's Use and Abuse of History in Midnight's Children', *Ariel: A Review of International English Literature*, vol. 25, no. 2, pp. 91-107, at 96-106.

[19] Ibid., p. 98.

6

Les fees ont soif: Feminist, iconoclastic or blasphemous?

Maria-Suzette Fernandes-Dias

In his 1993 book, *Blasphemy*, David Lawton is of the opinion that blasphemy in the arts is healthy because it 'often registers the irruption of a new reading community'[1] and marks such a community's rite of passage. Women's writing has been an important site of blasphemy in the twentieth century. Blasphemy has provided a formerly marginalised group with a medium though which to assert its rights against an existing social and cultural order that abhors transformation and resists it. It does this by wielding the power of religious constructs about the sacrosanctity of dogmas and beliefs, the naturalness of civil codes of ethical and moral propriety, and the necessity of judicial provisions like repressive censorship and blasphemy laws. This chapter examines a literary scandal that marked Quebec's rupture from traditionalism and religious institutionalism, and the emergence of its post-Quiet Revolution feminine identity.

The scandal of *Les fees ont soif* erupted in 1978 — more than a decade after the Quiet Revolution (1960–66) and Quebec's rejection of traditionalist spiritual values, classical education, church-controlled and inspired social welfare institutions and its rural, agricultural heritage, and its assertion of a new Quebecois identity. Feminine emancipation was still in its embryonic stage. The Catholic Church, despite its waning political clout, exercised nevertheless, considerable influence on the behaviour of women.[2] A decade of secular outlook had not been long enough to dismantle traditional constructs about the role of women and centuries of cultural and social conditioning about male superiority, or to undo the imposing omnipresence of retrograde patriarchal ideologies in newly established secular institutions. Frustration, coupled with the emergence of a second wave of feminism in Western Europe and the USA, catalysed the surfacing of an almost militant and utopian feminist movement in Quebec. In 1976, Quebec witnessed the emergence of *L'Autre Parole*, a publication by women who identified themselves as Catholics and feminists and asked for the de-gendering of religious practices and discourses to include the presence and the voice of women. Louky Bersianik's *l'Eugelionne*, published the same year, parodies sacred male writings, especially the Bible and the writings and theories of Freud and Lacan, satirically denoted as Saint Siegfried and

Saint-Jacques-Linquant. *L'Eugelionne* challenges, deflates, and deconstructs androcentric ideology, its sexist discourse and practices, its misogynist reality, and its harmful dichotomies.

Owing to its representational power to encompass physical and sexual difference within the existing patriarchal discourse and to deconstruct negative myths and images, theatre provided feminist collectives with a transgressive and performative space in which to pursue their quest for a female identity. Well known examples of this feminist iconoclastic fervour are plays like *Si Cendrillon pouvait mourir (If Cindrella could die)* (1975) and *La Nef des sorcières (A Clash of Symbols)* (1976), which directly attack stereotype female role models.

Quebec decries *blasphemy*

On 16 May, 1978, the Arts Council of Montreal informed the director of the Théâtre du Nouveau-Monde, Jean-Louis Roux, about their decision not to fund *Les fees ont soif*. The president of the council publicly called this play 'a piece of shit', 'trash' and challenged local newspapers to publish three pages of its script. The day after this declaration, *La Presse* published an extract of the play and by the end of the month, the editor of *Devoir*, Michel Roy, called for a censor. By June, the debate over the play mobilised public opinion, igniting another *Querelle de Tartuffe*.[3] While rehearsals continued, organisations such as the Association of Theatre Directors, the Human Rights League, Quebecois Writers' Union, and the International Institute of Theatre filed petitions against a potential censor. The only female member of the Council, Mme Thérèse Lamarche resigned in protest against the council's decision. On 11 November, when the play was advertised to be staged, the battle seemed won. However, the crusade had just begun. The play premiered on 25 November amidst protests by the extreme right, with reparation vigils organised by the Archdiocese of Montreal and congregations even picketing the theatre *en masse* to recite the rosary while the play was being performed. Three days later, the Archbishop of Quebec, Mgr. Paul Grégoire, denounced the play for its vulgarity and its frivolous portrayal of the Holy Virgin as 'a puppet, an invention of male domination, a figment responsible for the alienation of women'.[4]

A judicial imbroglio ensued. Following a plea lodged by Emile Colas on behalf of Young Canadians for Christ, Quebecois Catholic Parents' Association, Farmers' Association and the Quebec State Council of the Knights of Columbus, the printed version of the play was banned by the High Court. In January 1979, the decision was reversed on the basis of a technicality and a petition signed by intellectuals, including Simone de Beauvoir, Julia Kristeva, Phillippe Sollers, Denis Roche and Christiane Rochefort. Colas, appealed to the Supreme Court and lost. More judicial proceedings followed until the Supreme Court declared, in 1980, that it would not hear any more cases against the work, stating that 'any injunction against a work of art having considerable social impact, should come from the Public

Prosecutor of the province, given that the work affects the whole society, not isolated individuals'.[5]

Since 1980, *Les fees ont soif* has been successfully staged several times — even during the papal visit to Canada in 1984 — and as recently as July 2005 during the *Festival de Fringe* in Montreal, without being decried as blasphemous or scandalous. In the literary and in the cultural paradigm, *Les fees ont soif* is considered as a prominent marker of the post Quiet Revolution assertion of the feminine identity and the social rupture from religious dogmatism in Québec. Why?

Les fees ont soif: feminist iconoclasm and blasphemy

In his book, *Sorcières* (1862), French historian Jules Michelet describes fairies as the proud and fantastical queens of Gaul, who brazenly turned their backs on Christ and his apostles and continued to dance. For this impudence, they were imprisoned in containers that would be opened only at the end of time. Drawing on this metaphor in *Les fees ont soif* (translated by Alan Brown as *The Fairies are Thirsty*), playwright, Denise Boucher, attempted to deconstruct the role played by myth, image and language in the formation of women's socio-cultural identity by creating an iconoclastic feminine trilogy of the Virgin Mary, the Mother and the Whore as a satirical counterpart to the Holy Trinity of the Father, the Son and the Holy Spirit, to depict how patriarchal tradition has incarcerated women in stereotypical roles of submission. The three characters rebel against their archetypal roles and invite the audience to 'imagine…imagine…imagine' a different world, recreated by women.

In *Mythologies,* Roland Barthes elaborates how societies create myths to legitimise power structures.[6] The rapport between power and myth being symbiotic in nature, power creates and legitimises the myth and the myth perpetuates itself while ensuring the official recognition of power. Thus, a myth is, according to Barthes, a social construct which presents itself as natural, but is in fact, fabricated by History through social and cultural conditioning.

More than just a system of theatrical representation, the archetypes of the Virgin, the Mother and the Whore constitute the foundations of an androcentric ideology that has strived to alienate the woman from her own history and her body. The originality of Boucher's play was to create with these archetypes, a functioning trinity capable of denouncing its fears, its deprivations and its stasis.

The Virgin, despite her status as a female religious icon, is more of a feminine model than a feminine creation. The patriarchy accords her power and authority, but only to serve as the model of the perfect, submissive woman. As Julia Kristeva illustrates in her article 'Stabat Mater',[7] the religious and secular representation of femininity in our civilisation is characterised by motherhood — the desexualised maternal representation of women — a myth reinforced by the dogma of the Virgin Mother.

Boucher sought to explore not the myth of the Virgin but the wife and mother repressed in her, as she explains in the foreword of her play:

> Since childhood, the image of the Holy Virgin walked in my body and my head. The woman hidden in her haunted me. Where would it be possible to meet her?…An entire bachelor culture had projected and transferred its fantasies of virginity on the mother of Jesus and all other women. An androcentric culture had only fabricated a single archetype of reference for women — that of the virgin. A woman who does not enjoy sensual pleasures, be it a mother or a whore. Women are thus exiled from the gratification of their bodies.[8]

A proponent of the same tradition as Kazantzakis, Scorsese and Gibson, Boucher tried to emancipate the Virgin Mary from the conflict between the contradictory elements of the human and the divine that co-exist as part of her personality. Adhering to the iconoclastic conviction that the Divine-Human beings remain essentially divine by overcoming their human impulses and urges and by seeking the 'higher mission' through constant prayer, Boucher induces her character of the Virgin Mary to expunge the divine and embrace the human by rejecting prayer and abnegation from her life: 'Once upon a time, one day…and that is today, I began to distort the Angelus'.[9] 'To make a statement, one must come down from the cross'.[10]

In the theatrical production, Boucher divided the stage into four distinct areas, offering a representational space to each archetype — Marie, the mother in a kitchen; Madeleine, the whore in a bedroom; and the Virgin Mary as a statue raised on a pedestal towards the back of the stage. In the foreground is the neutral space, a space free from patriarchal influence, where the three characters discover themselves, express themselves freely, and develop their solidarity. More than the depiction of the Virgin, flanked by her supposed alter egos, Marie the wife and mother and Madeleine the whore, it was Boucher's transgression from the terrain of art — or rather her subversive use of art — to attack the overpowering influence of the church on the behaviour of women and the sanctity of the dogmas of the Virgin and the Holy Spirit, that drew the wrath of the clergy.

The statue of the Virgin is portrayed as holding a thick and heavy chain, a parodied representation of the rosary and making a mockery of the Litany of Loreto:

> I am an image
> I am a portrait
> I have my feet planted in plaster

I am the queen of nothingness
I am the door to an abyss
I am the unconsummated marriage of priests (…)
I am the mirror of injustice
I am the throne of slavery
I am the elusive sacred vessel
I am the obscurity of ignorance (…)
I am the help of the useless
I am the tool of weaknesses
I am the decayed symbol of rotting abnegation
I am more oppressive and more repressing than all words (…)
I am the imagined image
I am she who does not have a body
I am she who never menstruates.[11]

The eternally idolised Virgin leaves her pedestal to occupy the same space as the housewife and the whore, to express her doubts and her aspirations. She agrees with Marie, the mother and wife, about the impossibility of articulating a feminine voice within constraints of a predominantly masculine discourse. Says Marie, speaking to her demented mother:

You who suffered for your subservience, why are you trying to force me into submission as well? (…) you liked the parish priests. They turned you away from your body. From your man. And from me. They robbed you of yourself. (…) They cheated you, mama. Their discourse does not belong to us. It does not possess the vocabulary to express what I feel, what I am looking for. It denies me my identity.[12]

Stepping into the neutral space, the Statue of the Holy Virgin continues:

They profess: 'Silence is golden' in order to crush under their feet, the silent female herds. I too have to shut up so that I can listen to Him always. I owe it to Him to sport the Buddha's grin, the Sphinx's head, the Virgin's eye.[13]

Pushing the limits of decorum and of what was considered as representable in a theatrical production, Boucher not only engages in vulgarising discussion about sexuality, incest and rape, but even involves the Holy Virgin in doing so. Like a frolicsome teenager, the Statue keeps singing repeatedly: 'Someday my prince will come for me'.[14]

As an almost shocking sequel to Madeleine the whore's drunken monologue about her depression and her growing aversion to her profession, the Statue moves to the neutral space, chanting a commercial for tampons:

On those dreary day, lady, thanks to Tantax, feel free! Go horse riding, play tennis, swim! Tantax is discreet. Tantax protects you. Tantax allows you the freedom of movement! Use Tantax! Be modern! Be free! Be Tantax![15]

The Statue incites the women, Marie and Madeleine, to articulate what was than considered 'unspeakable' and joins them in voicing in a nursery rhyme, their womanly fears of solitude, ageing and independence in a male dominated society:

Statue: Fear
Marie: Fear of going mad.
Madeleine: Fear of being alone.
Marie: Fear of growing ugly.
Madeleine: Fear of becoming too fat.
Statue: Fear of knowing too much.
Marie: Fear of being touched.
Madeleine: Fear of laughing too much.
Marie: Fear of weeping.
Statue: Fear of speaking out.
Marie: Fear of making a fool of myself.
Madeleine: Fear of being a hussy.
Marie: Fear of becoming frigid.
Madeleine: Fear of an orgasm.
Marie: Fear of not having an orgasm.
Madeleine: Fear of being free.
Marie: Fear of my husband.
Statue: Fear of mice.
Statue: Fear.[16]

To reinforce her metaphorical accusation against a system that legitimises the use of abuse as a means of controlling women, Boucher had the actress playing the role of the Holy Virgin, also playing the role of the rapist of the whore and justifying: 'Raping a prostitute does not amount to rape'.[17]

In an almost ironic theatrical twist, the Virgin and Marie take the centre stage to condemn the judiciary and lament the judicial fiasco that ensued as a result of the rapist's trial:

Marie: The trial has all the elements of a masquerade. All the humiliation, all the misery of a dispossessed woman.

Statue: The judge came across as objective. The lawyers as well. None of them felt implicated. (…) None of them recognized in the victim the image of their mother, their daughter or their spouse. Patrimony remained unaffected. As if to say that our heritage permits the rape of women.

> During the trial, the question that aroused the most interest and the
> anxiety and made us forget even the accused, the question that became
> the deciding one for the acquittal of the accused was: 'Did the victim
> resist?'[18]

Some of the lines articulated by the Virgin in this scene are tainted with crude and scandalous *sous-entendus* about sexuality; for instance, the statue of the Virgin says: 'No matter where. No matter when. No matter how. A tail can thrill. Everyone knows that.'[19]

In Luke 12:10, blasphemy against the Holy Spirit is decreed as unforgivable, but Boucher did not consider it as a stumbling block to her feminist iconoclasm — she makes the Virgin call holy prophets 'eunuchs in flesh and mind',[20] deplore her role in the story of creation as the sacrificing mother, call the Holy Spirit a bird, and denote herself as the 'Immaculate of all male obsessions' and the 'queen of the mute':

> I was given a bird as a husband. My son was robbed from me through
> all the ages. He was given a celibate, jealous and eternal father. I was
> sculpted in marble and made to crush the serpent with all my strength.[21]

Questioning the dogma of the Immaculate Conception is interrogating the dogma of original sin and the virgin birth and amounts to attempting to dismantle the very foundation of the Christian monotheist civilisation. As Leonard Levy demonstrates in *Blasphemy*, 'The virgin birth was always a likely subject for blasphemous ridicule from Taylor's mad utterances in the seventeenth century, to Paine's sarcasms, to Yeat's "Stick of Incense"'.[22]

In the denouement of *Les fees ont soif*, in which each of the characters rebels against her culturally imposed social role, the Virgin breaks her plaster cast, drops her rosary and releases the serpent, the symbol of sexual desire, a creature cursed by God in the story of Creation, and expresses her disgust of the existing order:

> I can't take it anymore. I won't take it anymore. No. No. I don't want
> this sarcophagus. I don't wish to be worshipped as a statue whilst I am
> being denigrated, despised and demeaned in every woman. I no longer
> want to be an alibi for this cursed race of old boys![23]

Commenting upon the iconoclasm in the play, feminist Claire Lejeune who prefaced the published version of *Les Fées ont soif*, describes the play as 'a diabolic Sabbath in which the sense of sin and the sacrosanct distance between the mother and the whore are simultaneously lost in public'.[24]

Defence against allegations of blasphemy

Elaborating on the characteristics of blasphemy, Lawton points out that those who have set out deliberately to blaspheme, 'set out to argue a system of belief or to commend a way of life, and what is taken to be blasphemy is often, in their view, incidental to their aims or a misrepresentation of them. They tend to feel and say that their words have been taken out of context'.[25]

The creators of the *Les fées ont soif* always avowed what Bakhtin would call, their 'carnivalesque' aspiration to undermine and destroy the hegemony of Quebecois paternalistic ideology and to elucidate feminine potentials as an alternate conceptualisation of reality. The music composer, Jean-François Garneau, fearlessly affirmed: 'Our entire culture is a culture of celibate men who have rejected women and children through the ages.'[26] Comedians Michèle Magny and Sophie Clement, who played the roles of the Mother and the Whore respectively, publicly asked: 'Up to now, why did our mothers maintain their silence on topics like rape, incest, prostitution and their own self privation of pleasure?'[27] As for the use of coarse language, Boucher deemed it necessary because stereotypes are not easily shattered.

While the Church claimed its 'right to respect' and affirmed its dedication to the emancipation of women, editor of *Le Devoir*, Michel Roy, expressed the opinion that Boucher could have achieved her objective on the dramatic, lyrical and ideological planes by withdrawing the passages that many believers considered as blasphemous.

The issue of blasphemy normally arises in a community that is divided, and it generally arises because the community is divided. For the readership and the viewers of *Les fees ont soif*, the boundaries between theatrical representation and reality began to blur. Even for Fr. Emile Legault, founder of the Companions of Saint-Laurent and a strong defender of theatre in Quebec, in a daring television interview praised the play as a 'marvellous theological intuition' but made the following observation:

> Five minutes through the play, I began to say to myself that the author was wrong in not presenting to us her characters as clients of a psychiatric clinic. If she had, then the Madonna would not have been the Holy Virgin *in person* but a mentally disturbed person who thinks she is the Holy Virgin.[28]

Dailies like *La Presse* reported the angry response from male protesters that the personalities portrayed in the play were a far cry of what their mothers or their sisters were. As for those who practised the oldest profession on earth, they did so 'out of their own free will because it paid fifty dollars a quarter of an hour, better paid than most factories'.[29]

And then, of course, there were rejoinders from agnostics, who felt it was time to re-examine the dogma of 'virginity of a mother',[30] and frenzied feminists from the Council for the Status of Women, who accused Quebecoise society of muzzling women and artists radically. Detractors representing this extreme, such as Micheline Carrier, retorted: 'There has never been an occasion for women to interpellate the Church without being reminded to respect the established order, because the Church refuses to engage in a dialogue with women as if to say that the Holy Spirit breathed only upon the male half of humanity.'[31]

A study of the religious history of Quebec indicates that the blasphemy law in Quebec, formulated in 1806, is very precise — the most severe form of punishment was, undoubtedly, cutting the tongue of the offender. Drawing on this analogy, Nancy Huston articulates the conclusion of her article on the reception of Boucher's play:

> In North America, almost twenty centuries after the birth of Christ, the belief still prevails that — just as the best way to keep a fish from smelling is to cut off the nose — the best way to keep a fairy from being thirsty is to cut out her tongue.[32]

From outrage to acceptance

The Quebecois society of the 1970s strove to reject *Les Fées ont soif* from its cultural discourse for its vulgar language and its treatment of then proscribed themes such as menstruation, prostitution, violence against women and women's rage and madness; from the social discourse for its religiously blasphemous import and its virulent onslaught on taboos and myths profoundly anchored in the history of the people; and from the artistic discourse for its amateurish melange of genres like poetry, theatre and opera. However, as is often the case with censorship and *succès de scandale*, despite its modest artistic quality and its espousal of what now seems to be a utopian cause of the feminism of difference, the play has found a niche in the literary history of Quebec as a daring attempt to create social justice for women by calling for a profound restructuring of society and of the way in which people think and experience the world. By stressing that 'the personal is political', breaking the silence over issues like rape and incest, and, of course, rendering the discourse with much potence by attributing it to the character of the Holy Virgin, this play made the social inequality of women a public and not merely a private problem.

How does one explain the public's nonchalance in the consequent years leading to the present, to the staging of what was once disparaged as blasphemous? Envisioning the humanity of the divine and evoking or expressing it in art is still considered as an attack on conventional piety as we have seen in the public's reaction to Scorsese's *The Last Temptation of Christ* (1988) or Mel Gibson's *The Passion of Christ* (2004). It is therefore understandable how a recognisably human dimension and an *avant-garde* feminist depiction of the Virgin as a woman compelled to suppress her corporeal desires, a mother who resents having to sacrifice and grieve for her son in silence in accordance to a higher plan ('I went through this excessive agony of making a child see the light of the day and the darkness of the unknown higher plan. Since I gave him life, I became in many ways responsible for his death as well'[33]), and as a rebel who finally breaks away from her role, challenged the beliefs and expectations of the Quebecoise Catholic community.

But with the passage of time, a community that was already divided and in a state of transition gradually lost the importance it accorded to religion as a factor of social cohesiveness. Therefore, an artistic creation that was once considered as morally and spiritually objectionable and had overstepped the metaphorical and ideological limits imposed by the traditional order, did not shock the Quebecois society anymore. The focus of the public has thus shifted from the alleged blasphemous content to the humour and the social message embodied in the play, which Ingrid Pux who played the role of the Virgin in 1995 when the troupe Majeure presented the play, describes as being 'topical because it shows women fossilised in stereotypes'.[34] Far from being an indictment against men, as it was viewed when it premiered amidst the re-emergence of feminism as 'feminism of difference', for the audience today the play, 'transmits the enduring message that the world can only change when women and men work together to bring about change instead of imprisoning the other in proverbial clichés'.[35]

I must confess, however, the moral conflict that assailed me while writing this chapter. Boucher's depiction of the Virgin scandalised me, for, as a Catholic, I have always revered the Holy Virgin for her emancipatory role in the history of redemption of Mankind. As a daughter, a wife and a mother, I look up to her not as a servile instrument in the fulfilment of a greater plan but as a role model exemplifying dedication, fortitude and courage — she is one of the reasons why I feel privileged to be a woman. Despite my reservations and my personal religious convictions, as a Bakhtinian, I laud *Les fées ont soif* for its artistic iconoclasm, which induced society to reconsider and re-evaluate its attitude towards women; and for its heteroglossic capacity to reflect a multitude of dissenting voices in a dialogic relationship, interrogating the predominance of a single repressive ideological discourse.

Endnotes

[1] David Lawton, *Blasphemy*, 1993, Philadelphia: University of Pennsylvania Press, p. 139.

[2] In *Les religieuses sont-elles féministes*?, Micheline Dumont speaks about the increase in the number of Quebecoise nuns (from 1850 to 1965, an increase from 650 to 43,274) and explains that taking orders was a form of individual emancipation, that the Church provided women who became nuns with an access to life which the Quebecoise society would have otherwise denied them. Micheline Dumont, 1995, *Les religieuses sont-elles féministes*? Montreal: Bellarmin.

[3] Querelle de Tartuffe (1693-94). As evidence that the clergy in the New World could be as controlling as that of the Old, the Church banned the proposed production of Molière's *Le Tartuffe*. Even 30 years after its creation, the play was still considered controversial in France. In the New World, the controversy was more of a battle of power between the state and the clergy than a battle over morality.

[4] Lise Gauvin, 'Introduction', in Denise Boucher, 1989, *Les fées ont soif*, Montréal: l'Hexagone, p. x. For a more recent version of the play, see Denise Boucher, *Les fées ont soif*, Éditions Typo, 2008. This play has also been translated in English by Alan Brown as *The Fairies are Thirsty*, Talonbooks, 2008. This translation can also be found in the *Anthology of Québec Women's Plays in English Translation*, Volume I (1996-1986), (edited by Louise H, Forsyth) Playwrights Canada Press, Toronto, 2006. An English translation can also be found in Plays by French and Francophone Women: A Critical Anthology (edited and translated by Christiane P. Makward and Judith G. Miller with an annotated bibliography by Cynthia Running-Johnson) The University of Michigan Press, 1994.

[5] Ibid., p. xi.

[6] Roland Barthes, 1957, *Mythologies*, Paris: Seuil.

[7] Julia Kristeva, 1985, 'Stabat Mater', *Poetics Today* vol. 6, no. 1-2, pp. 133-152.

[8] Boucher, op. cit., p. 39.

[9] Ibid., p. 46.

[10] Ibid., p. 52.

[11] Ibid., p. 60.

[12] Ibid., p. 77.

[13] Ibid., p. 85.

[14] Ibid., pp. 47, 48.

[15] Ibid., p. 53.

[16] Ibid., p. 53.

[17] Ibid., p. 92.

[18] Ibid., p. 93.

[19] Ibid., p. 93.

[20] Ibid., p. 77.

[21] Ibid., p. 50.

[22] Leonard Levy, 1993, *Blasphemy*, New York: Alfred Knopf, p. 534.

[23] Boucher, op. cit., p. 95.

[24] Levy, op. cit., p. 28.

[25] David Lawton, 1993, *Blasphemy*, Philadelphia: University of Pennsylvania Press, p. 2.

[26] Jean-François Garneau, 1978, Texte liminaire de l'édition originale, *Intermède* quoted by Lise Gauvin, 'Introduction', in Denise Boucher, 1989, *Les fées ont soif*, Montréal, l'Hexagone, p.10.

[27] Garneau, op. cit.

[28] Legault, quoted in Edmond Robillard, 1978, 'Forum des lecteurs' *Le Devoir*, 18 December (my italics).

[29] E. Robillard, 1978, 'Opinions', *La Presse*, 15 December.

[30] Bernard Larivière Saint-Colomban, 1978, 'Arts et Spectacles – Lectures', *La Presse*, 15 December.

[31] Micheline Carrier, 1978, 'Forum des lecteurs', *Le Devoir,* 28 December.

[32] Nancy Huston, 1981, 'Blasphemy in "Nouvelle France" Yesterday and Today', *Maledicta,* vol. 5, no. 2, pp. 163-169.

[33] Boucher, op. cit., p. 83.

[34] As reported by Renée Larochelle in her preview, '"Théâtre. Les fées ont soif". Au fil des Événements", Université Laval', dated 12 October 1995 of the performance to be staged on 13 and 14 October, 1995, at Café theatre des Fourberies. http://www.scom.ulaval.ca/Au.fil.des.evenements/1995/45/011.html (Viewed 26 August 2008.)

[35] Larochelle, op. cit.

7

The body of Christ: Blasphemy as a necessary transgression?

Carolyn D'Cruz and Glenn D'Cruz

This chapter was originally prefaced with an audio-visual presentation showing key scenes from Martin Scorsese's film, The Last Temptation of Christ, *cut to the folk hymn, 'Go Tell Everyone', which is reproduced below. The video segued into a short duologue, which dramatised the ambiguity inherent in God's call. The presentation concluded with the same hymn accompanied by images of the poor, the marginalised and the powerful.*

> God's spirit is in my heart
> He has called me and set me apart
> This is what I have to do, what I have to do
>
> He sent me to give the good news to the poor
> Tell prisoners that they are prisoners no more
> Tell blind people that they can see
> And set the downtrodden free
> And go tell everyone, the news that the kingdom of God has come
> And go tell everyone, the news that God's kingdom has come.[1]

Did you hear the call?

What call?

I think it's the call from God.

You think? If it is the voice of God shouldn't you know?

But it could be the voice of the devil fooling me to believe it is God. How will I ever know for certain?

You won't.

In the *Last Temptation of Christ*, Martin Scorsese's Jesus heard voices. He was not always sure if it was the voice of God calling him, setting him apart to redeem the world from sin, whether it was the work of the devil leading him into temptation, or whether it was just his own basic corporeal voice of desire. In any case, Scorsese's Jesus struggled between the pull of a divine plan on the one hand, and temptations of the flesh as part of living a typical life on earth on the other. In contrast to the many filmic images of Jesus that episodically rise from the dead on our television screens at Easter time — images embodied by the likes Max Von Sydow, Jefferey Hunter and Robert Powell — Scorsese's image of Jesus, as he puts it, does not 'glow in the dark'. Scorsese wanted to present the world with a Jesus whose human side was not effaced by his status as a deity. Adapting his filmic text from Nikos Kazantzakis's novel of the same name, Scorsese underscores the struggle that Jesus experiences *as a man* coming to terms with the temptations of 'ordinary' life. He experiences these temptations as strongly as the voices that call him to a duty not to himself but to others.

It is possible to read *The Last Temptation of Christ* as a text that responds to Scorsese's own calling. When Paramount Pictures initially agreed to proceed with the film in 1983, the studio executives asked Scorsese why he wanted to make the film; he replied: 'So I can get to know Jesus better.'[2] This would come as no surprise to Scorsese scholars, as one can hardly miss the Catholic themes and iconography in films such as *Mean Streets* and *Raging Bull*. Indeed, many academic commentaries on *The Last Temptation of Christ* note similarities between this film and its predecessors, arguing that the entire Scorsese canon dramatises the struggle between the sacred and the profane, the body and the spirit. As Rolando Caputo notes:

> Scorsese has so doggedly and publicly pursued this 'long treasured project' [*The Last Temptation*] that there is almost a hidden implication that he would have us believe most of his previous films were mere sketches for a canvas, of which *Last Temptation* is the final unveiling ... In retrospect, and not surprisingly, many of Scorsese's films are a little bit of *Last Temptation,* or as Kay more aptly states it, he is 'synthesising all his cinematic Scorsesisms into one film.[3]

Furthermore, it appears that Scorsese heard his own calling to get to know Jesus better well before he became a film director. He was brought up Catholic, served as an altar boy and wanted to become a priest before studying film at New York University. As a 'true believer', so to speak, Scorsese was attracted to Kazantzakis's novel because he found the novelist's representation of Christ accessible. While recounting an episode in his film when Christ says: 'Lucifer is inside me, he's saying I'm not the son of Mary and Joseph, I am the son of God, I am God', Scorsese says:

> So he thinks it's the Devil inside him saying this, and he believes he is the worst sinner in the world. I felt that this was something I could relate to: this was a Jesus you could sit down with, have dinner or a drink with.[4]

If we were to give any weight at all to authorial intentionality, as so many people do, we would be more than hard pressed to accuse Scorsese of wanting to make a blasphemous film.[5] As far as intentions go, Scorsese recalls a priest telling him that Kazantzakis' novel was read in Catholic seminaries in order to provoke debate and discussion. Scorsese states: 'this is what I hoped the film would do'.[6] Defending Scorsese against charges of blasphemy, Jonathan Rosenbaum remarks: 'the religious doubts about Scorsese, one should stress, are not doubts about religion, but on the contrary, doubts which could only exist within a system of religious belief'.[7]

But regardless of Scorsese's authorial intentions, despite his careful framing of *The Last Temptation* as a *fictional* text, he was bound to offend the self-appointed guardians of Christianity over the way the story of Christ should be told. It ought to be common knowledge that as a text, *The Last Temptation of Christ* will be read in a variety of institutional and discursive circumstances and contexts that generate different meanings. Cinemagoers, for instance, might be interested in the film's aesthetic qualities, seminaries might use the film as a pedagogical tool, and equally some viewers might find the thought of Jesus Christ having sex on film titillating. As we will see, Christian fundamentalists used the film to galvanise their constituency against what it saw as moral corruption. So, if Scorsese was intent on provoking 'debate and discussion' on his particular religious calling, he could not escape doing so among a cacophony of other receivers of the call.

In this sense, Scorsese's struggles presented through the non-'glow in the dark' Jesus are not unlike our own. Perhaps each of you has heard a calling. Perhaps it is a religious calling and you are certain it is the voice of God. Or perhaps, in accord with the seemingly secular context of the modern academy, you might prefer to think of a calling as the voice of conscience or reason. But for some people, like us for example, even the voice of conscience and reason does not adequately capture the 'spirit' of the call to which we are responding to today. Now neither of us, the authors of this chapter, are religious in the strict sense of the term, although we have extremely divergent relationships to the heritage of Christianity. Yet the call that we underscore here and now cannot escape the messianic tone of at least one thread of Christianity's heritage: the coming of justice. Our philosophical guides for grappling with this heritage and call are located in works by Emmanuel Levinas and Jacques Derrida in particular. We will come back to these guides later. For now, let us focus on our aesthetic guide, Martin Scorsese and his fictional, cinematic re-telling of the story of Christ, which gives the hypothesis of this chapter its impetus: the contention that so-called 'blasphemy' might be a necessary transgression against the fundamentalist Christian Right, and as an important consequence, an essential ingredient for creating a more just society.

For the record, we do not believe that the film is actually blasphemous, if we take blasphemy to mean 'a contemptuous or profane act or utterance, or writing concerning God'.[8] Christ is tempted by flesh in the film, but he does not succumb to it. He wonders if he is merely mortal, but eventually accepts his divine calling.

But this is beside the point. The point is that the charges of blasphemy were made by a tightly organised, relatively powerful group of Christian fundamentalists — most notably the National Federation for Decency led by Donald Wildmon in the United States — who were able to disrupt the very production of the film, years before it even made it to the screen.

In charting these attempts to censor the film, we get an idea of just how influential fundamentalism can be in determining who gets to speak about Christ, and how Christ must be spoken about in order to speak legitimately. It also shows who gets to define blasphemy.

In his book, *The Man the Networks Love to Hate*, Donald Wildmon recalls that when he first heard about Paramount's plans to fund Scorsese's *Last Temptation*, he orchestrated a nationwide campaign to prevent the film's production. He exhorted Christians to express their outrage by bombarding Paramount with letters, phone calls and postcards of protest. 'Thankfully', Wildmon states, 'this flood of communication convinced Paramount, which had already spent $2 million on the Last Temptation project, to cancel its plans'.[9] Paramount's withdrawal from the project generated apprehension throughout the film industry, and for a short while, it seemed that the film would find no producer.

Five years later, Scorsese secured the backing of Universal, a subsidiary of the Music Corporation of America (MCA), on the proviso that he would produce, direct and develop his subsequent projects exclusively for them. The company gave *The Last Temptation* 'a budget less than half of the average Hollywood film'.[10] Universal tried a number of methods to defuse religious controversy, and went as far as hiring conservative religious opinion makers as consultants for marketing the project (the consultants later resigned after their calls for revising two thirds of the script went unheeded). Still controversy could not be defused. This time, the fundamentalist response was even more extreme, and widespread. In fact, Christians of various denominations joined the fundamentalist protest all over the world (some even bombed a Parisian theatre). Needless to say, very few protesters had actually seen the film. Nonetheless, the scale of the protests against the movie was unprecedented. Wildmon engaged in a media blitz that saw him appear on network television shows such as *Oprah* and *Good Morning America*. He sent 250 copies of the script to what he calls 'influential' Christian leaders, and recalls that his organisation, the American Family Association (AFA),

> recorded a three-minute Last Temptation-related radio spot that was soon airing on 800 Christian radio stations nationwide. We also hurried to produce a 30-minute television program attacking the movie. It aired on more than 50 Christian stations and cable networks. We urged people to protest by writing and calling MCA/Universal. Our AFA phone number

also appeared so people could call and request a special petition asking local theatre owners, out of respect for Christians in their community, not to show the film. But this was only the beginning. In July I wrote to 170,000 Christian pastors and asked them to promote the protest effort in their churches. I also sent out more than three million letters to Christian lay people.[11]

Following the example set by Wildmon and his organisation (by now re-named the American Family Organisation), other fundamentalist organisations such as the Campus Crusade for Christ, under the direction of Reverend Bill Bright, 'offered followers a 'Last Temptation Battle Plan', complete with information packet and video on the life of Christ'.[12]

As David S. Olson notes in his recent account of the American Family Organisation's campaign against *The Last Temptation of Christ*, the fundamentalist protest was effective. Three Republican Congressmen attempted to pass a resolution that the film be withdrawn from circulation, and the film lost money at the box office because many cinemas refused to screen it. (It recovered a little over half of its production costs).[13] Indeed, only cinemas associated with MCA would actually screen the film.[14] It is still illegal to watch the film in Chile, and when the film was released on video, the Blockbuster chain refused to carry it. Controversies surrounding the film were re-ignited in the mid 1990s when it first appeared on national television in Britain and Canada. In fact, according to the Independent Television Commission, *The Last Temptation* held the record for the most complaints received by a television station in 2003. This record of 1554 complaints was broken only recently in June 2005, when *Jerry Springer — the Opera* attracted more than 15,000 complaints when aired on the British Broadcasting Association.[15] Clearly, when the Christian Right embarks on a campaign to censor particular representations of Christ, one thing is certain: millions of Christians throughout the world will dismiss texts that they have never seen, even though they might be spiritually and theologically engaging.

So, why did the fundamentalists protest so much? What incited one Reverend Bright to describe the film as 'absolutely the most blasphemous, degenerate, immoral, depraved script and film that I believe it is possible to conceive'?[16]

To begin with, it seems that *representing* Christ with the fascinating possibility that he too struggled with doubts, fears and passions, like other human beings, was far more shocking than the supposed 'true' flawless Christ told through the Bible's gospels. The irony is that this overtly *fictional* representation of Christ allows audiences to grapple with Christ's story in ways that traditional Hollywood depictions of Christ do not. As Jonathon Rosenbaum puts it: 'serious engagement with doctrine is considered blasphemy, yet Hollywood representations of Biblical incidents are viewed unproblematically, even though they are dependent on a series of almost arbitrary and often absurd representational conventions'.[17]

Predictably, the fundamentalists also objected to the presence of women at the Last Supper. But more than anything else, they objected to the portrayal of Christ as having sexual impulses. He is depicted, in the infamous 'dream sequence', as making love to Mary, sister of Lazarus. Notwithstanding the fact that this sequence is presented as Christ's last temptation — the desire to produce a family and make a life with them, as so many other human beings do — the Christian Right was intent on preserving Christ's call to sacrifice himself for the sins of the world as completely unequivocal. If the presentation of a doubting Christ makes this film blasphemous, then we certainly do believe that blasphemy is a necessary transgression for redeeming some of the sins of the world today. For without having doubt about the sanctity of our calls — without pausing to ask how we might distinguish the calls of God from those of the Devil — what sort of responsibility would we be taking for our ethical behaviour?

This is not to suggest a nihilism or relativism in the making of ethical decisions. It is rather to acknowledge that ethical decisions are caught within conceptual distinctions such as Go(o)d and (D)evil, which, like all antithetical values, are not independent and complete entities in themselves, but knotted together in the very acquisition of their meaning.[18] While Nietzsche exploits the exposure of the conceptual complicity between Good and Evil in his campaign against morality, thinkers like Derrida and Levinas, as we will see below, explicitly link the non-totality of conceptual opposites to the opening toward the Other. This opening toward the other is known as the ethical relation. The Other for Derrida and Levinas cannot be known in advance, so in order to be responsive to the call of the Other we must endure the passage of *suspending* all reliance on a programmatic, universalised morality.

The scandal over the film clearly illustrates that responding to the Christian heritage is governed not so much by who hears the call, nor even who answers, but whose voices acquire *power* to not only name the call, but act on its behalf. This kind of fundamentalist response to art as outlined above begs a *terrifying* comparison with George Bush's recent proclamation that 'God told me to invade Iraq'. For what Bush shares in common with the fundamentalist Right who frequently sabotage particular representations of Christ is both a forcing and forging of who gains propriety over the Christian heritage. Crucial differences between artists as opposed to the fundamentalists and Bush are situated in the fact that the former explicitly portray an *interpretation* of their own *singular* relationship to Christ without claiming their representations as Gospel, as it were. Both the Bush administration and the Christian Right act as if they are the 'chosen people' responding to the call of God. We are asking here today, if all of us here and now, whether Christian or not, or whether from any other religious denomination for that matter, are obliged to take responsibility for what takes place in the name of such a call.

As mentioned earlier, if there is a call from the Christian heritage that we want to reaffirm here and now, it is a call for justice. Yet, in doing so, we are forced to reckon with all the atrocities that occur in the world today in the name of justice. Now, while we might not have the means or power to expropriate the term back from its current world stage appropriators, we do have the ability to respond to a certain spirit of justice that ties Christ's message to what Derrida, after Levinas, situates as the ethical call of the Other. For Levinas, ethics inheres in the face-to-face relation, where the self stands accused by the face of the other *before* its own concerns with self over-coming. It is the 'nakedness of the face' that confronts the self as a summons to responsibility in the encounter of the other's death. Levinas wrote:

> The other man's death calls me into question, as if, by my possible future indifference, I had become the accomplice of the death to which the other, who cannot see it, is exposed; and as if, even before vowing myself to him, I had to answer for this death of the other, and to accompany the other in his mortal solitude. The other becomes my neighbour precisely through the way the face summons me, calls for me, begs for me, and in doing so recalls my responsibility, and calls me into question.[19]

This ethical relationship to the Other is not subsumable within a universal ethics, as it is intrinsically a *singular* relation. Unlike Kant's categorical imperative or Mill's utilitarianism, Levinasian ethics do not have recourse to rules and maxims that guide behaviour. Like the Pharisees who Jesus castigates in the gospels (Matthew 23:23, Luke 11:42), contemporary fundamentalists promote strict adherence to the literal 'truth' of the Bible, thereby invalidating interpretations of the holy scriptures that emphasise the practice of justice over sanctimonious observance of the law.

Without detailing the intricate dialogues between Derrida and Levinas regarding how the Other gets situated in the language of ontology,[20] let us focus on the fact that Derrida reinforces this *singularity* of the ethical relation when he distinguishes justice from law.[21] For while law aims to be universal and rule-bound, answering the call for justice must attend to the singularity in which *each* of its calls are made. Moreover, Derrida situates law as something that is deconstructible, because it is institutional, conventional, calculable, legible and to use a famous Derridean term, 'iterable'. Justice on the other hand, is 'infinite, incalculable, rebellious to rule' and undeconstructible. For Derrida, maintaining the space between law and justice is necessary in order for the singularity of the Other to be given room to interrupt the universality and generality of calculated laws. In other words, the decision between what is just and unjust is never insured by a rule as justice comes in the form of a singular idiom. As John Caputo,[22] has noted, Jesus is exemplary here. Through the gospels that tell us of Jesus making the blind man see, of saving the whore from being stoned to death, and of raising Lazarus from the dead, we find the ethical resonance of the face-to-face relation, where Jesus attends to the Other's command *each time* he is called: singularly.

In presenting Jesus in all his *human* frailty (yet without discounting his divinity), Scorsese opens a space from which we can perceive ourselves struggling over the receiving end of a call. Who's calling you? The Bush alliance? The casualties of war? Or your neighbour in her everyday struggles? Do you respond to a programmatic, universal 'Ethics', or are you finding yourself increasingly attuned to countless calls from singular others who suffer? These questions are not supposed to be easily answered. As outlined in what Derrida calls the aporias of justice, our role in judging the answers to these questions cannot take place by a mere instrument that calculates. Each decision in the name of justice requires a 'fresh judgment' to be made in a 'reinstituting act of interpretation'.[23] If we are serious about responding to the heritage of Christ, then this requires a unique interpretation that no 'coded rule can or ought to guarantee absolutely'.[24] Furthermore, a free decision must go through the ordeal of the undecidable, which is not merely the tension between two decisions, but the negotiation with that which is beyond calculation; an impossible decision. If Christ did not struggle between his divine calling and life on earth, there would have been no sacrifice at all, but the mere robotic motions toward a destiny that had no business with free will. Yet the passage through the undecidable does not mean that we therefore forgo the making of the decision; this would reduce action to an equally inert disposition. The final aporia of justice that Derrida outlines concerns the 'urgency that obstructs the horizon of knowledge'.[25] The immediacy and urgency in which incoming calls from others are received demand that a decision must be made no matter how much time and information one has at one's disposal. We must respond and act in the here and now as Christ responded to the downtrodden then and there. Such a treatment of justice — the call for a fresh judgment, the ordeal through the undecidable and the urgency of the decision — is a far cry from the programmatic doctrine of Christian fundamentalism. If the struggles of Scorcese's Jesus give us a character that is more relatable and accessible to our own ethical problems today, then perhaps the blasphemy Scorsese is accused of is a necessary transgression for reacquainting ourselves with Jesus as an ethical activist. As an accessible character, Scorsese's Jesus also invites us to ask where our own ethical calls come from, and judge what temptations we might succumb to, and what sacrifices we might make as we attempt to heed the calls. For, without struggling with these questions and agonising over our responses to them — as Scorcese's Jesus did — we would be fleeing from a responsibility for passing on the heritage that is committed to bringing the good news, so to speak, to the oppressed.

So, just as my father sent me

Now I'm sending you out to be
The spirit throughout the world, the whole of the world

Endnotes

[1] 'Go tell every one' was sung at folk masses in the UK in the early seventies. We are unable to trace the author of the song.

[2] Martin Scorsese in David Thompson and Ian Christie (eds), 1990, *Scorsese on Scorsese*, London: Faber and Faber, p.120.

[3] Rolando Caputo, 1989, 'Forbidden Christ', *Cinema Papers*, vol. 71, p. 7.

[4] David Thompson and Ian Christie, op. cit., p. 117.

[5] Debates about authorial intentionality have a long history and emerge in various forms in discourses of philosophy, aesthetics, literary theory, psychoanalysis, Marxism and poststructuralism. Our own relation to the concept of intentionality is guided by Foucault's 'What is an Author?' and Derrida's 'Signature Event Context'. Neither philosopher denies intentionality its place in contributing to a text's meaning, but both question the ability of intentionality to act as final arbiter of interpretation. Michel Foucault, 1977, 'What is an Author', in D.F. Bouchard (ed.), *Language, Counter Memory, Practice: Selected Essays and Interviews by Michel Foucault*, D. F. Bouchard and S. Simon (trans.), Ithaca, New York: Cornell University Press, pp. 113-38. Jacques Derrida, 1988, 'Signature, Event, Context', in G. Graff (ed.), *Limited Inc*, S. Weber and J. Mehlman (trans.), Evanston, Illinois: Northwestern University Press, pp. 1-23.

[6] Martin Scorsese in Thompson and Christie, op. cit., p.124.

[7] Jonathan Rosenbaum, 1988, 'Raging Messiah: The Last Temptation of Christ', *Sight and Sound*, vol. 57, no. 4, pp. 281-82.

[8] *American Heritage Dictionary*.

[9] Donald Wildmon with Randall Nulton, 1989, *The Man the Networks Love to Hate*, Wilmore: Bristol Books, p. 194.

[10] L. Keysen, 1992, *Martin Scorsese*, New York: Twayn, pp. 166-186; this quotation, p. 168.

[11] Wildmon, op. cit., p. 200.

[12] Majorie Heins, 1993, *Sex, Sin and Blasphemy: A Guide to America's Censorship Wars*, New York: New Press, p. 167.

[13] David S. Olson, 2001, 'The New Religious Right Versus Media Wrongs: AFA Fights Temptation', *Journal of Film and Video*, vol. 53, no. 2/3, p. 6.

[14] Steven C. Dubin, 1992, *Arresting Images: Impolitic Art and Uncivil Actions*, New York: Routledge, p. 92.

[15] 'Springer Protests pour in to BBC', BBC News (Online), 6 January 2005. http://news.bbc.co.uk/1/hi/entertainment/tv_and_radio/4152433.stm. (Viewed 31 October 2005.)

[16] Wildmon, op. cit., p. 201.

[17] Rosenbaum, op. cit., pp. 281-82.

[18] Friedrich Wilhelm Nietzsche, 2003 (1886), *Beyond Good and Evil: Prelude to a philosophy of the future*, London: Penguin.

[19] Levinas, Emannuel, 1989, 'Ethics as First Philosophy', in S. Hand (ed.), *The Levinas Reader*, S. Hand (trans.), Oxford and Cambridge: Blackwell., pp. 75-87; this quotation, p. 83.

[20] For an introduction to the dialogue, spanning near to thirty years, between Derrida and Levinas, see S. Critchley, 1992, *The Ethics of Deconstruction: Derrida and Levinas*, Oxford and Cambridge: Blackwell.

[21] Derrida, J. 1992, 'Force of Law: The Mystical Foundation of Authority', in D. Cornell, M. Rosenfeld, D. G. Carlso (eds), *Deconstruction and the Possibility of Justice*, M. Quaintance (trans.), New York and London: Routledge, pp. 3-67.

[22] John Caputo, 1993, *Demythologizing Heidegger*, Bloomington, Indianapolis: Indiana University Press, p. 205.

[23] Derrida, 2002, 'Force of Law', op. cit., p. 23

[24] Ibid., p. 23.

[25] Ibid., p. 24.

Section III

Reinterpreting Freedom of Expression

Multiculturalism and religious pluralism pose a particular set of political issues for a liberal society. On one interpretation, all that freedom of religion requires is freedom from persecution. Yet, a stronger requirement suggested for many is that a liberal society should make allowances for the religious group. For instance, it has been argued that allowances may be made to enable the member of a religious group to participate in religious observance, and to maintain their integrity in meeting religious duties. An even stronger claim is that tolerance in a society with religious pluralism requires more than mere exemptions to laws, but respect for their beliefs. As Peter Jones (1990) puts it, '"respect for beliefs" is a principle that is especially relevant to a pluralistic society in which different groups of people hold fundamentally different beliefs. It holds that, in such a society, not only should people be allowed to conduct their lives in accordance with their most deeply held beliefs, they should also not have to endure attacks upon those beliefs'. Such a principle, however, is seen as deeply at odds with the liberal principle of freedom of expression.

Providing an analysis of what he calls the 'monologue of Liberalism', Jasdev Singh Rai presents the perspective of the Sikh community that was involved in protests over the play *Behzti*. Rai rejects the dichotomy between freedom of expression and religious fundamentalism and orthodoxy implicit in Nash's interpretation of the dangers of multiculturalism. What Sikhs were protesting about was not blasphemy, but the misrepresentation of their religion from the perspective of the West, and the deliberate intention to offend. Rai makes a case for the Indic model of tolerance. Plurality of meaning does not exist in Indic civilisation as two separate entities but subsumed as a whole—what might seem like conflicting dichotomies to the Western observer, like the sacred and the profane, coexist without any problem. Conflict arises when attempts are made through art to impose a hegemonic view on individuals or when what is cherished as sacred by a community is publicly discredited or desecrated. To bring about change in what some may perceive as oppressive dogmatism, one does not need to blaspheme or offend a religion, but rather resort to intellectual debate and critique.

Jeremy Shearmur explores the limits of J. S. Mill's justification of freedom of speech in terms of the interrogation of religions' claims to truth. While supporting Mill's position, Shearmur offers arguments against an expansive interpretation of the requirements of freedom of speech. He takes the position that offence is a harm to be avoided. More specifically, Shearmur advances a (tentative) theory about how we might classify ideas, in terms of the degree and kind of criticism to which they might be subjected, and also suggests that those of us who operate in a sphere in which ideas are routinely submitted to a high degree of critical scrutiny, should legitimately exercise a degree of paternalism — in the sense of not necessarily treating other people's ideas in the manner in which they are, *prima facie,* advancing them, unless they are fully aware of what the implications of so doing may mean. Typically, people have beliefs that they implicitly take to be correct and organise their lives by. In going about their lives, they are not offering their ideas up for public scrutiny in terms of truth and falsity. He argues that we are only entitled to challenge them when we are invited to do so, or when such views impinge significantly upon us or those about whom we care. This suggests that the acceptability of vigorous attacks upon, or questioning of, people's views is context dependent. The implication of the argument from offence is that cartoonists and artists do wrong when they ridicule religious beliefs, or use them as the basis for 'aesthetic play'.

8

The monologue of liberalism and its imagination of the sacred in minority cultures

Jasdev Singh Rai

The particular evolution of Western civilisation has forced upon its artists a responsibility that becomes invalid and obscurantist when transposed upon the cultures of Indic civilisation. The fundamental distinctions between the two civilisations offer different challenges to the artist. But Western hegemony in the arts often clouds critical thinking and encourages the generalisation of inherited western experiences and concepts as universal and transcendent rather than as particular to its own cultural evolution. The arts and the theatre have enjoyed an uninterrupted progress in Indic civilisations for over 3000 years. In that period, subjects such as freedom of expression, boundaries, and sacrilege have been considered in this ancient and pluralistic civilisation, and even articulated in the ancient text of arts and theatre, *Natyashastar*.

What does the sacred mean in other civilisations, and can it be treated in the same context as the sacred in Western civilisation? In other words, firstly, can civilisations be treated to similar artistic explorations, and can art have intrinsically a uniform role across cultures and civilisations? And secondly, can the Western format of the institution of arts and its temple, the theatre, enjoy the same immunity from the normal etiquettes of engagement in Indic cultures as it does in Western civilisation?

The editors' comment: 'In recent years, issues surrounding the rights of minority cultures to recognition and respect have raised new questions about the contemporariness of the construct of blasphemy and sacrilege. Controversies over the aesthetic representation of the sacred, the exhibition of the sacred as art, and the public display of sacrilegious or blasphemous works have given rise to heated debates and have invited us to reflect on binaries like "artistic and religious sensibilities", "tolerance and philistinism", "the sacred and the profane", "deification and vilification".' This offers an opportunity to open Western discourse on freedom of expression to a different construct of critique in which words such as 'blasphemy' lose their meaning and concepts such as binaries are uncomfortable juxtapositions. There is a paradox in the parody of the passionate

Western artist struggling against the fabricated demons restricting freedom of expression that he/she assumes exist within ancient civilisations such as Indic. The depth and breadth of freedoms in Indic civilisation have evolved over a much longer period than the experience of freedoms in the West and need to be appreciated in the context of different political and social philosophies that have been prevalent in South Asia.

A principle perspective in the West is a dualist worldview, and inherent in Western civilisation are the concepts of evangelic universalism in almost all fields. A driving force within the imposition of Western philosophical paradigms in the public space is an assumption that at any given time some basic principles or ideas occupying the public space in that particular period are universal without contest: that they are absolutist, from which people deviate at their peril, or the standard toward which others need to strive. Usually only one philosophical paradigm or conceptual framework dominates and determines the public space. For instance, in medieval times, Christian dogma was the universal absolute truth, while post-Enlightenment, secularism and science are the paradigms of truth. It is in this secular paradigm that freedom of expression is often held as an absolute, and from which the purist accuses people of deviating from, or of compromising.[1] It is within this context that the sacred and the profane exist in Western civilisation and the contest between the artistic and the restrictive is played out in various forms of art. In this binary world, the Church once considered it a triumph to uphold laws against blasphemy, hence restricting freedom of expression. The opposite has now been legitimised in the public space, where the theatre's efforts to push the boundaries of expression even through offence[2] are seen as a triumph against the traditional restrictions of the Church.

However, to impose this Christian, Western dynamic upon other civilisations and cultures is at best naive, and perhaps constitutes a political statement. There is a fundamental difference between Western and Indic civilisations. The essential philosophy of Indic civilisation destroys generic dualism and absorbs it. It enables multiple philosophical paradigms and conceptual frameworks to occupy the public space at the same time. It also abhors evangelic and assertive universalism and perpetually deconstructs it. Moreover, most Eastern philosophies devalue anthropocentrism. Since dualism is destroyed, the dichotomy of sacred and profane has little relevance in Indic cultures. Therefore, the appreciation of the 'sacred' has to proceed within different perspectives. This chapter argues that the 'sacred' is the creative in Indic civilisations, standing independent of the concept of the profane; and offence is seen as the failure of theatre rather than its triumph over restrictions. Moreover, protection of what is 'sacred' from offence is part of the embedded political philosophy of pluralism.

The British play, *Behzti*, which attracted considerable indignation from the Sikhs in Britain and was ultimately forced to close down, was set within the contesting binaries of western philosophy. Its producers had assumed that the Western conceptual and historical evolution of freedom of expression as a universal norm is absolute. They failed to see that the play had transgressed the boundaries of success and entered the arena of failure, as well as the hegemonic politics in their perception of Indic societies as operating within the same binaries.

Principles and pluralism in Indic civilisation

As a generalisation, the bulk of Eastern philosophy, with some exception such as the Nyaya and Vaisesika schools,[3] absorbs and devours dualism within most of its strands. The perpetual conflict for hegemony between opposing universalisms becomes redundant in Indic civilisation. The artist is free in Indian civilisation, because the civilisation itself is essentially free from dogma. This is the obvious thing that escapes the Western liberal artist when Indian cultures are 'orientalised' and treated under the rubric of the dualist struggle in terms of which the main body of Western civilisation comprehends reality. Edward Said, who introduced the word 'Orientalism'[4] in relation to perceptions about the Islamic world, charged the West with failing to understand other cultures and of imposing its own worldview to make sense of others; this misunderstanding was partly romantic and partly demeaning. Such an approach perverts the understanding of alternative cultures, and eventually it leads to the leading Western-educated minds in other cultures internalising the myth created by the West of themselves. Similarly, Western liberalism has generally failed to comprehend the non-dualist world view of the East in practical everyday life. Although many Western intellectuals romanticise it 'intellectually', they rarely understand its practical expression, and often simplify the seeming contradictions in Eastern cultures in Western dualist contests of good–bad, freedom–oppression.

Multiple and sometimes competing complexities fusing into one strand are a feature of the dominant Vedanta school of which the Advaita (meaning non dualist) Vedanta[5] of Adi Sankara[6] has inspired most of Hindu thinking. In Vedic thinking, there is not only Brahma the creator, and Shiva the destroyer, but also Vishnu the preserver. One creates, the other destroys, the third preserves. What is destroyed is created again, preserved and destroyed and it goes on. Time and space become irrelevant, as does history. There is harmony among the three rather than conflict. Underlying all this is the still, unmoving Brahaman,[7] the Eternal in whom everything finally collapses into, who has set this drama, the *Lila*, an illusion of cycles perceived subjectively by each human mind. Thus, Hindu philosophy obfuscates certainty and undermines fundamentalism anchored in divine revelation.

In the ordinary tapestry of Indian life, Rama, the god of virtue and charity, can sit with Kali, the god of destruction and sacrifice. The *Dharmasashtra*, the text of chants of moral duties can be read with the *Kama Sutras*, the texts of pleasure, in the same temple. Varanasi, the holiest place of worship on the Ganges is not very far from Khajurao, where the temples have bestiality, orgies, homosexuality and heterosexual positions carved on temple walls. The sacred and profane are not seen as in conflict with each other. The tapestry is flattened, all existing in the same domain, the same corner, walking and breathing together without threat from the other or threatening the other.

In the Sikh philosophy, Satguru, the eternal teacher is called by so many attributes and character names that the name loses meaning, becoming *'anaame'*[8] (without name) in the Dasaam Granth, the text written during the period of the tenth Sikh Guru, Guru Gobind Singh. The *anaame* is the benevolent architect of the tranquillity of a quiet beach, and also the alleged demonic destroyer who created the Tsunami[9] as explained in the Guru Granth Sahib, the textual guide of the Sikhs compiled by the ten Sikh Gurus.[10] Everything functions within *hukam*,[11] the laws, but no one quite understands why things happen, ultimately.[12] Bad and good are in people's minds. We can venture conjectures on the mechanics, but to understand 'the why' is beyond ordinary language and discourse. No one can know the ultimate truth; therefore no one can claim to have knowledge superior to that of others.[13]

Dialogue and critical discourse is an intrinsic feature of Indic philosophies. Consequently Indian philosophies and cultures are used to disagreements and critical views. But in critique and dialogue, offence is avoided in Indic cultures. For instance, within Sikhi, the trinity of Hinduism (called Trimurti) is not dismissed with a language of condemnation, but it is made irrelevant through subtle critique.[14] The human can outwit the trinity gods and make a direct connection with the Eternal. The pantheon of Hindu gods is thus made irrelevant. But, in the Sikh scripture, *Sri Guru Granth Sahib*, the language is never offensive, never commanding, just as it never is in Indic traditions. It initiates a debate within the individual to come up with the desired inference. The one eternal divine reality of Sikhi and the multiple gods of some sections of Hinduism have coexisted in the same territorial, social and political space without either system waging a crusade against the other.

The sacred and profane exist within the same context, in the same dimension, in the same space. They are not demarcated by territory or barriers. Differences exist in people's minds. Therefore, there is no battle for the artist to overcome or external forces to challenge, except people's minds. The success of the artist is to introduce a dialogue within the mind.

But this is where the *Natyashastar*[15] places sanctions, as does Kautaliya's *Arthashastra*. Both prohibit deliberate offence. The reason becomes apparent when other aspects of Indian civilisation and the theory of arts are considered. The *Natyashastar*, written about 2500 years ago, is the text of theatre and arts. The *Arthashaster*, also written around the same time by Kautaliya, is a text of statecraft and politics, written at least 1500 years before Machiavelli's *The Prince*.

Most Indic philosophies believe in an eternal drama. Creation is engaged in a drama, the *lila* (Sanskrit), constructing, deconstructing in perpetual cycles operating concurrently.[16] *Lila* is the key concept that enables Indian thinker to escape from universalism and anthropocentrism. There is nothing special about Man. All creation is engaged in this perpetual drama. Some day, humans will become extinct and may rise again. All human ideas are conjectures as no one can penetrate the ultimate reality of the drama. On the other hand, our perceptions are illusions, *maya*, which are real for us, but in the wider context, part of illusion within the *lila*.

This enables an enduring plurality and the freedom from hegemonic tendencies. The philosopher is under no compulsion to be an evangelist and spread his inspirations or impose his world view. In Indian tradition, the *guru* (the guide) waits, and the disciple comes to him. Different gurus have different perspectives. The Nyaya school[17] is highly analytic, as opposed to the intuitive and even blind belief system of some schools. It uses principles of human reason to deconstruct. The Samkhya school is atheist.[18] It believes that only what we can see, feel and reason, exists. The Vedanta, the most popular school in Hindu society, believes in the Brahaman,[19] the creator and the creation as *maya*, an illusion. Yet, the different schools co-exist in the same town, and in the same Kingdom.

Stated within the acceptable norms of dialogue, nothing is shocking and nothing is really suppressed in Indic civilisation. There is nothing that invites the wrath of the 'Church', as there is no Church. Since there is no concept of the sacred and the profane as distinct entities, everything is sacred. All life, all creativity and all action are sacred. Even rejection of a divine order or a God isn't considered blasphemous, unholy or a sacrilege. In fact, the Samkhya school of Hinduism is atheistic and has coexisted as an alternative philosophy of reality without tension between it and other systems.

Hindu civilisation makes a subtle difference between philosophy and pragmatic everyday life. The differences are manmade. People pray to stone gods, but the philosopher engages in dialectic beyond gods. Beliefs exist in perpetual dialogue with others, with the environment, and with the abstract perception of truth. The individual is free to choose his god and his version of reality, his method of perception and form of sacredness. The individual's engagement is voluntarily. No church or doctrine forces a particular world-view upon the individual. But the culture imposes that he or she accepts and respects the personal space of the other. What one individual considers sacred may seem ridiculous to the other. This degree of pluralism survives by each person and community respecting the other for what they are, not what they can be in one's terms.

In this free-for-all world, order is maintained in society through some regulation. Civil regulation is part of society, made sacred, but never so universalist as to warrant crusades to convert other systems. There are at least four versions of the *Dharmasutras,* [20] (also named Dharmashastra) the texts of duties, but there have never been conflicts or wars over 'which' *Dharmasutra.* Whenever domination occurs, it is asserted out of pure desire for power and not in some vague belief in one single absolutist idea of the cosmos and life. There are laws, but they are often made by the hegemonic caste or group. These are not absolute laws. They are enacted and imposed consciously by a section of society for its own benefit, sometimes hideous and unjust laws which function to create privilege. The upper caste claims authority from the ancient sages for these laws and repression of others. But if the Brahmins created the caste for their own power, the *sanyasi* (ascetics) made the casteless system outside the civil. In traditional India, the towns and villages were often regulated by the Brahmin with rules codified in Manu's laws.[21] However, the dissenter could legitimately walk out on this and into the almost bohemian and non-materialist life of the *sanyasi*, with their camps and dwellings in forests. The *sanyasi* could wander into the towns and villages without fear, but did not stay there to avoid living under civil laws. One version of the Hindu text, *Ramayana* was written by Valmiki, a *sudre* (of the low caste), yet Brahmins, not so long ago, cleansed themselves even when the shadow of a *sudre* prevailed on them.

But one almost universalist concept in Indic civilisation is to limit the scope of gratuitous offence as a weapon of critique, in order to maintain this fiercely pluralistic society. This is the principle that requires the arts and the theatre to avoid offence for the sake of offence, ridicule for the sake of ridicule, or 'profanity' simply to make a point. The sacred is not universal but individual to the person or the community. Each person and each community of believers creates his/her own space outside others. That space is its 'essential' and, therefore sacred. And each creates its own rituals, practices and causes. The rules of dialectic allow critique but not offence. Offensive acts towards or offensive representations of another's sacred is a political statement. It is the equivalent of robbery, impropriety or intended humiliation.

If people were to ridicule the other's choice, make mockery, deliberately offend, and purposely destroy the 'sacred' imagination of another, society would break down into a series of violent retaliations and power struggles. This is the basis of self regulation in Indian civilisation. The distinction between critique and offence is embedded in culture. Since another's god is not imposing any laws upon one's own value system, there is no reason to embark on a campaign of humiliating the other's god or the other's beliefs. There is no mileage in parody of the sacred, since the submission to a god or a system is voluntary.

This principle of civility allows the atheist of the school of Samkhya to live as neighbour in the same street as the believer in the elephant god, Ganesh. The person who sacrifices to Kali (goddess of destruction) and the Sikh who rejects this multitude of gods and idol worship and the Muslim who believes in a revealed religion, the Christian who believes in a son of God and the Buddhist who does not ponder about a creator, can coexist. This coexistence would break down if the humanist put up plays offending the others in his or her assumption of superior values, or the Christian stamped on the elephant god as devil worship, the Sikh spat on the idol of Kali, and the Muslim tore down the crucifix of Christ under pretext of freedom of expression. Indian society would simply tear itself apart. Plurality survives on rejection of universality but respect of the other's sacred space.

One of most spectacular living examples of this plurality of beliefs, philosophies and ways of lives is seen at the three-yearly festival of Maha Kumbh Mela, rotating between four cities in India. The Hindu Pantheon, from the *nanga sadhus* (naked holymen) to the rigidly caste-ist and puritanical Brahmins, come together in a gathering of millions. Nothing creative can shock in the Maha Kumbh Mela. In this grand spectacle of Indian civilisation in performance, there is no absolute ceiling, no divinely ordained universal restrictive laws, and no desecration as understood in Western civilisation. It is a world of believe and let believe.

Perhaps the very concept and terminology of religion is misplaced in Indic cultures. Hinduism has the *Dharmasutras*, the texts of natural duties, the *Shilpasashtra*, the texts of science and architecture, the *Arthasashtra*, the text of politics and statecraft, the *Kama Shastrar*, the text of pleasure, and the *Natyashastra*, the text of theatre and arts as well as many other smaller Vedic texts. But they also coalesce. There is the wide-ranging Manu's laws,[22] which deal with individual moral life, inter-personal interactions, community relations, commerce, politics and in fact most aspects of life. They are part of the so-called sacred cannons of Hinduism. How can these broad fields be classified as religion? They are part of a civilisation that does not differentiate between the religious and the political, between the secular and the spiritual. Indic philosophies tend to work on the premise of a holistic approach and interdependency.

In Sikhi too, the distinction between religion and politics, worship and action, science and spirit, simply do not exist. They are artificial atomistic distinctions created by modernity and when applied to Sikhi, they confuse interpretation and meaning of the Sikh teachings. The word that Indic systems use to describe themselves is *'dharma'*.

The word *'dharma'* does not have a direct transliteration in English. Sri Krishna Kant, Vice President of India in 1997, made a clear distinction between *dharma* and religion.[23] He described *dharma* this way:

> First and foremost it [*dharma*] means living in harmony with nature and natural laws. It means to live by moral and ethical principles of the society without surrendering the freedom to question them. The term *'Yuga Dharma'* signifies that *Dharma* itself is continually evolving and not rigid or inflexible. The continuous evolution of *Dharma* has been through debate, and the triumph of logic, consensus and harmony. Most importantly, *Dharma* is not linked to any religion or set of beliefs.[24]

The Krishna society describes *dharma* as 'the inseparable quality that makes a thing what it is. A stone's *dharma* is to be hard, water's is to be wet, fire's to be hot, sugar's to be sweet'.[25] The Mahabharat, one of the sacred texts of Hinduism, describes: (*'dhaaranaat dharmam ityahuh dharmo dhaarayate prajah,'*) 'They call it *dharma*, since it upholds; it is *dharma* that upholds the people (of the world)'. That which upholds, supports or sustains this universe, without which the universe would disintegrate, is *dharma*.

The Guru Granth Sahib, the living textual Guru (Guide) of the Sikhs does not use the word *mazhab*, which translates as 'religion', but the word *'dharam'* (a Punjabi word for *dharma*) as the context of its teachings. There is now a body of work in India which refutes the use of the word 'religion' in reference to Indic systems, and which considers the word to be appropriate to Abrahamic traditions, with a restrictive meaning. The word *'dharma'*, in my own writings is described as the essence of modern science with the spiritual dimension intrinsic. Thus, it is the elusive truth which science is trying to search and which Indic traditions have been speculating and searching for a long time. Religions, on the other hand, tend to end up in proscriptive truths. (Truth, that is, so-called.)

Therefore, parallels with Western civilisation become irrelevant and irrational. Indic systems never strive to create a single way of thinking or a single 'truth' or system of understanding reality. The civilisation is most at ease when there is pluralism. From this perspective, statements such as 'binaries like artistic and religious sensibilities, tolerance and philistinism, the sacred and the profane, deification and vilification' lose their meaning and context.

The challenge from the universalists

Indic civilisation has seen an invasion of its systems at least three times, and all from the Abrahamic universalist creeds. First Islam crusaded against India's idols, and then it embarked on an economic and sometimes oppressive program of converting people to its revealed set of universals. The Sikhs, the Marathas and Rajputs (Hindus) rose against the Mughals to stamp out their intolerance. Then Christian zealots and missionaries and neo-scientists came with the Empire, openly mocking and ridiculing the gods of the Hindus. Mahatma Gandhi used this offensive and oppressive behaviour of the colonist as one of his campaign logics to drive out the British. The humanists (an atheist version of Abrahamic creeds) gained enough Indian converts and caused mayhem through secular democratic theory (Indian Congress Party) and the communist party. There has been a tension between the 'reformists' and traditional India since independence. But gradually, ancient India is pluralising the liberal universalist. Since all human thought and ideas are conjectures, the very idea of a set of some secular principles being more sacred and universal than the ideas and practices guiding worship of the elephant god is an antithesis of Indic philosophy. More than three thousand years of cultural pluralism has survived by restraining from imposing.

In post-colonial India, modernism with its universalist tendencies, has cast a long shadow in the social, political and arts fields. It has influenced mainly the educated classes. Traditional philosophy is not taught in schools, and people are left to find out about it through religious institutions or general literature. It is only in the last two decades that some critical thinking is emerging on the different conceptual foundations. It is quite common to find that 'educated' Indians think in Western dualist concepts and Western ideas of freedom of expression. No lesser a person than Vice President Krishna Kant commented on this: 'The Western education system forced us to think in Western ways.'[26] The most likely reason may be discerned from Lord MaCauley's words in February 1835 when he wrote his rationale for a new education system for British India (during the Empire): 'We must at present do our best to form a class who may be interpreters between us and the millions whom we govern; a class of persons, Indian in blood and colour, but English in taste, in opinions, in morals, and in intellect.'[27] There hasn't been a fundamental reform of the Indian education system since. It is common to find the average Indian brought up on traditional education and knowledge, reacting differently than the educated classes to similar issues. One of them is freedom within the arts. Interestingly, a modernised universalist and united but intolerant form of Hinduism has also emerged from the educated classes which David Ludden ascribes to the influence of modernity.[28] It is expressed as political Hinduism of the Hindu Mahasabha, an umbrella organisation of Hindu movements which started in the early twentieth century in reaction to British colonialism, and which gave rise to the Bharatya Janata Party (BJP).

Critique and conflicts within Indic discourse

In Indic civilisation critique is encouraged, a dialogue of disagreement is encouraged and a discourse of rejection of the other's belief through debate (textual, verbal, and visual) is promoted. In fact, the *Upanishads* are critiques written and discoursed over centuries. However, there is a balance between offence and critique which has been observed in Indian civilisation for centuries.

When it breaks down, it leads to violence and disruptions. This became evident in the modernised version of Hinduism of the BJP, with its intolerant universalist and united formulation of Hinduism. But ancient India rejects them just as it dislikes the secularist enforcer.

There have been breakdowns and conflicts between different groups in Indian history. They have been conflicts for power. In the Hindu pantheon, even gods fight. The gods of some people win wars over the gods of others. The gods of some are plagiarised. But the culture reverts back to its pluralistic stability and mutual respect. For instance, the Sikh Scripture, the *Guru Granth Sahib* subtly critiques the Hindu pantheon. The Hindus treat the *Granth Sahib* with reverence. The *Granth Sahib* does not offend but critiques, thus respecting, but not agreeing with, the Hindu pantheon.

The arts and particularly theatre is a field in which critique and disagreement has been expressed for centuries. However, this has generally followed guidelines established by the ancient text, the *Natyashastar*.

Indian arts and theatre, the *Natyashastar*

In ancient Indian arts theory, the entirety of existence is itself theatre. The constructed theatre of man is only another drama within it. It therefore evolves, dissolves and plays within the larger theatre of life, ideas and philosophies.

The *Natyashastar* (or *Natyasastra*) of Bharata (the writer/s), the oldest text of arts and theatre in India, propounds a sophisticated theory of theatre and of the performing arts. The *Natyasastar* stands as one of the greatest books from the ancient literature of Indian civilisation and brings the theories of the other *shastras* into drama. It is a detailed text on the theory, practice and rules of performing arts. Five main principles summarise the *Natyashastar*. These principles are *Artha, Rasa, Abhinaya, Sahmita* and *Natyadharma*.[29]

Artha is the sentiment or the substance that the author wants to convey, that is, the message of the text. In Indian theatre, the text is extremely important, written within the wider philosophy of *maya* (illusion of reality) as *lila* (drama). It is not absolutist. It engages human life and the wider drama of existence. The message, the substance, strives to impact through *Rasa*.

Rasa is the essence. *Rasa* cultivates the receptive faculties of receivers activating a whole range of responses whose aim is a condition of *sahmita* (wholeness). *Rasa* is not a sudden revelation;[30] it results from a gradual revelation. The performer and the audience become engaged in the whole performance. But *bhavas,* or states of mind, have to be aroused. The *Natyashastar* recognises two distinct *bhavas*. The *sthayibhavas,*[31] of which there are nine, are dormant in human nature and aroused by external stimuli, and the *vyabhicaribhavas,* of which there are 33,[32] and which are transient and fickle.

Abhinaya is the variety of props and techniques that give visual form on the stage. This is the function of the actor and the director.[33]

Sahmita is the concept of wholeness. A particular event or a story may be performed, but the story is in the context of the holistic view of life, the intertwining facets of human existence that are essential in Indian philosophy. As Yarrow states from the Natyasastra: 'Art is not diversion, escape, amusement: it is means to wholeness of vision and to the integrated function of perception in more than ordinary modes.'[34] *Sahmita* also concerns the intrinsic knitting together of *artha*, the *rasa,* and *abhinaya.*

Natyadharma, the rules of drama, determine how, when and what can be put on stage in one form or other. The rules require that the play avoid grim realism, tragic ends, sexually explicit actions, political revolt and offence.[35] Although theatre in India has made some dramatic departures over time, for instance, plays have put tragic and grim ends (for example, the tragic love operas *Heer Ranjha, Sohni Mahiwaal* and the Tamil classic *Shilappadikaram* [36]), contained politically subversive messages (in the dramatic political poetry of folk singers called *Dhaadis* in Sikh uprisings against Mughals, and in *Nil Darpan,*[37] an 1860 play that exposed British colonialism's effect on indigo workers and was banned by the British subsequently leading to the *Censorship Act* of 1876), and have been sexually explicit (such as the temple dances of Devadasis, which shocked the British), the principle of avoiding offence was retained throughout. However, according to Kautilya's Arthashastra, the guide to State craft, entertainers were permitted to make fun of the customs, castes or families and the practices and love affairs of individuals.[38] The fine distinction between ridicule, fun and gratuitous offence was maintained. The early Indian cinema stuck close to the five principles of *Natyashastar*, and modern Indian cinema still avoids offence.

The other aspect of theatre and arts in Indic civilisation is that, unlike Western theatre, the inherited Roman amphitheatre, it generally lacked distinct theatre enclosures with an audience captured in a walled setting. The temple itself was theatre. Theatre travelled to the ordinary person, into the villages, in remote places and in big cities.[39] It blended.

The performance could last for days, which made the task of the performers extremely difficult as they had to retain the *rasa* (essence) from day to day, keep the audience engaged, and get the message across. The challenge was to deal with difficult critique without offending, but leaving a deep impression that asked the audience to think for a long time after the performers had left. The play avoided immediate offence, but succeeded in leaving a sentiment and a dialogue within the recipient.

Thus, the traditional Indian audience is sophisticated, having inherited a pattern of theatre which rejects universality and sustains the general principles of plural life in Indian cultures. Traditionally, Indian theatre has been conscious of the freedom of conscience that allows for a pantheon of beliefs and choices. This gives the artist complete freedom in creativity. Theatre understands that each person and community creates its own sacred space as its identity and its creative activity. The creation of these variable and innumerable forms of creative sacred spaces gives rise to forms of art and expressions of the individual, deliberately transported out of the domain of explanation or reason in many instances. Disparate systems co-exist within a healthy dialectic of critique and doubt. But the art is in learning the boundaries of critique, so the arts never become offensive. This is understood within traditional theatre, which can be provocative without being offensive. The play succeeds if it can engage the audience through *rasa*, with the *artha* (the sentiment) that invokes thought rather than anger. It fails if it causes offence and provokes violent response or anger.

Modernity and Indian arts

In this ancient and highly sophisticated civilisation, modernity has created disruptions. Many Indians educated within Western systems are oblivious of the history and theories of the *Natyashastar*, and have transformed Indian theatre to a mirage of Western theatre. Indian life has been 'invaded' by western cultural forms.[40] Theatre is bound by the limits of time and it uses Western theatre theory to be provocative. But the audience of the villages and the traditions are used to a different sophistication in theatre. They do not like the brutal form of theatre of the West. They can appreciate the subtle and entertaining form of Western theatre. But they react adversely when it provokes with offence, because this breaks one of the most sacred principles of Indian plurality, 'respect and be respected', the dialectic of critique without the politics of desecration and hegemony.

It is an irony that the Western liberal cannot teach the traditional Indian freedom of thought as it is intrinsic in Indic civilisation, so he/she reverts to teaching the Indian freedom to offend! But an important question is 'offend what and offend for the sake of what?' If criticism and disagreement is allowed and since no system of belief assumes a position of infallibility, what exactly is offence trying to achieve?

To offend implies a self elevated sense of superiority as the racist in the street does. To offend assumes one knows better than the other. But, according to Indic civilisation all human knowledge is ultimately a myth, a creation of human imagination. The truth remains elusive. The Indic civilisation does not support the belief that there is an objective knowledge out there to be decoded definitively through the empiricism of science. Even science is a human construction, a certain way of looking at things, a methodology. In the Indic context, why is the myth of the liberal any superior than that of his predecessor, the Christian or the Muslim? And how are the myths of the Muslim any superior to that of the Christian or the Jew? How are the humanist's ethics any more real than those of the animist or the so called superstition of Ganesh, the elephant god? The humanist calls his creed rational liberalism, the Christian fundamentalist claims his creed to be a divine revelation that cannot be faulted. The extremes of the two exist in tension and compete to claim authentic legitimacy. The use of the weapon of offence in this duel is understandable as neither concedes ground or acknowledge the other to have legitimacy too. When the dialectic breaks down or is restricted, the politics of violence and offence takes over.

The new religion of Western civilisation is a certain construction of human reason, a particular worldview. The liberal is as fanatical as his predecessor, the Christian believer. Just as the Christian wanted to spread the message across the world, and force it down the throats of the rest of the unwitting world, the liberal assumes a similar crusade driven by a belief in the universality of his ideals. When examined in context, the genesis of Western liberal thought from the Enlightenment appears to have failed to address the essential problematic feature of medieval Christian dogma. The sinister fanaticism, the certainty, the universalism that gave rise to the crusades, colonialism, slavery and oppression, has crept through intact into the new liberal creed. Negri's 'Empire'[41] is a great expose of the neo-colonialism of liberalism. All that has changed is that faith in the certainty of divine revelation has been replaced by faith in the certainty of human reason. The West stumbled towards freedom from the oppressive restrictions of the Church. But it shows little if any recognition that the 'other' (that is, Indic civilisation) has had freedom for at least three millennia and has no sanction against criticism, no system of inviolable oppressive ethics, no concept of the proscriptive, no problem with freedom of expression and no concept of the sacred as defined in relation to the profane. The distinction between sacred and profane does not exist in Indic theatre.[42] There isn't comprehension that Indic civilisation does not have a sense of religion in the context of Abrahamic religions. It appears that hegemony seems to empower interpretation and comprehension of the other through one linguistic tool and worldview.

In the Indian context, the profane is the universalist, because it attempts to undermine the basic Indian concept of pluralism. When the sacred is deliberately treated with disrespect, rather than critique, it is seen as the beginning of political universalism, a concept Indian civilisation has successfully contested and defeated time and again through its known 3000 years of civilisation. This was at the heart of the response of the non-Westernised Sikhs in UK to the crude theatre of *Behzti*.

Behzti, the contest of civilisations

We come to the practical: the real drama of *Behzti*. There were at least three plays in the entire saga: the serious play by Gurpreet Bhatti, the semiotic play by the Birmingham Repertory Theatre (or its director), and the drama out in the street — a clash between two civilisations.

Bhatti's play was simple and straightforward. Written from an orientalist perspective of Sikhi and full of cultural clichés common in liberal fraternity and the Westernised sector of Sikhs, the play tried to deal with the humiliation of women in a religious context. Lacking any deeper understanding of Sikhi, she interposed Christianity as a model of religion upon Sikhi and the Sikh Gurdwara as the institution. The characters involved the president of the Gurdwara and people around him. The play's theme is sexual corruption and financial greed. He is killed by one of his victims. Ms Bhatti admitted that this was pure fiction and without any basis in reality.

The Sikh public is weary of these negative stereotype plays which seem to be the ones that get financial backing and mainstream opportunity for production. However, the Sikhs are used to parody and to jokes about them. Indians joke about Sikhs as the English joke about the Irish. The Sikhs even join in these jokes and joke about themselves. Moreover, fictionalisation of life in theatre is something Indians (and Sikhs) are used to. The Sikh tendency is to ignore these, as they initially did with Bhatti. It is possible that some British-educated Sikhs may have been offended by this type of negative portrayal production and might have written to the theatre or local council. But that is as far as the protest would have gone. The majority of Sikhs, born in India, would simply have brushed off the production. Drama is fiction. There have been controversial and provocative productions by other young Sikh writers in the past, but the Sikhs have simply ignored them or found them amusing. A playwright called Harwant Bains produced a play in which a Sikh cuts his hair on stage and mocks the 'religion'. He tried his best to get publicity by provoking the Sikhs. He went on to claim to have had threatening phone calls, possibilities of demonstrations, etc. The Sikhs simply ignored him. Fiction is fiction. His production died a quiet death.

Moreover, the theme of humiliation of women is not new in Indian theatre, or to the Sikhs. The attempted disrobing of Draupadi the wife of the Pandavs in the epic Mahabharata, the sacred Hindu text about dharma and virtue in war, is a classic narrative in Indian culture. Sikhi, like other Indian philosophies, makes no distinction between the religious and the secular. Inevitably, a narrative of a Sikh man humiliating women would involve the principles, or lack of them, of his *dharam* (moral duties). *Dharam* and 'religion' are two different words with different meanings, as described earlier. Indian philosophies call themselves *Dharma* and not 'religions'. But colonialism insisted on a particular category, and hence forced a dichotomy upon Indic cultures. The dichotomy between the religious and the secular is meaningless in an Indian cultural context.

Indian theatre has dealt with the theme of women's humiliation successfully for millennia without offending the audience and yet leaving the message of the writer deeply imprinted in the minds of the audience. The Sikhs expected that subtlety from Bhatti. Many traditional Indians expect writers of Indian origin to know of the traditions in Indian theatre. But disjunctions in cultures and community become apparent in instances such as this which are a theatre of their own. Ironically, neo-Western Indians, ingrained with universalist liberalism, think they are 'educating' their 'provincial' community while the community assumes that such Indians have a critical understanding of their civilisation. These conflicting assumptions were evident in *Behzti*.

Behzti went a bit far. Not the play, the *artha*, written by Gurpreet Bhatti, but another play in the background. This was the *abhinaya* playing silently, whose sole aim was to offend. *Abhinaya* is the variety of props and techniques that give visual form on the stage. The props used to give form to the play were not fiction nor did they have any relevance to the play. It was a semiotic theatre reminiscent of colonialism, triumphalism and power. This was the director's play; the director wanted to provoke for the sake of provoking, offend for the sake of offending. The director had power, the public's money behind the theatre, and a mere two centuries of fundamentalist Western liberal rhetoric. The director tried to bring an Indic civilisation system into the dual context of Western historical experience and the recently discovered freedom of expression. The director tried to construct the concept of sacred and profane, the triumph of reason over 'religion', an assertion of crude freedom over conjectured proscriptive restrictions. The director tried deflating the icon that is central in the Sikh system and tried to make the essential in Sikhi mundane and irrelevant. The director was on his own little crusade to teach the Sikhs about freedom of theatre and to gain publicity in his attempt. But, for the Sikhs, the play had gone beyond *rasa* into offence. It was no longer attempting to stage Bhatti's play, but the Director's perversion. The *artha*, the *rasa* and the *abhinaya* had no cohesion, or *sahmiti*. As far as the Sikhs were concerned, it was no longer theatre but the director's 'safe zone' of intentional humiliation: the offence that was disallowed in *Natyashastar*. This was no longer theatre nor a creative act, but a political statement. From their perspective, theatre had failed and entered into the politics of neo-colonialist presumption.

The Sikhs, like most Indians, are sophisticated in receiving theatre. Thousands of years of cultural orientation are not lost merely by migrating to another country. Controversy, criticism, subtle deconstruction, bad language, sexual perversions, character assassination, etc, are all acceptable as part of fiction, but political humiliation and deliberate offence is not acceptable. It broke the *natyadharma* and failed to create *rasa*.

The director brought the Gurdwara and the Guru Granth Sahib's text into the stage where rape and corruption were being staged. From an Indian perspective, this was no longer theatre, but a political statement. At best, it was a misguided political statement imagining a battle between artist's freedom and religious dogma. This has no history or relevance in Indic civilisation. Indian civilisation recognises the artist's total freedom, but also the artist's responsibility towards wider pluralism and the freedom of the individual to his sacred art. It was also clear from the play that the writer had no real knowledge of Sikhi, the institution of Gurdwara, or the benign teachings of Sri Guru Granth Sahib, the living textual guru of Sikhs. The director treated the living created iconology of the Sikhs into his dead world of intellectual discourse, the post enlightenment war between the Western concept of human reason and its assumed irrelevancy of the Abrahamic God in Western public life. At best, it was ignorance of the 'other' because there is no such conflict in Sikhi or Indic civilisation.

Sikhs protested. It is interesting that on the twelfth day, British born non-practicing young Sikhs emerged from the pubs in Birmingham, saw the pain of their community and took matters into hand. They attacked the theatre. Although brought up in Britain, they do not share the British middle class reverence for the Western theatre as a 'sacred' place. The theatre stage has replaced the Church pulpit in the West. At one time in Western history, the pulpit was the safe stage from which war could be waged against ideas of heresy and blasphemy. Now it is the theatre which is the safe stage from which war can be waged against the very concept of ideas being called heresy or blasphemy. But this historic Western conflict between Church and State, between Church dogma and scientific thinking, between Christian proscription and Western liberalism, the perpetual tension of duality, receives little empathy within the civilisation of Indians. Indians have inherited a tapestry of plurality of coexisting imaginations without restriction, and in the minds of Indians, theatre is the drama beyond the confines of the building. The 'magic' 'epic' or 'divine' world co-exists with the everyday (Yarrow).[43] In the Indian mind, there is nothing sacred about theatre if it breaks from the *natyadharma* (the rules of engagement in theatre). Once a performer moves away from *dharma*, he/she forfeits the assumption of sacred 'freedom'.

The Gurdwara as the 'sacred'

Since everything is *maya*, an illusion of realities that emerge and then vanish, drama is played in the context of the wider world. According to Sri Guru Granth Sahib: 'This world is an illusion; it dies and it is re-born — it comes and it goes in reincarnation.'[44] The Sikhs believe that every second is a new creation. The past dies, its memory only constructed, the present is real for a nanosecond and the future hasn't arrived, it is just conjecture.

The Hindus carry out a special service called *Arti*. It is worship of the creativity of nature but represented in a plate. *Arti* is very sacred. The Sikh gurus critiqued this. *Arti* is the entire world. Everything is in a creative state, dying and reliving. The individual needs to break from the confines of buildings into the broader space that exists around him or her. The sacred space is the wider world, not in a confined theatre or building.

But then, why is the Gurdwara sacred? The Gurdwara is not sacred in the sense of demarcated territory. It is the sovereign territory of *Guru Granth Sahib*, a text to other people, but which is treated as a human person when it is read. Derrida's philosophy of the differ/ance may help to explain this phenomenon. The Guru Granth Sahib was written by the Sikh Gurus themselves and is in *raags* (musical format) and cannot be changed, added to or modified. The text is considered as the spoken word without the lag that Derrida conjectures, without the censor of the human mind, without that corruption that takes place between the hidden and the stated. One of the practices in Gurdwaras is to recite the Guru Granth Sahib without an intervening interpretation. The Gurdwara is the residence of the guru. The Sikhs identify themselves with the *Guru Granth Sahib*, treating it as a living, speaking and engaging entity. It makes no sense to others, but that is the essence of Indian plurality. It is the creative act of every Sikh treating a text as a living person.

The Sikhs do not see the theatre as a sacred territory where the rules of the wider society can be suspended and offence created. But, brought up with pluralism, they respect the Western institution of the apparent 'free' theatre. However, they do not expect this historic western tension played as freedom to colonise their own cultural space. They do not mock it nor humiliate it. Coexistence requires negotiation of mutual respect, not assuming a right to offend the other's sacred. But when the director of the theatre went beyond the Western cultural sphere and dragged in the created sacred of another to humiliate in the theatre's safe territory, the theatre forfeited that respect and war was declared. Like the colonist who used indigenous co-opted intermediaries to legitimise their rule, the director justified his act by pointing out Bhatti's origins in a Sikh family. The Western theatre commands respect from people like the Sikhs as long as it stays within its own boundaries. Once it crosses into the territory of others then it has to respect the rules of the 'other', otherwise it can only enforce its respect with the aid of the coercive power of the State to suppress the people whose otherwise benign indifference is provoked into protecting their own. The Sikhs stood outside the theatre for twelve days quietly protesting, puzzled by the transgression of the director and the theatre's production manager's refusal to engage in a dialogue. Dialogue is at the heart of Indic civilisation. The theatre production manager refused 'dialogue'. The manager set up a monologue a few days prior to the play being shown, and then, like the imperialist, decided that the community had to learn 'freedom of the theatre'. The director's crusade, like a colonist, to 'teach' an ancient civilisation the West's newly acquired concept of freedom was an absurdity in itself. Like the French who pursued culture evangelisation in East India in the seventeenth century, only to be thrown out, like the missionaries who caused havoc with their soul-saving crusades in ancient civilisations, the manager-director of the Birmingham Repertory Theatre was on a mission, little realising the comedy of the producer's own position. The director's freedom is that of the adolescent emerging into puberty, full of bravado, threatening without the wisdom of experience. The Sikh has inherited centuries of freedom with the sophistication of critique and drama without crossing the limits of offence.

It is notable that the Sikh representatives who defended the Sikhs' objections to the play in public statements,[45] made a clear distinction between the *artha* and the *abhinaya*, stating that they had no problems with the substance of the play, but objected to the depiction of the Gurdwara and symbolism of *Guru Granth Sahib*, both of which are their sacred institutions separate from those of others.[46] In contrast, almost all articles and comments by leading figures from the arts and media, including the petition by 700 leading luminaries of British arts conflated everything into 'freedom of speech'[47] and 'refusing debate'[48] or 'the right to challenge religion'![49] Most of the articles and statements attacking Sikhs seemed to lack any rationale or analysis and depend more on histrionics. It is still not clear to Sikhs who this debate was supposed to be with, as the audience was largely white middle class and some British educated Indians who rarely if ever go to Gurdwaras. The community that this debate was supposed to be initiated in was enraged by the disrespect shown to the *Guru Granth Sahib* and the Gurudwara, the 'Rasa' had broken down.

In context, *Behzti* brought two civilisations into contact but in unfortunate circumstances. From the perspective of Indic civilisation, the West's much protected and prided freedom of expression extending to freedom to offend[50] in arts and theatre[51] is but an old conflict being played between those in power and those without power that started in the Roman amphitheatre with its captured audience in a walled confine. The Romans ridiculed the weak in the bloody games in their amphitheatre. After them, the Church saw its right to be free to offend human reason from the theatre of the pulpit. In the twentieth century, human reason assumes a new born right to offend religious doctrine from the theatre of arts. This has no relevance in Indic civilisation which is based on the principle, 'believe and let believe'. Freedom of conscience and expression is a fundamental aspect of the non-dualist Indic civilisation. It allows critique and dialogue but stops at gratuitous offence to preserve and nurture its essential plurality. The wider play in *Behzti* was the interaction between two different civilisations with different historical evolution of ideas and political dynamics of freedoms, and with different philosophical developments. One which sees the right to offend as its sacred duty, while the other which, in the words of Yarrow, 'needs to be recognised...for the subtlety and power of its grasp of the nature and operation of individual and communal effects as embedded in its performance tradition and in Natyasastra'.[52]

Endnotes

[1] In a letter to the editor of the *Guardian* newspaper (UK) 23 December 2004, 700 of UK's leading figures from the arts world wrote: 'We must defend freedom of expression', and, 'It is a legitimate function of art to provoke debate and sometimes to express controversial ideas. A genuinely free, pluralist society would celebrate this aspect of our culture'. Shelley King, David Edgar and 698 others: 'We must defend freedom of expression', http://arts.guardian.co.uk/news/story/0,,1378818,00.html

[2] Nicholas Hytner, the artistic director of the National Theatre, told the BBC that theatre's role was to provoke powerful feelings: 'The giving of offense, the causing of offense, is part of our business,' he said. Alan Cowell, 'Rape, religion and artistic freedom', *International Herald Tribune*, 29 December 2004. http://www.iht.com/articles/2004/12/28/features/bhatti.php

[3] The Nyaya school of Hinduism is an analytic school which believes in the duality of mind and body. The Vaisesika school is atomistic. S. Radhakrishnan, 1989 (1978), *Indian philosophy*, vol. 2, New Delhi: Oxford University Press.

[4] Edward Said, 1978, *Orientalism*, New York: Vintage Books.

[5] Arvind Sharma (ed.) 2004, *Advaita Vedanta: An Introduction*, New Delhi: Motilal Benarsidas.

[6] Adi Sankara was a Hindu monk who articulated the *Advaita Vedanta* (end of Vedas writings). In modern times, Swami Vivekananda popularised Adi Sankara's work in the nineteenth century.

[7] The word 'God' may obscure its understanding.

[8] In Jaap, Sahib, Dasaam Granth (the text of the tenth Sikh Guru).

[9] *Sri Guru Granth Sahib*: (*Avar na ko māranvārā.*) 'There is no other Destroyer than the Eternal,' p. 391, line 2.

[10] The Sikhs have had ten human Gurus, one after the other from 1469 to 1708. They compiled their teachings during their lives. This compilation in 1430 pages, mostly written in ragas, is called the *Sri Guru Granth Sahib* and is revered as a living text, in the form of human by the Sikhs. The first eight pages are the poetry of the first Guru, Guru Nanak, called the Jap, in which the Guru sets out the philosophical context of Sikh teachings. From pages 14 to 1353 are the collection of hymns in 31 ragas. The last pages are the poetry of some main spiritual people from around India whose teachings were consistent with those of the Sikh Gurus.

[11] *Sri Guru Granth Sahib*: (*Hukm hukam chalā rāhu.*) 'The order orders the paths to follow'. Jap, p. 2.

[12] *Sri Guru Granth Sahib*: (*Kiv kar Akha kiv salahi kio varni jana.*) 'How can we describe, how can we explain what happens, how can we know?' Jap, p. 4.

[13] *Sri Guru Granth Sahib*: (*Nanak, akhan sabh ko akhai ik dui k siana.*) 'O Nanak, many speak of the eternal truth to others, each one claims to be wiser than others'.

(*Vada sahib, badi nai, kita ja ka hove*) 'The great master with the most superlative names, ultimately knows what has and will happen'.

(*Nanak, je ko apou janai, agai gaia na sohai.*) 'O Nanak, one who claims to know everything, shall not be gifted with knowledge beyond his immediate world'. Jap, p. 5.

[14] *Sri Guru Granth Sahib*: (*Eka Mai Jugat Viai tin chele parvan*) 'One source conceived the entire existence and authorised the three';

(*Ik sansari ik bhandari ik lae deban*) 'One the creator, one the sustainer and one the destroyer' (talking of Brahma, Vishnu and Siva);

(*Jiv tis bhavai tivai chalavai jiv hovai furman*) 'Whatever is desired so will happen, they merely follow the order';

(*Oh vekhai ona nadir na avai bahuta ehu vidan*) 'The eternal watches them, but they cannot see the ultimate Source, that is the greatness of this mystery'. Jap, p. 7.

Therefore, in Jap, Guru Nanak subtly asks the audience: Why go through gods who can do no better than the human?

[15] Chandra Bhan Gupta, 1954, *The Indian Theatre*, Munshiram Manoharlal Publishers: New Delhi, p. 107.

[16] *Bhagvat Gita*

[17] Radhakrishnan, op. cit., pp. 29-175.

[18] Ibid., p. 248.

[19] Ibid., p. 430.

[20] The four were, *Apastamba, Gautama, Baudhayana* and *Vasistha*, P. Olivelle, (trans.), 1999, *Dharmasutras, the Law Codes of Ancient India,* Oxford: Oxford University Press, Contents and p. xxv.

[21] Manu was the lawgiver of ancient India who codified civil rules of behaviour and claimed divine authority for these. It is considered that Manu became the *nom de plume* for a series of lawgivers. However, Manu did not claim universal imposition for these laws, and hence they had no meaning in the world of *sanyasis*.

[22] W. Doniger and B. Smith, 1991, *The Laws of Manu,* London: Penguin Classics, Penguin Books.

[23] 'In modern day language, *Dharma* is equated quite unfairly with religion', Sri Krishna Kant, Vice President of India, 1997, Convocation address, Sri Sathya Sai Institute of Higher Education, p. 3. http://www.sssu.edu.in/pdf/CG_Address1997.pdf

[24] Ibid.

[25] Teachings of A.C. Bhaktivedanta Swami Prabhupada, website owned by Bhaktivedanta Book Trust, http://www.krishna.com/en/node/492

[26] Kant, op. cit.

[27] T.B. MaCauley, Minute dated 2 February 1835. Bureau of Education, 1965 (1920), *Selections from Educational Records, Part I* (1781-1839), H. Sharp (ed.), Delhi: National Archives of India, pp. 107-117, http://www.columbia.edu/itc/mealac/pritchett/00generallinks/macaulay/txt_minute_education_1835.html

[28] David Ludden, 2006, *Making India Hindu*, Oxford: Oxford University Press, p. 21.

[29] E.W. Marasinghe, 1989, *The Sanskrit Theatre and Stagecraft*, Delhi: Sri Satguru Publications (India Book Centre).

[30] Ibid., p. 185.

[31] Ibid., p. 186.

[32] Ibid., p. 186.

[33] Ibid., p. 197.

[34] R. Yarrow, 2001, *India Theatre, Theatre of Origin, Theatre of Freedom*, Richmond, Surrey UK: .Routledge Curzon, p.118.

[35] Chandra Bhan Gupta, op. cit., p.107.

[36] 'The Ankle Bracelet',,Yarrow, op. cit., p. 113. Yarrow holds that tragic ends and realism is consistent with Sanskrit theatre.

[37] Bhatia Nandi, 1963, *Acts of Authority/Acts of Resistance: Theatre and Politics in Colonial and Postcolonial India*, Michigan: University of Michigan Press, chapter 2.

[38] L.N. Rangarajan, 1992, *Kautilya, The Arthashastra*, New Delhi: Penguin Classics, Peguin Books.

[39] Yarrow, op. cit., p.12.

[40] Ibid., p. 27.

[41] M. Hardt and A. Negri, 2001, *Empire,* Harvard: Harvard University Press.

[42] Yarrow, op. cit., p.12.

Ibid., p. 13.

[43] Ibid., p. 12.

[44] Sri Guru Granth Sahib, p. 138.

[45] 'But Gurdial Singh Atwal, a Labour councilor and representative for the Council of Sikh Gurdwaras, said: 'It has caused a great hurt, and shows a lack of respect. The Sikh community had a small demand: rather than setting it in a gurdwara, set it in a community centre.' T. Branigan, 2004, 'Tale of Rape at

the temple sparks riot at theatre', *The Guardian,* 20 December,
http://arts.guardian.co.uk/news/story/0,,1377285,00.html

[46] 'But many Sikh representatives argue that the issues have been misunderstood. Harmander Singh, a spokesman for the advocacy group Sikhs in England, said concerns about the setting of the play had gone unheeded for days before the violent protests. Sikh representatives had suggested that the play would be far less offensive if the setting were changed from a temple to a community center, a proposal the theater rejected.' Cowell, op. cit.

[47] Sir Christopher Frayling, chairman of the Arts Council said: 'It sends out a message that there are certain subjects about which they must never speak.' Terry Kirby, 2004, 'Violence and vandalism close theatre', *The Independent,* 21 December, http://www.independent.co.uk/arts/theatre/news/article25779.ece

[48] Petition: 'We must defend freedom of expression'. 'It is a legitimate function of art to provoke debate and sometimes to express controversial ideas. A genuinely free, pluralist society would celebrate this aspect of our culture'. Letters, signed by 700 leading illuminaries in the arts: 'We must defend freedom of expression', *The Guardian,* 23 December 2004,
http://arts.guardian.co.uk/news/story/0,,1378818,00.html

[49] Dominic Dromgoole, 2004, 'Theatre's role is to challenge religion', *The Guardian,* 20 December 2004.
http://arts.guardian.co.uk/features/story/0,,1377489,00.html

[50] '"Artists" power to move brings with it a duty of intellectual integrity. Within the limits this duty imposes, however, they must be free to offend — and this freedom, too, is sacred.' Editorial, *Times,* 21 December 2004.

[51] Nicholas Hytner, the artistic director of the National Theatre, told the BBC that the theatre's role was to provoke powerful feelings: 'The giving of offense, the causing of offense, is part of our business', he said. Cowell, op. cit.

[52] Yarrow, op. cit., p. 21.

9

Blasphemy in a pluralistic society

Jeremy Shearmur

In this chapter, I will tentatively address a difficult issue: what we should make of blasphemy today, in a society like Australia?[1] My discussion falls into three parts: considering blasphemy under the headings of truth, ridicule, and play. I also discuss some different dimensions to the character of the offence. I conclude with a discussion of some particular problems about blasphemy posed by the fact that we are living in a pluralistic society, in the face of which I make some specific — but inadequate — recommendations. I am happy to call them 'inadequate' just because my aim, at the end of the paper, is to open up what seem to me some difficult problems rather than to resolve them.

In my preparatory research, I came to the conclusion that the more that one looks at some of the issues connected with blasphemy, say, at their history, the more complex they turn out to be. The consequence is that if, as in the present chapter, one is trying to speak in general terms, one becomes acutely aware of just how thin the ice is upon which one is treading. As a result, it is bound to be the case that, in addition to provoking the kind of critical reaction that I am intending to provoke, and which I am hoping will lead to a fruitful response to the issues which I am setting out to raise, I may also provoke all kinds of gnashing of teeth on the part of those who have specialised knowledge on issues that I deal with very briefly. All that I would say in my defence is that I am acutely aware of my fallibility and, as a former student of Karl Popper's, I am aware of the need for criticism, which I look forward to receiving in due course.

Let me start by saying a *very* little about a key problem. It is: What is the character of blasphemy as an offence, and why was it thought appropriate to punish it? My concern here will not be with its legal status,[2] but with what the underlying concerns have been. There seem to me to have been several lines of argument. I will mention but five.

The first, as, say, we meet it for example in *Leviticus* 24, 16-18, is that the punishment, even with death, of the blasphemer is simply seen as a command of God, which is to be followed as such.

The second is that blasphemy is understood as a substantive offence against God. Here, humans who make accusations of it, and uphold the law in relation to it are, as it were, acting in His defence, or in defence of His reputation.

The third is slightly convoluted. It is that blasphemy is understood as something which, if unpunished, will threaten those who do not punish it with the judgement of God. Punishment of the blasphemer is, here, seen as a reaction to the threat of the collective punishment by God of those who fail to punish blasphemer.

The fourth is the idea that an attack on religion is problematic because of what are thought to be its social consequences, i.e., the destruction of civil order. This played a significant role during one period of British law, as is illustrated by the following statement by Lord Chief Justice Hale:

> ...to say, religion is a cheat, is to dissolve all those obligations whereby the civil societies are preserved, and that Christianity is parcel of the laws of England; and therefore to reproach the Christian religion is to speak in subversion of the law.[3]

Finally, there is a more typically modern understanding. This is the notion of blasphemy as an offence against the sensibilities of believers, and, further, as something which because it so offends, is problematic because it is liable to lead to a breach of the peace.

Let me now move to the discussion of blasphemy, as such. I need briefly to explain why I am discussing the issue of blasphemy under the three heads to which I have referred: truth, ridicule and play.[4] I do so because, historically, one can note people as having been charged with blasphemy for activities that fall conveniently under these somewhat different headings, and I wish to argue that the issues that they raise are somewhat different, too.

Historically, one element in blasphemy has been a simple contesting of the truth of various religious claims. This, for example, was one element in the charges against Thomas Aikenhead at the end of the seventeenth century and against G. W. Foote in the latter part of the nineteenth. In earlier times, people who had wished to contest the truth of Christianity, were sometimes punished — but for impiety. In the context of an orthodox Christianity feeling under threat from Socinianism and Deism,[5] Aikenhead's youthful mixture of contestation of and irreverent comment about Christianity was taken horribly seriously, and he was executed.[6] Foote, the editor of *The Freethinker* in the 1880s, combined denial of the truth of Christianity, and fierce argument to that effect, with the use of ridicule.[7] In the context of one of the trials of *The Freethinker*, Lord Coleridge declared:

> I lay it down as law, that, if the decencies of controversy are observed, even the fundamentals of religion may be attacked without a person being guilty of blasphemous libel.[8]

This is generally accepted in Western countries today; but, for example, it may be contentious for some Muslims. Foote, however, did much more than this. And that takes us to the second category, of ridicule. One of the features of *The Freethinker* were various hostile cartoons about the life of Jesus, and more generally illustrating in a satirical manner various themes from the *Bible*. The latter included an unsubtly illustrated version of the verse from Exodus 33, verses 22-3: 'And it shall come to pass…that I will put thee in a clift of the rock…and I will take away my hand and thou shalt see my back parts'.[9] *The Freethinker*'s cartoon, as the previous quotation from Lord Coleridge implicitly indicated, raises the issue: Is the use of ridicule as part of an attack on religion acceptable?

Third, and of particular significance in our current context, is what I will term the playful or aesthetic use of blasphemy. By this I mean blasphemy committed not as part of a disagreement with, or an attack on religion (although it is not clear that it would be used in such a manner by a devout religious believer), but, instead, as used for literary or artistic effect. An obvious example here is Salman Rushdie's playing with themes from Islam to literary effect, in his *Satanic Verses*. We may here, similarly, consider the work of art, *Piss Christ*, and also, say, in a much more minor key, parodies of the Creed, and so on, produced by William Hone for political purposes in the early nineteenth century.[10] The key idea here is that religious material is played with, or used for effect, in ways that believers could reasonably find offensive, but where the motivation of those making use of this material is not to attack religion. With this before us, let me now turn to the body of the paper, and to the issue of truth.

Truth

Truth seems to me usefully looked at in terms of the kinds of consideration that John Stuart Mill advanced in his *On Liberty*. I should state explicitly that my concern, here, will be with the social consequences of epistemological fallibilism[11] rather than with the specifics of Mill's views; Jonathan Riley has argued powerfully that Mill's own arguments are best seen in the wider context of his social philosophy, and that seen in that light, Mill is to be taken as arguing for a more liberal view than that which is presented here.[12] If it is being claimed that various religious doctrines are true, then some kind of case has to be made for them. What is involved here, may seem to get us into the territory of various traditional arguments for the existence of God, such as the 'cosmological argument'. But what is actually offered in the context of religious proselatisation may be rather different.

Now if any such claims are being made as to the truth of religious doctrine, we get straight into the issues which J. S. Mill discussed.[13] He argued that all of our knowledge is fallible, and that if we are aiming for truth, our best course of action is to submit our claims to open critical scrutiny. In this context, he was then able to develop arguments against the suppression of opinion. To Mill's argument, it might be objected by the believer: 'but *our* religious views are not fallible'. However, those who agree with Mill can respond: 'but you have certainly not furnished us with telling arguments that show you views to be anything but fallible.[14] And your tendency, across history, to kill or to imprison those who have objected to your claims, does not exactly speak for their strength — for if the arguments were strong, why should they require support from the hangman or the jailor'.[15]

It seems to me that, here, the case for allowing the public contestation of religious doctrines is unanswerable. Not only is the Millian case a powerful one, but since the Reformation we have lived in a society in which religious truth is contested. If there are Catholics and Protestants — to say nothing of Muslims and Jews, and also non-believers — who are members of a single society, then clearly there is disagreement about religious truth.[16] Indeed, the very beliefs of these groups implicitly or sometimes even explicitly involve the view that the other religious beliefs are incorrect. If we are living in a society that is pluralistic in this sense, the notion that the discussion and the contestation of religious ideas should be suppressed would seem an absurdity. (It is, however, worth noting that Jewish criticism of Christian claims, particularly its claims about itself as a supposed fulfilment of the Old Testament, was frequently suppressed.[17]) Given that all the groups to whom I have referred — contemporary Judaism apart — are universalistic and attempt to convert others, this is surely an invitation to contestation.[18]

Today, Christendom accepts the case for openness of argument. (Although one wonders sometimes what the more dogmatic believers would do, if they could get their hands on the reins of enough political power.) It is not clear that this case for openness of argument is accepted by all Muslim clerics. Attitudes there, at least in terms of the views of some clerics, seem closer to those that were common in Western countries several centuries ago, although there are, of course, also liberal Muslims. There is also room for debate as to just what is supposed to be accorded what kind of protection, and it is quite another matter what anyone actually becomes concerned about (the Rushdie case had strong political elements to it). At least in principle, to voice disagreement about some key issues is problematic, even if all that is involved is intellectual engagement. Of course, in practical terms, no Muslim is going to be able legally to take action against Christian ministers who may say things within their religious congregations that are at odds with Islam. Further, Muslims have, I think, to face the fact that if they choose to live in a society like Australia, they are living in a society in which the open *intellectual* contestation of their beliefs — whether by sceptics, or by those who favour other religions — will take place. Further, if such contestation is conducted along the 'decent' lines that Lord Coleridge suggested, other citizens will expect that those engaged in such contestation will, if necessary, receive full protection from the law.

Some limitations of the truth-based argument

It is, however, worth pausing to consider what the intellectual issues to which I have referred actually amount to. For this intellectual case has limitations; in particular, it does not seem to me to offer the basis of a case for 'freedom of expression'. (Clearly, someone might say: 'but the case for freedom of expression does not depend on arguments like Mill's, but, instead, relates somehow to ideas about human agency, or is simply a "right"'. But it is just not clear on what basis such a right could be established if, say, it involves a purported entitlement to behave in offensive ways towards others.)

Let me return to the fallibilistic argument from Mill. As far as I can see, all that is required for the fulfilment of the kinds of requirement that Mill set out, is that there be some place where such contestation can take place, and that the results of debates about such matters be freely available in the society.[19] What this means, is that there need to be journals in which such matters can be discussed, and places where people interested in such things can meet. This is a very different matter from some entitlement to bombard other people with challenges to their views when they do not wish to encounter them,[20] or, say, a right even to demonstrate as opposed simply to the advancing of arguments. More generally, an awareness of human fallibility seems to me in principle compatible with restrictions on the dissemination of information which has not been exposed to some appropriate form of inter-subjective scrutiny. This might, however, today be accomplished without the suppression of opinion, by way of the requirement that certain kinds of material be published only in a setting in which an indication can be given of the basis on which others disagree with what is being advanced. For example, rather than the making of claims about, say, holocaust revisionism illegal — which may itself backfire[21] — there could be a legal requirement that the material be posted only to web pages that allow for responses by scholars who disagree with the case being argued.

Let me also offer some further considerations against the taking of Millian arguments in an expansive way. There is much that goes to constitute our day-to-day lives that might quite fairly be called necessary fictions. We typically have a view of the world, and of ourselves, which we implicitly take to be correct and live by, and which we are not interested in having challenged. Most people, if they are not suffering from depression, are moral heroes in their own internal narratives; and all of us operate within a framework of assumptions — many of which will not, in fact, be true — which we certainly do not wish to have challenged, unless we choose to open them up to such challenges. Some of those reading this will, like myself, be academics, and this means that certain things that we do will be subject to fairly constant challenge and criticism. More generally, the cultures in which academics live and by which our ideas are broadly informed are subject to certain kinds of challenge and scrutiny. But typically — and, I think, quite properly — the ideas that constitute the assumptions under which we live on a day-to-day basis, are not usually submitted to such scrutiny. In part, this is because one can, as it were, hardly live in the open — with all aspects of ourselves and our conduct exposed to the critical scrutiny of others all the time. In part, it is because many of these ideas are simply things that we use while getting on with other, more pressing, matters. At the same time, one of the features of life in Australia which I have come to value — as compared, say, to the USA — is that there is a degree of accountability here to one another, in our ordinary culture, for what we believe.[22]

Now, the ideas on the basis of which we live may well be incorrect or misguided. Sometimes, we may become annoyed with other people because of what they believe and act on. But broadly speaking, it seems to me that we are not entitled to challenge them (unless we are invited to do so), unless it is the case that those ideas and their actions (or failures to act) impinge significantly upon us, or upon others with whose well-being we have a legitimate concern. In this respect, while intellectual contestation is important, there is no case for the view that one is simply entitled to harangue other people, unasked, about their ideas or view of the world. (Or rather, there is a sense in which one may do this, in respect of people who are friends of ours, provided that they have the option to stop being our friends if they find this wearing!) Such ideas — consider, say, whether or not they think that eating meat is wrong — in effect become like the tastes of these other people: things that we simply live with provided that they neither positively harm others in ways that we find intolerable, nor make us really uncomfortable. If they harm others,[23] we may feel it our duty to open up a discussion about them. If they simply make us uncomfortable, we may need to modify how we interact with these people (for example, just moaning about them to friends who agree with us), or possibly even break off contact with them.

This may seem a somewhat timid viewpoint, and you may even object to it. But if you do, just ask those who know you, how many of your views about things they think to be incorrect, and ask yourself: 'would I like to be constantly open to contestation about them?' Alternatively, you may yourself be committed to some form of proselytisation; for example, for some religious view, or for some form of environmentalism. If this is the case, it is worth bearing in mind just to what extent you may be infringing upon the kinds of informal rules that we normally live by concerning such matters, and thus pausing to consider just how obnoxious you may be. If you *are* going to do this, however, it seems to me that what is good for the goose is good for the gander. You should recognise that not only may people (understandably) start to avoid you, but you may legitimately expect them to make you aware of the range of objections to your views, if they are not too polite to do so.

This is a somewhat difficult matter. For consider, say, the Protestant who thinks that if you are not saved, you will suffer in Hell.[24] How, such a person might say, can they be expected to conduct the ordinary niceties of life with you, without drawing this to your attention — and repeatedly, because so much hinges on it? They would surely do this, if you were in physical danger; and how much more important is your fate in Eternity? But just as that person may feel that he or she cannot engage in polite social chit-chat with those on the edge of a precipice, so the objects of their concern may find that they really cannot take constantly being engaged with on this subject. The only courses of action may be to agree not to raise the issue, or to separate.

There is, however, also another aspect to all this. It is that, as academics who are used to the cut and thrust of discussion, we typically come to know what we are letting ourselves in for if we enter into it. For each of us, there will be certain kinds of standards to which we know that we will be held accountable in our various professions and the sub-areas of these that we inhabit. I can, by now, make a pretty fair judgement as to what the (different) standards are, to which different groups of philosophers, of political scientists, of historians of economic thought, and so on, will hold me accountable if I give a paper to them. Further, if I make some claim — say, about the arts — in a gathering of people who deal with the arts professionally, while I cannot judge quite how what I say will be appraised, I will have at least a rough idea about the *kinds* of things that might be thrown at me.

Such knowledge, however, is typically acquired by us gradually through our lives, and sometimes somewhat painfully. I can still recall coming to university, as a gauche young man who simply did not know how these things worked, and how painful the first few steps were. I have also had the (at times difficult) experience of operating within different disciplinary contexts. By contrast with all this, we may forget that other people may not have this kind of experience behind them. As, say, we are sometimes reminded when a capable but academically inexperienced mature student joins an introductory course in the subject that we teach, people may have specific views which they believe to be true, but where their asserting them as true does not mean quite what it would normally in academic contexts. If I make claims that I assert to be true, this opens me up as an Aunt Sally, for everyone to have a go at. If people do not have an academic background, they may not realise what they are getting into if they make similar claims in an academic context. But, on the other hand, unless we are anthropologists or sociologists with an interest in these issues, we are not likely to have any real knowledge as to how their claims about the status of such views are made and negotiated in different areas of even our own society.

I would, in this kind of situation, suggest that we should exercise something the name of which I hardly dare speak, namely, paternalism. That is to say, it seems to me that, unless it is clear that the people in question wish to have their ideas contested as we would have our claims contested, their views be treated more like the expression of tastes. This will typically not be *fully* adequate to the cognitive character of those views, and there is a risk that we may be insulting to them. But perhaps better this, than the exposure of their ideas to the full force of the critical apparatus that we, given our training, may be able to bring to bear upon them. This, while fully legitimate in its place, may be inappropriate if used in a contest in which people are not accustomed to it, or do not realise what they are getting themselves into. I am reminded of a conversation that a good friend of mine reported that he had with his partner. They had some disagreement about their personal affairs, and he said to her: 'We should talk this out.' *She* said: 'No way — you, as a philosophy lecturer, are a specialist in arguments. I would not have a chance, even if I was right about everything.'

Just as in this case, it seems to me that in the kind of situations about which I have been talking, respect for other people as persons may mean that we should treat their views as having a somewhat different status from what they may present them as having. After all, *we* may be quite used to discovering that ideas which we have cherished, and have worked on for a while, turn out just to be no good. Given our professional training, we typically have the resources to cope with such things, even though the experience may not be pleasant. However, it may not be something that other people, without these resources, can easily cope with at all. It is certainly not clear to me why coping with it should be thrust upon them, without their indicating positively that they wish to get into such a situation.

Accordingly, there seems to me a case for the protection of some ideas from criticism — although it is not one which compromises what I might call the minimalist Millian case for there being a public sphere in which any idea may be contested (including, of course, ideas as to what such a sphere should be like). At the same time, it is important to note that the case for the moderation of criticism was made in the face of the vulnerability of the people whom I was discussing, and also under the assumption that what they were doing was not having adverse effects on others. The (interesting) social task here would be to create ways of behaving which protect the vulnerable, but which do not shelter the powerful.

From intellectual engagement to ridicule

So far, I have been dealing with issues of truth and falsity, and of the contestation, back and forth, of particular claims. But what of ridicule? Is it ever appropriate to ridicule or to insult things about which other people have deep feelings?

Here, it seems to me, we get onto more difficult ground. For if, say, a Christian believes that God, the all-powerful creator of the universe, gave his Son not only to suffer the humiliations and pangs of mortal life, but to die a gruesome death for the sake of each of us — then to poke *fun* at this, seems simply grotesque. It certainly is not something that can rest upon a J. S. Mill-style defence. May anything be said in its favour? Two interesting lines of argument here were advanced by the English Freethinker G. W. Foote, who ended up being imprisoned for blasphemy in the 1880s.

First, consider those who are not believers. They may find the hegemony of the ideas to which they are constantly and oppressively exposed, simply intolerable. I recall, here, a comment made by a distinguished sociologist of education, who was Jewish, and who undertook an ethnographic exercise, over a period of three years, in a fundamentalist Baptist school. He later recalled that, he hit a problem:

> ...in one of the phases of research, the last phase, the write-up. Obviously, my ox had been gored. As a non-Christian at Bethany I experienced repeated proselytising by students, parents, teachers, and the superintendent of the school. I felt that I had been assaulted by the most arrogant people I had ever met in my entire life...Obviously, all of this had gotten to me in more ways tha[n] I understood; it was coming out in my writing, though I didn't want it to. I did not want chapter one, let alone chapter two, three, four, five or six, to be redolent of the anger suggested by terms such as 'assault' and 'arrogance'.[25]

In this case, the sociologist could get away from the group which he had studied. But what if one were a member of a minority group, who were endlessly the targets of something similar from the wider culture?

In this setting, at the very least, it would be fully understandable to let off steam, to other members of one's group, about the kind of things to which one was subjected. This, indeed, was pretty much Foote's explanation for one of the things that his newspaper did: for running his cartoons, poking fun at passages from the Bible. His argument was that the material was sold in a newspaper for Freethinkers; it was not forced upon religious believers, and it would be pretty clear to the believer what the character of the journal was, should they come across a copy.

Foote, however, offered another line of argument, too. Let me present it, in his own words:

> Christians may, of course, urge that their *feelings* on such a subject as religion *are sacred*, and a few superstitious Freethinkers may concede this monstrous position. I do not. The feelings of a Christian about Father, Son and Holy Ghost, are no more sacred than my feelings on any other subject. I have no quarrel with persons, and I recognise how many are hurt by satire. But the world is not to be regulated by their feelings, and much as I respect them, I have a greater respect for truth. Every mental weapon is valid against mental error. And as ridicule has been found the most potent weapon of religious enfranchisement, we are bound to use it against the wretched superstitions which cumber the path of progress. Intellectually, it is as absurd to give quarter as it is absurd to expect it.[26]

I do not know what you might make of this. In some ways, for Foote to take this line in a situation where he might well go to jail for it, and indeed did, was courageous. At the same time, it is also clear that such satire need not be on the side of what is right, even though it may be horribly effective. Consider, in this context, the use by the Nazis, and by the regime in the Soviet Union, of art and representations which dehumanised those with whom they disagreed. Not only were those — often very powerful — representations exercised in the interests of views which were, surely, wrong, but they also served to dehumanise people, in ways which opened them to what became ghastly treatment. All told, there seems to me something to be said for treating people with decency, and respecting their sensibilities, even in cases where we think that they are deeply wrong.

Such concerns, however, look to me pressing only in the case of ordinary people, and those who do not exercise power. The powerful can, surely, well look after themselves — although even there, there is surely something to be said for recognising the human in everybody. If we accept this argument, then there is also reason to accord them a certain kind of respect — which would include not submitting those things about which they have the strongest and most tender feelings, to the full force of our abuse.

Play, or the aesthetic use of blasphemy

So far, our concern has been with those who wish to take issue with the content of religion. But if we consider blasphemy in contemporary contexts, this seems to me not, typically, what we are concerned with. Instead, what has been thought problematic, has been the use of religious ideas for aesthetic reasons or, to put it bluntly, a certain kind of playing around with them.

Consider Salman Rushdie's *Satanic Verses*. Here, he made a certain amount of mileage, for his own aesthetic purposes, with themes from Islam: the so-called 'satanic verses' episode itself, which related to the supposed interpolation —

and then deletion when their character as illegitimate interpolations was revealed
— of some verses into the text of the Koran, which legitimated the role of some
local gods as intermediaries between people and God. In addition, Rushdie played
around with the idea of the denizens of an imaginary brothel, who boosted their
custom by naming themselves after the wives of the Prophet. Was Rushdie's
aim to attack Islam, in something like the way in which Foote did Christianity?
Surely not; it was more a matter of his using these ideas, as instruments in his
novel.[27] Similarly, one might say, the artist responsible for *Piss Christ* was
playing around with Christian symbolism.

What is to be said about this? Clearly, there are legitimate uses of religious
material, not only in a devotional context, but — because of the extent to which
our culture and language is (still) permeated with them — for the purpose of
playfulness and parody. Two things, however, are worth noting. First, such
usage is parasitic upon the public, cultural significance of the material. The
reason why a form of words that draws upon well-known passages from the
Bible, or from the Creed, or upon religious symbolism, may make the impression
that it does, is because of its resonance with the material from which it is drawn,
and the kinds of public associations that it has. Second, there is the problem of
the offence that it may cause.

It might be said: 'No offence is intended — the artist had his or her own
private intention.' This, however, will not wash, because of the public
significance of the material. After all, the aesthetic weight of the material is
drawing precisely upon its public, in this case religious, meaning.[28] What is
more, people have to take into account the public meaning of what they are
saying. If, say, someone gets up and yells 'Fire, Fire' in a crowded, darkened
cinema, it is possible that they may have had their own particular intentions —
for example, they might be giving an impromptu performance of some free verse.
But this is no excuse; unless there is a very distinctive preparation of the people
who will be receiving the material,[29] such that this serves to diffuse its normal
social meaning, it is clear how it will be interpreted. And the poet will justly
suffer the consequences of their action, if they don't do so.

In the course of the discussion of the Salman Rushdie case, John Updike is
reported as having said: 'it is perhaps in the nature of modern art to be
offensive...In this century if we are not willing to risk giving offence, we have
no claim to the title of artists'.[30] But bear in mind what it is to be offensive.[31]
First, if someone is offensive to you, they may surely risk retaliation, and if they
thought about it, they might well realise that this is what they should expect.
Why, after all, should the rest of us be expected to sit there and have people
behave offensively towards us, without reacting to it? This, of course, then leads
to that element in blasphemy cases in which people are taken to have committed
an offence, because their conduct is liable to lead to a breach of the peace.

Second, being offensive — especially to the defenceless — may simply be a horrible thing to do. Once, say, people understand just what kind of offence certain kinds of conduct, or the improper use of Aboriginal designs, may give to the people in question, it is surely inexcusable to persist in giving offence. It is a horrible action, and also made worse by the sheer lack of power of the people on whom it is inflicted. However, it is not at all clear, say, that the kinds of offence that may be given to ordinary Muslims, or to devout Catholics or to conservative-minded evangelical Christians is any less. Just think, in the latter cases, of how they might experience what is taking place. As I mentioned before, in their view, the creator of the universe chose to humble himself, take on human form and to suffer, so as to bring about the salvation of all who would accept this gift…and *this* is then mocked, turned into a travesty, or used as a prop for the purposes of comedy. I am not advocating the jailing of the people who might behave in this way. But it seems to me that we should think twice about the idea that such activities can easily be defended as part of a supposed right to self-expression. However, should we go along with such ideas we face a problem; one that I am not sure how to resolve.

Blasphemy in a pluralistic society

When Salman Rushdie wrote, he knew full well what he was doing. The knowledge that he displayed — in playing around with the 'satanic verses' episode and even in his use of the names of the wives of the Prophet — required some real knowledge of Islam. But it should equally have been clear to him that what he was doing would have been found highly offensive by some Muslims. Clearly, there was much more to the episode than this. There was a strong political element to the attention that his work received, and Muslims could find much other material that would give offence, but which was not singled out for condemnation in this way. Many of his Western readers, however, might have found these aspects of his work unusual, and while — especially if they came across some commentary upon them — they might have been able to understand them, they would surely not have experienced the kind of emotional reaction that some Muslims may have felt.

One obvious problem however, is that now that we are a pluralistic society: in Australia, there are many faiths and sensibilities, and even societies which are relatively homogenous are affected by what is done elsewhere. Just what protections are needed, and what should be protected?

In the face of the Rushdie case, one reaction in the UK was that some Muslims there wished for Rushdie to be had up for blasphemy. They swiftly discovered, however, that in Britain laws against blasphemy related only to the Christian religion — and even, it might appear, to the doctrines of the Church of England. There was, then, a call for the widening of blasphemy law, so that it would apply to other religions. This, however, poses a problem; namely, what should count for this purpose. Think about this in an Australian context: Christianity — in all its forms? Islam — bearing in mind that, for Shiites, the twelfth (occluded) Imam would also require protection? Judaism? Aboriginal beliefs? But what about Jehovah's Witnesses, the Mormons, and New Agers, to say nothing of Little Pebble?[32]

There is also a further problem here: namely, just *what* the *content* of that which receives such protection will be. It is often — and surely rightly — said that, say, Aboriginal cultures are not static, but evolving. The same, surely, might be the case for what others hold to be Holy. But this poses a problem: if what is so recognised acquires special protected status, it can surely become the subject of politics. In an early episode in the Garfield cartoon series, Garfield, a fat striped cat, was made to say something like: 'One good thing about being a cat is, any food you touch, becomes yours.' The Holy, or what plays a key role in your culture such that it demands protection, might equally become the vehicle for a not dissimilar kind of acquisitive opportunism.

In addition, as I noted earlier, one feature of religious pluralism is that the key tenets of many religions commit their devotees to denying the claims of the devotees of other religions. It is just not clear that there can be respect and mutual tolerance, if you take the claim to the truth of your own beliefs seriously, and it is integral to your own views that the other people have got things terribly wrong.

Finally, here, although I can address this question only very briefly, there is an interesting problem concerning whether, with regard to these matters, there is an area between the private and the public.[33] I earlier referred to one line of argument in Foote, in which he argued that the cartoons in the *Freethinker* were produced for an audience of secularists, and that this should have been clear from the character of the publication. It is possible that the same might be argued, in respect of the *Gay News* blasphemous libel case. Here, a short poem by James Kirkup, depicted a Roman centurion expressing his love for Jesus, by means of various forms of sexual activity conducted with his just-dead body.[34] It would seem as if the poem was intended to express a genuine devotion, but its public meaning was highly offensive, and Mrs Mary Whitehouse, of the British National Viewers and Listeners Association — a crusader for morality — brought a private prosecution against it for blasphemous libel, which was successful.[35] One might ask, however: but should not the fact that it appeared in *Gay News* indicate that it was produced for, as it were, a niche market, such that those who might find this offensive would understand that it was not for them? But in this particular case, the reaction of their own readers, and that of those working on the paper towards the poem, suggested that this defence might not be open to them,[36] even if it could be defended in a wider context.

Where does all this leave us? I am initially inclined to say that, in a pluralistic setting, there is good reason for ditching the crime of blasphemy. At the same time, there is surely a case for prohibiting by law offensive behaviour that is liable to provoke a breach of the peace. At another level, it would seem to me that it is reasonable to regard as morally offensive the production of things that would deeply offend harmless people: consider, again, the deliberate violation of things that Aboriginal people hold as sacred, but now generalise this to the core concerns of others. At the very least, this should mean that we don't fete work which gives such offence, or express solidarity with it if it is criticised. This does not mean that we should silently acquiesce to calls for the death or imprisonment of those who produce it.

I said, above, that I am inclined to offer that response. But there are problems about it, not least this question of what, and to what extent, things get protection, and who gets to decide. It is surely only core concerns that should receive such protection. But who gets to decide what people's core concerns are? And does the protection that might be accorded to the core concerns of major religions, really extend to, say, the fantasies of some group of ratbags who thinks that aliens have kidnapped them a space ship, and then returned them to Earth with remarkable news for mankind?

I am left unsure about what we should do concerning these matters. One might say: be respectful of work that has a public meaning as sacred, in the cultures within which our work is produced and in which we would expect it to be disseminated. And over and above this, be mindful of the sensibilities of the vulnerable. But such a response is clearly inadequate, and I am happy to leave *this* problem to others, to see what they make of it.

Andres Serrano, when his *Piss Christ* was attacked, commented that he thought that its destruction was an act of 'desecration'.[37] Clearly, I might be tempted to take any criticism of my paper in similar terms — if I were not, in these matters, influenced by Karl Popper, who stressed fallibilism and the importance of holding everything open to criticism, and who argued that it is good for us, even if we don't enjoy it.

Endnotes

[1] I would like to thank Geoff Stokes for conversation and for some most useful comments on a draft of this paper, from some of which I was not able to benefit on this occasion, for reasons of space, and also to David Wall and the editors for some useful criticism and suggestions.

[2] On which, see Reid Mortensen, 1994, 'Blasphemy in a secular state: A Pardonable sin?', *UNSW Law Journal*, vol. 17, no. 2, pp. 409-31. A useful brief overview of blasphemy laws in different states and territories is provided at: http://www.caslon.com.au/blasphemyprofile2.htm.

[3] Quoted by Mortensen, ibid., p. 411.

[4] There is also of course the issue of blasphemy as expletive; but this I will not discuss here. For a rather different classificatory approach, see Anthony Fisher and Hayden Ramsay, 'Of Art and Blasphemy', 2002, *Ethical theory and moral practice*, vol. 3, pp. 137-67.

[5] Socinianism, named after Lelio Francesco Maria Sozzini (1525–1562), was a sixteenth and seventeenth century religious movement, which called into question the deity of Christ, and emphasised, by contrast, the unity of God. It is sometimes regarded as an early form of unitarianism. Deism, a loose movement influential in the seventeenth and eighteenth centuries, while accepting the existence of God and his role as a creator, rejected revealed religion in favour of a sceptical and rationalistic approach, and also rejected the idea that God subsequently intervened in his creation.

[6] See, notably, Michael Hunter, 1992, '"Aikenhead the Atheist": the Context and Consequences of Articulate Irreligion in the Late Seventeenth Century', in Michael Hunter and David Wootton (eds.) *Atheism from the Reformation to the Enlightenment*, Oxford: Clarendon Press; and also W. Cobbett, T. B. Howell et. al. (eds), 1819, *A Complete Collection of State Trials*, xiii, London, pp. 917-40. For background, see also the other articles in the Hunter and Wootton collection, and also J. A. I. Champion, 1992, *The Pillars of Priestcraft Shaken*, Cambridge: Cambridge University Press.

[7] Foote's fascinating *Prisoner for Blasphemy*, London: Progressive Publishing, 1886, is available on the internet at: http://homepages.ihug.co.nz/~freethought/foote/blasphemy/0bcontents.htm. Foote is discussed at length in Joss Marsh, 1998, *Word Crimes*, Chicago & London: University of Chicago Press.

[8] Quoted in Marsh, ibid., p. 160.

[9] It is reproduced in Marsh's *Word Crimes*, ibid., p. 142.

[10] For some discussion of which, see Marsh, ibid.

[11] That is to say, that aspect of Mill's views about toleration, that stems from the stress that he placed on the idea that human knowledge was fallible, that currently accepted views may not be correct, and so on.

[12] See Jonathan Riley, 2005, 'J. S. Mill's Doctrine of Freedom of Expression', *Utilitas,* vol. 17, no. 2, pp. 147-79.

[13] It is striking from the discussion in Hunter and Wootton, that at times the production of apologias for the truth of Christianity against imagined opponents gave rise to people taking the imagined opponents' case seriously and finding it telling.

[14] For critical discussion of claims to infallible knowledge in the Shi'ite tradition of Islam, compare the work of Abdolkarim Soroush, 2002. Some of his essays are available in English in his *Reason, Freedom and Democracy in Islam*, Mahmoud Sadri and Ahmed Sadri (eds), London etc: Oxford University Press.

[15] Clearly, an argument might be made for the suppression of material on the grounds that it might mislead the immature. But it is not clear that, for example, the history of the suppression of heresy or of Jewish objections to Christianity, can really be placed in that category.

[16] This oversimplifies, in that there was, historically, the recognition of a kind of pluralism within Islam, as in the milet system of the Ottoman Empire (cf. http://www.eurozine.com/articles/2004-03-25-ivanov-en.html), and also in Christendom at such times as Jews were not being persecuted. In addition, in the period immediately after the Reformation, a system was adopted in which the religion of a country was simply settled by the choice of the ruler.

[17] Cf, for example, Richard Popkin 'Jewish Anti-Christian Arguments as a Source of Irreligion from the Seventeenth to the Early Nineteenth Century', in Hunter and Wootton (eds) *Atheism from the Reformation to the Enlightenment*. Isaac Troki's *Faith Strengthened*, for example, something that it is tempting to say should be compulsory reading for all evangelical Christians, is currently difficult to obtain in printed form (although a version is now available on the internet at: http://faithstrengthened.org/). It is striking that Hans Joachim Schoeps was able to remark in the 'Foreword to the Second Edition' of his *The Jewish-Christian Argument*: 'This book made its first appearance in 1937, behind closed doors, as it were, for the authorities at that time in power in Germany allowed its sale only in Jewish bookstores and to Jews. Then, when it was noticed that it was a "dangerous" book, it was prohibited completely.' See his *The Jewish-Christian Argument*, London: Faber, 1965, p. xiv. See also Richard Popkin, 2006, *Disputing Christianity: The 400-year-old Debate over Rabbi Isaac Ben Abraham Troki's Classic Argument*, Amherst, N.Y.: Humanity Books.

[18] At the very least, if one is offering arguments that are supposed to convince others, this opens up the possibility of contestation; for example, to the effect that the arguments are not valid or are not telling.

[19] I am offering this as an argument as to what follows from epistemological fallibilism, not as an interpretation of Mill. There has been argument about just what follows from Mill's own arguments, with some (for example, John Skorupski, 1989, *John Stuart Mill*, London: Routledge) taking the line that I am commending here, while others (for example, Jonathan Riley in his 'J. S. Mill's Doctrine of

Freedom of Expression') argue that Mill's own argument leads to a defence of more expressive activities, such as demonstrations.

20 But where, obviously, if they offer arguments or try to convince others that they are right, they deserve everything that they get in response.

21 Compare, in this context the controversy in 2004-05 opened up by the Iranian President Mahmoud Ahmadinejad's remarks about the Holocaust. It is striking that the Pakistani academic Ijaz Hussain, in an opinion piece 'COMMENT: Who is more civilised: Iran or the West?' was able to make what read like a reasonable case for Ahmadinejad's views, by way of describing the legal suppression of dissent about the Holocaust in several countries, and providing a list of people or organisations which had questioned it. He did not, say, refer to works which contest such claims, such as Deborah Lipstadt's *Denying the Holocaust* (New York: Free Press, 1993), or to the various publications on the David Irving libel trial against Lipstadt in the UK. Ijaz Hussain, 2006, 'COMMENT: Who is more civilised: Iran or the West?' *Daily Times*, Pakistan, January 4 2006; see http://www.dailytimes.com.pk/default.asp?page=2006%5C01%5C04%5Cstory_4-1-2006_pg3_5)

22 The tradition of freedom of religion in the USA seems to be taken as a freedom to live without ones religious ideas being challenged and this — or so it seemed to me when I was living there — extended to beliefs about many other matters, in a manner that contrasts with day-to-day life in Britain or Australia.

23 Clearly, what counts as another may be contentious — say, with regard to vegetarianism, or, say, the treatment of some socially unpopular minority — but on the face of it there is a difference between how something is to be appropriately handled if it is broadly socially contentious in the society in question, as compared to ones having what is very much a minority viewpoint in the society in question. (For example, pleas for vegetarianism in a society of meat eaters need to be made in journals rather than at the dinner table.) Even issues that are contentious may need to be treated in a circumspect manner: if, say, the vegetarian chooses to eat with meat eaters in a society in which there were lively divisions and debate about vegetarianism, it would hardly be appropriate for them to accompany the meal with a running commentary about sentience, slaughterhouses, and quotations from Peter Singer.

24 Cf., on this, Joseph Alleine, *Alarm to unconverted sinners etc*, London: Nevil Simmons, 1993 etc.

25 Alan Peshkin, 1992, 'Experience Subjectivity', Qualitative Interest Group, College of Education, University of Georgia, 1992 conference proceedings, Keynote Address. http://www.coe.uga.edu/quig/proceedings/Quig92_Proceedings/peshkin.92.html (Viewed January 21, 2005).

26 Quoted from Foote, *Prisoner for Blasphemy* (see note 2).

27 The ideas of which Rushdie made use were familiar enough, and had not been thought of as particularly contentious, in discussions of Islam. See, on this, and on many of the other complexities of the Rushdie case, the discussion in Michael M.J. Fischer and Mehdi Abedi, 1990, *Debating Muslims: Cultural dialogues in postmodernity and tradition*, Madison, Wis: University of Wisconsin Press.

28 I have in mind here something along the lines of the view developed by Quentin Gibson and used by him and others in the context of textual interpretation in the history of political thought; cf. James Tully (ed.) 1988, *Meaning and Context*, Princeton: Princeton University Press.

29 Or, say, unless they were a recently arrived visitor to the country who could quite reasonably not be expected to appreciate the significance of what they were saying.

30 Quoted in Daniel Pipes, 1990, *The Rushdie Affair*, New York: Birch Lane Press/ Carol Publishing Group, p. 108.

31 Of course, what is offensive is something which will change over time and will also be context-dependent, which introduces further problems that I cannot even attempt to deal with, given the space at my disposal.

32 'Little Pebble' is the name of the leader of a Catholic religious group, who in 2005 was in court to answer charges relating to sexual conduct towards an under-age member of his flock. For a site which gives some indication of the charges against him, see http://users.bigpond.net.au/wanglese/pebble.htm (Viewed January 3, 2006); for the group's web page, see: http://www.shoal.net.au/~mwoa/ (Viewed January 3, 2006).

33 I would particularly like to thank Geoff Stokes for discussion on this point.

34 The poem is reproduced at http://gaytoday.badpuppy.com/garchive/events/070502ev.htm (Viewed November 3, 2005).

35 See, for a brief report, http://news.bbc.co.uk/onthisday/hi/dates/stories/july/11/newsid_2499000/2499721.stm, which includes a picture of Mrs Whitehouse. (Viewed November 3, 2005.)

[36] It is striking, however, that from Rictor Norton's personal account of the background to the publication http://www.galha.org/glh/214/norton.html, not only was there considerable protest from within the readership of the journal, from people who found it offensive, but Norton indicates that they 'did not relish defending a poem that we frankly realized was rather sick', even if it was sincere.

[37] See 'Andres Serrano talks with Judith Ahern', *Photofile* 53, April 1998, pp. 8-13; see p. 13. Serrano claimed that he saw it as a desecration 'not toward the mage but toward Christ himself'. But this seems to me simply an indication of the degree to which — not unlike the poet in the cinema — his personal interpretation was of kilter with the public meaning of what he had produced.

Section IV

Self-expression and Restriction

The argument in this section considers artistic creation and self-expression achieved within restriction. It is hard to see that the value claimed for artistic expression, of showing the world anew, or of expressing the common concerns of humanity, requires that art should be unrestricted. While it might be assumed that artists must work without restriction in order to express themselves, 'fetters' do not necessarily constrain what may be represented. For instance, films that respect modesty may also express sexual longing and consummation. Restriction is a condition for creativity, and is a framework within which creativity is recognised.

As artist and curator, Christopher Braddock coordinated the exhibition *Votive: sacred & ecstatic bodies* including the works of Ian Breakwell and Cathy de Monchaux (Britian), Pierre & Gilles (France), and Megan Jenkinson (New Zealand). The exhibition responded to controversy surrounding Tania Kovat's exhibit *Virgin in a Condom* at the Museum of New Zealand Te Papa Tongarewa in 1998 and the work of Andres Serrano, Braddock writes about issues of blasphemy in artworks that engage with collisions between sacred imagery and the body. This chapter addresses complex relationships in the artworks between, on the one hand, attitudes of devotion and, on the other, severe critique of the Church. The artists exhibiting in *Votive* transgress, but avoid obvious attacks through an emphasis on religious ecstasy and sensory qualities of religious symbols, rather than their meaning. Braddock argues that the gallery provides a context for the exploration of devotional forms excluded from the Church.

The next two chapters explore externally, and internally imposed censorship. Post revolution Iranian cinema has been subject to heavy censorship particularly in the manner in which the romantic relationships between men and women are represented on screen and the language that is used in the script — un-Islamic, profane, blasphemous or sacrilegious utterances, acts and gestures are forbidden. In a culture that upholds religious norms stringently and where idolatry and imitating the creative act of God is considered to be highly sacrilegious, Michelle Langford is surprised that no official sanction has been imposed against producing films but instead, cinema is used as a vehicle for promoting the State's agenda of educating people about Islamic values. While the lack of 'fundamentalism' may be surprising, it is clear that the state still seeks to control the social construct of the pure and the impure within these films. However, Langford's analysis of Iraqi cinema shows that even stringent controls do not necessarily undermine an artist's ability to express themselves, or to critique the State.

Many Australian Aboriginal societies utilise secrecy as a fundamental norm for regulating speech. In Yolngu society, a person requires 'the right' to speak on a topic, and the anthropologist Ian Keen has reported that this secrecy is supported by self censorship, even when a person knows information, they may refuse to acknowledge that they have this knowledge. Silence presents a means of negotiating the sacred and preserving the sanctity of Indigenous knowledge. In Indigenous Australia, collective experiences of a community are sacred and cannot be recounted. Stories are the only way by which such a sacred world may be represented, but stories embody ancestral beings and places and are sacred in their own right so they should not be needlessly evoked.

In our final chapter, Caroline Josephs, a writer, makes a very personal exploration of this system. In identifying with the Yolngu and giving credibility to their religious accounts of the land, she interprets the silence surrounding such stories not as censorship but as respect, or awe, in the face of the sacred, and as a means of negotiating the relationship she has with others. By employing various forms of storytelling — braiding genres of personal, cultural, conceptual storytelling — the author covers three aspects of silence in relation to one particular story — the Wagilag Sisters Story. Josephs weaves what she cannot say about the Yolngu Wagilag Sisters story into her own story of 'coming to know' the story and the place of their dance.

10

Blasphemy and the art of the political and devotional

Christopher Braddock

A breakdown in the unity of state and church has altered the context in which blasphemy might be understood. Rather than viewing blasphemous libel as intrinsically linked through the Ecclesiastical courts within the unity of State and Church, the emphasis has shifted to the individual in society whose freedom of artistic expression is constrained instead by the secular laws of defamation and obscenity. In this light, artists such as Andres Serrano and Tania Kovats embrace a freedom to use dramatic and visually confronting binary oppositions in their works of art.[1] Andres Serrano juxtaposed the crucifix with urine, and Tania Kovats, a statuette of the Virgin Mary with a condom. Such iconography provokes the possibility that these artworks might function as simultaneously political and devotional: powerfully critical of church institutions, while aesthetically operating as symbols that evoke reverence. In this context it is significant that, in the debates that followed the controversies surrounding these works of art, the arts establishment emphasised the division between church and state in justification of the artists' right to freedom of expression, and the difference between temple and museum was highlighted in discussion about the contextual setting of the museum as a place in which 'blasphemy' could not occur. Artistic intention, and the context in which these works are witnessed, are debated as factors in determining the possibility of blasphemy within the divide of state and church, museum and temple.

In this chapter I will argue that interpretations of graphic Medieval images of the body that avoid binary opposition are useful in a reappraisal of the controversy surrounding artworks such as Serrano's *Piss Christ* and Kovat's *Virgin in a Condom*. This raises questions about the role of devotional images. Do they exist primarily to reinforce the strict teachings of the church or can they be used to examine those beliefs? If we accept the latter as a possibility, could these confrontational images signify divine revelation in the body, the very essence of the Incarnation?

Locating 'blasphemy' in the polemical

The beginning of the twenty-first century has brought into focus issues of right-wing religious fundamentalism (be it Islamic or Christian) even more sharply. The dangers and dilemmas of essentialist religious paradigms have joined a list of vitally important global issues to be reckoned with, arguably as important as global poverty and global warming. It is in this light that bearing-witness to blasphemy becomes part of a debate about tolerance within a pluralistic society.

As Kyla McFarlane described in the catalogue for the exhibition *Votive: Sacred and ecstatic bodies,* [2] in the last decade, Australia and New Zealand bore witness to artwork seemingly crossing the boundaries that constitute blasphemy:

> In October 1997, Melbourne's National Gallery of Victoria closed an exhibition of works by American artist Andres Serrano after two physical attacks by members of the public on his photograph *Piss Christ* (1987). This incident followed earlier claims by Christian groups and senators in the USA that the work was indecent and obscene.[3] Serrano had received funding from the National Endowment for the Arts and, following a complaint from the American Family Association, Senator Jesse Helms proposed that indecent or offensive works should not continue to receive funding. New York Senator Alphonse D'Amato also condemned the work in Congress. His outrage, and that of Helms, was publicly echoed by many constituents.[4]

Serrano's work is a photographic enlargement of a small commercially produced crucifix immersed in Serrano's own urine. Without the title of the work to indicate the substance of piss used to create the image, the viewer might revel in the sublimely romantic connotations of a misty atmospheric sky at sunset striking at the heart of the crucifixion story with its hope of resurrection after death. But Serrano's titling ensures that the viewer has to confront the dilemma that this *is* a vat of urine.

A severing of the unity of state and church has reinforced the freedoms of the individual to roam across boundaries making a question of ownership of religious symbols and their employment difficult to answer. The Catholic Archbishop of Melbourne, Dr. George Pell, who considered *Piss Christ* blasphemous, applied unsuccessfully for a Supreme Court injunction to prevent the National Gallery of Victoria from exhibiting the work. Justice Harper cast doubt on the need for the common law of blasphemous libel in Victoria, saying that Australia 'need not bother with [it]' because contemporary Australia is a pluralist, tolerant society.[5] Justice Harper distinguished the Victorian position from the English law stating that blasphemous libel is 'an anachronism of English history from a time when the State was intrinsically linked with the Church, through the Ecclesiastical courts, and the unity of State and Church was not transported to the Australian Colony. This position is supported by the fact that Victoria does not recognise an established Church under section 116 of the Australian Constitution'.[6] Now that the state and the church are no longer inseparable, the question of authority and how religious iconography is employed appears to shift to wider concerns of freedom and artistic expression as constrained by the laws of defamation and obscenity. A calculation of the level of offence experienced by the viewer moved to centre-stage.

McFarlane points to a similar reaction of public outrage with respect to Tania Kovat's *Virgin in a Condom*:

> In a matter of days, Tania Kovats' *Virgin in a Condom* (1992) was stolen by a visitor to the Museum of Contemporary Art in Sydney. Exhibited as part of 'Pictura Britannica', a show of work by young British artists, it provoked numerous letters of protest and complaints from incensed Christians and Muslims when it toured to Te Papa/Museum of New Zealand the following year.[7]

Virgin in a Condom is a strikingly polemical work. On the one hand, the seven and a half centimetres tall mass-produced statuette *is* a religious object made for the purpose of evoking the Virgin Mary's divine intercession and has been covered with an object used, more or less exclusively, for covering erect penises or a variety of sex toys, such as 'butt-plugs'. Clearly, many viewers understood the work as presenting an analogy to the Virgin Mary as a dildo. As I will argue, a reappraisal of these binary interpretations might suggest that, on the other hand, the statuette is religiously shrouded or concealed, visually resembling a work such as Piero della Francesca's *Madonna della Misericordia* (circa 1445) , in which the Madonna protects the people with her mantle. This condom as shroud evokes notions of the polarised role models for women within Catholicism: that women are unfairly torn between virgin and whore in the archetypal models of Mary, the Mother of God, and Mary Magdalene, the redeemed whore. As well as this, the sculpture strategically provokes discussion about the Catholic Church's prohibition of contraception by the use of condoms. Neither of these issues, by the way, had any prominence whatsoever in the New Zealand media coverage surrounding the controversy over *Virgin in a Condom's* presence in Te Papa. The lack of media coverage on these key issues highlights an assumption that artists intend to shock rather than engage in public debate. Such an assumption overlooks the possibility that artist's may intend to provoke public discussion on these issues, or to explore unconventional views on religion within a museum context. I will return to this point in discussing the role of the museum as providing a space for unconventional views of religion below.

The perceived polemical nature of the work contributed to *Virgin in a Condom* becoming, arguably, the most publicised work of art in the history of New

Zealand, Tania Kovats would not reply to any invitation to participate in the exhibition *Votive: Sacred and ecstatic bodies* that I curated in Wellington in 2002. Her Australasian experience, which included receiving abusive mail and death threats, had been so traumatic that she wanted nothing more to do with us. Her representative, the London-based Asprey Jacque Gallery, indicated that the direction of her work was changing to the extent that another inclusion in a religious project would misrepresent the artist.

Arguments surrounding the accountability of public expenditure in public institutions such as galleries form strong undercurrents to these debates about the control and use of religious symbols. In contrast with the National Gallery of Victoria, Te Papa Tongerewa Museum of New Zealand stood their ground. They refused to remove *Virgin in a Condom* from the *Pictura Britannica* exhibition and backed their right to be an artistic conscience of society. In the words of the concept curator, Ian Wedde, the museum had to be a free space for several kinds of expression. It had to be available 'for the expression of divergent and controversial views'.[8] Some of these controversial views may be unorthodox religious or theological perspectives.

Serrano contends that *Piss Christ* stems from his religious upbringing, and that the work upholds his religious conviction that the body can be seen as a means for obtaining religious redemption. As Serrano puts it:

> The photograph, and the title itself, are ambiguously provocative but certainly not blasphemous…My Catholic upbringing informs this work which helps me to redefine and personalise my relationship with God. My use of such body fluids as blood and urine in this context is parallel to Catholicism's obsession with 'the body and blood of Christ'. It is precisely in the exploration and juxtaposition of the symbols from which Christianity draws its strength.[9]

Who then, should decide whether something is blasphemous? The church or religious group who claims ownership and control, or the artists themselves?

One standard model for the interpretation of art involves consideration of the artist's intentions. Within a context of the divide between state and church and the concomitant freedom of the individual, such a model seems apt. Our knowing that Serrano sees himself as working within the parameters of his own faith seems to alter our immediate impression that this is a case of blasphemy. It is as though, given his Christian upbringing, Serrano feels entitled to use the religious images as he pleases, and that, as a Christian, he was incapable of blaspheming. This idea of membership giving entitlement to use images however you like raises questions about how 'membership' is determined, and whether there can be levels of membership and entitlement.

A conflicting position about how we should interpret a work of art appeals to the conventional meaning of the symbols. If we read the image at face value, it is still his piss, a human by-product of waste not normally associated with the reverence of God. The media recently condemned American soldiers for the blasphemy of urinating on the Koran during the military campaign in Iraq. If this is clearly an act of blasphemy in relation to what is held sacred to Muslims, and was correctly interpreted as an attack on the sentiments of the Muslim prisoners they had captured, we would not expect a Christian to engage in a similar act with respect to their own faith. This raises the question of what role the gallery plays in providing a context for interpreting a work of art, and its appreciation.

The context of witnessing blasphemy

Is viewing *Piss Christ* in an art gallery different from contemplating or worshipping the image in a church? According to an institutional theory of art, the identification of something as art influences the manner in which something is interpreted. Such a theory of art is proposed by George Dickie where a 'work of art' must satisfy the dual conditions of an artefact made by 'a person who participates with understanding in the making of an artwork' together with a confirmation of its status as an artwork 'by some person acting on behalf of the Artworld'.[10] According to Dickie both conditions are necessary to confirm the status of a work of art. From this perspective, does the institutional context of the museum reserve a place for artistic critique that is separate from those contexts within which we plausibly interpret something to be blasphemous? In other words, does it reserve a space that permits artists to manoeuvre across parameters of critique and devotion? This is a significant question as it has implications for the role of the gallery as providing a space for alternative views of religion and for the practice of religion.

Serrano's work can be compared to Ian Breakwell's *Deep Faith* (2001), which was included in the *Votive* exhibition. In *Deep Faith*, a slide projection features an X-ray of the throat of a woman who had swallowed a small crucifix which had lodged in her throat. Breakwell found the X-ray while he was an artist-in-residence at the Cardiff Anatomy Unit. The gradual and repeated dissolving of a second slide over the first featuring the words 'deep faith', a reference to the 1972 pornographic film *Deep Throat*, sexualises the work's imagery. This overlay of images hovers between acceptance of Christian doctrine, indeed an obsessive consumption of the Body of Christ, and the sexual act of fellatio. This reference plays on devotional allusions, toying with the notion of complete acceptance of Christian doctrine, while aligning this with a sexual act. The image also has a violent subtext, with the figure becoming an intrusive lodgement in the throat. As McFarlane comments:

This association of the figure of Christ with the interior of the body also echoes Serrano's submersion of a similar figure in his own urine in *Piss Christ*. In both works, the body of Christ is strongly associated with the functioning of the human body, at the beginning and end of digestive process. In the former, the figure is taken into the throat and remains uncomfortably lodged there, whilst in the latter, it is associated with expulsion of waste.[11]

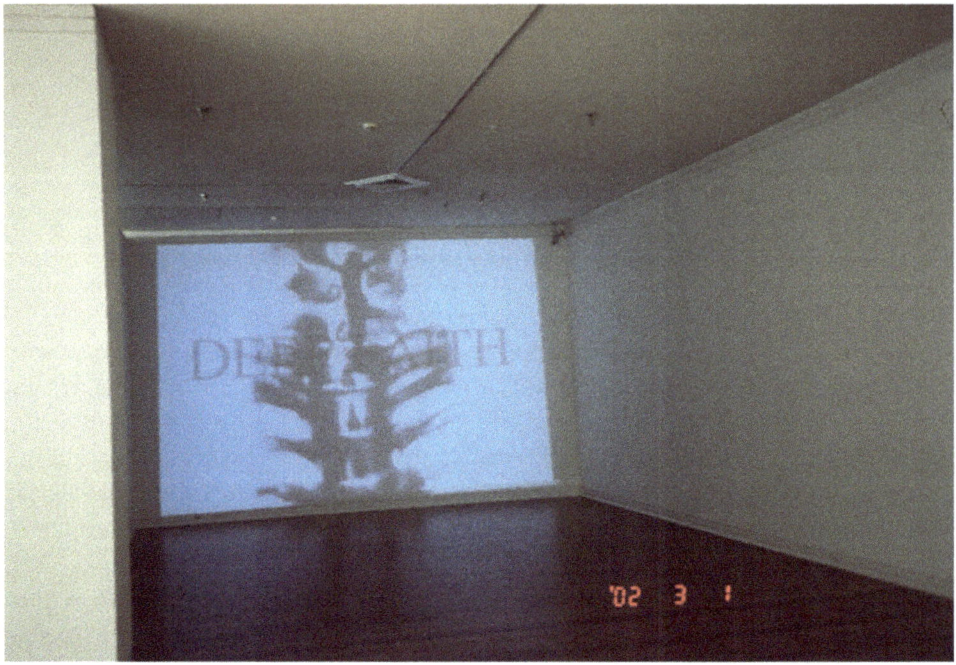

Ian Breakwell, *Deep Faith*, 2001, copyright The Estate of Ian Breakwell

Mediated by photographic processes and presented within the museum, do *Piss Christ* and *Deep Faith* operate outside of the realm of devotion, and only as a critique of the teachings of the Church? Do they, in other words, simply critique from the sidelines?

As an artist, the question of where these artworks are witnessed was on my mind when my work was included in an exhibition in New York City entitled *The Divine Body*.[12] The venues for the exhibition covered an array of institutional settings. The gallery at Columbia, the Cathedral of St John the Divine, and a theological seminary: art, worship and pedagogy. The distribution of the art works seemed to have been dictated by economic imperative. Those of higher economic value, such as the Andres Serrano and the Eric Fischl, were provided with the security of the Columbia's gallery, while other works were spread out across the other venues. It occurred to me to ask: 'What would have happened if *Piss Christ* had been exhibited in St John the Divine?' There might be people who think *Piss Christ* is not blasphemous in a museum, but blasphemous in a place of worship. To the best of my knowledge the work has never been exhibited in a place of worship. But, would this be blasphemous? What would happen if my cibachrome photographs of naked tattooed models were exhibited in St John the Divine? These works explore white-trash inspired tattoos inscribed close to nipple, buttock and pubis, intimately photographed. The works aim to provoke a collision between the practice of tattoo outlawed within most Judaeo-Christian circles and an edification of the body.

And the question of placing *Piss Christ* in a church struck at the heart of a dilemma in viewing both *Piss Christ* and *Virgin in a Condom*. On the one hand, I see them as overly simplistic slogan-like artworks that *are* blasphemous in their collision of clearly defined sacred and profane imagery; I would not photograph the Koran floating in a pool of urine. And, on the other hand, my acceptance of an institutional theory of art inclines me to think of the context of the art gallery as a site of questioning and critique, not a site of devotional practice. Yet, Breakwell's aestheticisation of the image — projected in a dimly lit space and viewed against the organ music of the late French composer Olivier Messian — clearly point to an atmosphere of reverence if not of devotion.

A conclusion that works of art accused of being blasphemous are so simply because they break religious dogma, or are exhibited in a sacred space, is problematic. The conclusion provokes questions about the role of religious symbols in ecclesiastical settings, and suggests that they exist primarily to reinforce the strict teachings of the church. A religious painting in a church could also examine or tease-out the nature of those beliefs. My earlier suggestion that the museum might reserve a place of artistic critique outside the realms of worship seems now too simplistic, and undermines the possibility of 'religious' art operating across the parameters of critique and devotion.

Religious law and sacred bodies

Ian Breakwell's video, *The Sermon*, 1984, which was also exhibited in the *Votive* exhibition, subtly explored interpretations of 'the law' in Catholic teaching and its relationship with the desires of the body. In so doing, Breakwell shifts our focus from a cleric reinforcing the law of the church to an individual overcome by a sense of blasphemy in how he occupies his own body. Kyla McFarlane writes in *Votive*:

> *The Sermon* is…[a] sardonic commentary on the effects of the law as stated by the institutional voice, it takes the format of a television sermon in a book-lined study reminiscent of the set of *Stars on Sunday*. The speaker, a seated priest, begins by calmly reminding the viewer that we have erred and offended against 'the laws' and that clarification is needed regarding areas of guidance. As the monologue progresses, however, his

avid pleasure in addressing the perverse and sinful becomes apparent, with the tone of the address moving from sage, fatherly advice to a frenzied tirade against the lusts of the flesh and original sin. The sermon is subject to a kind of leakage, as a perverse desire meets with the rigidity of the institutional voice...Breakwell's spoken text is littered with references to bodily fissures and seepages, such as 'the rupturing of membranes' during birth, or the leaking of sperm from a condom perforated with holes so that the marriage act can still be performed within the guidelines of the faith whilst collecting semen for laboratory tests. Or, finally, the gutting of the stomach of the depraved. Absurd and viscous, *The Sermon* ironically describes the impress of the body and its filthy excesses on the intellectual rigour of the law. In attempting to contain and restrain, the law itself becomes perverse and obsessive. By the video's end, desire and the law become blurred to the point of misrecognition.[13]

In the video, bodily function, and our relationship with the body, is inscribed with the categories of the pure and the impure. The body is thought of as a kind of temple, which requires us to treat it in a certain way. Yet the attempt to achieve purity is undermined by the body itself; its own secretions defile it.

Julia Kristeva argues that categories of abomination such as food taboos or corporeal alterations, topologically correspond to one's being able to have access to a place — the holy place of the Temple. Impurity, therefore, has a relationship to what happens outside the Temple. But this relationship is not contingent on a physical existence of the Temple: for Judaism, the Temple's function remained the same when the Temple was destroyed.[14]

Kristeva's notion of the Temple enfolds onto our own bodies, in biblical terms, the body as a Temple of the Holy Spirit: 'A mouth attributed to the anus: is that not the ensign of a body to be fought against, taken in by its insides.'[15] This describes a possibility for blasphemy and sacrilege in how we occupy our bodies individually, and by our relationship to other bodies. Seen from this perspective, *Piss Christ* contravenes the boundaries of the self's clean and proper body, just as Ian Breakwell's *Deep Faith* aligns throat and penis, as a symbolic protest against an intrusive moral theology.

Beyond the dichotomies of abjection and transcendence

Kristeva's project seeks to redeem the female body from categories of abomination, from existing outside the Temple, due to functions that include menstruation and lactation. And here it is helpful to imagine a fictitious artwork by Serrano that elucidates Kristeva's position, let us call it *Menstrual Blood Christ*. A crucifix submerged in menstrual blood indexes the sexualised female body, identified as abject, and describes a problematic position for women in relation to the holy place of the Temple.

Serrano himself comes close to such a work with *Milk, Blood*, 1986. Two vats, one of milk and the other of blood, are photographed butted up against each other. Only the central vertical edges of the glass vats are visible so that the image is abstracted and not dissimilar to some abstract colour field paintings. Serrano's *Milk, Blood*, while engaging in binary opposites on a visual level, encourages a more diffuse worry.[16] For Anthony Julius, this work provides an opportunity to reflect on the cultural connotations of bodily substances: 'They are similar: milk nurtures, blood animates. They are different: we ingest milk, we celebrate its flow, we obtain it with a caress; we may not ingest blood (save symbolically, or else to save our lives), we fear its flow, we obtain it painfully, invasively...Like *Piss Christ*, the work is mediated by photography and presents the same tensions between presentation and substance. We are seduced by the formal, almost minimalist (Rothko) nature of the work but simultaneously confronted by its substance'.[17]

Where Kristeva seeks to redeem the body from categories of abomination, Carolyn Bynum Walker's research on the female body and religious practices in the later middle ages (1200–1500) promotes a bodily (incarnational) manifestation of spiritual revelation that, I suggest, avoids binary opposition.[18] She points to graphic physical processes being revered such as: 'Holy people spat or blew into the mouths of others to effect cures or convey grace. The ill clamoured for the bath water of would-be saints to drink or bathe in, and preferred it if these would-be saints themselves washed seldom and therefore left skin and lice floating in the water.'[19] Following Francis of Assisi, who kissed lepers, several Italian saints ate puss or lice from the poor or sick, thus incorporating into themselves the illness and misfortune of others.[20] Bynum Walker cautions us against reading into medieval source material an assumption of the binary that control of the body equates to a rejection of sex. She argues that 'Medieval images of the body have less to do with sexuality than with fertility and decay. Control, discipline, even torture of the flesh is, in medieval devotion, not so much the rejection of physicality as the elevation of it — a horrible yet delicious elevation — into a means of access to the divine'.[21]

Two sixteenth-century religious paintings support this rejection of the body as abject, and the connection between sexuality and abjection. Leo Steinberg argues that, in Lucas Cranach's *Holy Trinity in a Glory of Angels* (c.1515-18) and Hans Schaufelein's *Crucifixion* (1515) (both of which depict Jesus with an erection), the erection is an iconographic symbol of the resurrection. A Dutch painting, the *Good Shepherd*, c.1550, from the church of St John in Schiedam, has Christ's genitalia as the central focus of the pictorial space. St. Augustus held that involuntary erections were a condition of original sin. Yet, in Christ's body, as the New Adam, an erection is willed and intended, a sign of the annulment of sin and death through the resurrection.[22] To suggest a singularly sexualised reading of such an image from the sixteenth century would be to misread the material, and to fall into the binaries of much contemporary discourse. Just as we do not need to read these binaries into the crucifixion–erection–motif, we may interpret a contemporary Virgin–condom–motif as having to do with fertility and an elevation of physicality as a means of access to the divine.

Mieke Bal explores such a turning of the tables. According to Bal:

The flesh that is so important in the Christian tradition takes on different meanings at different moments in history. From the perspective of an engaging late twentieth century [and now the twenty first century] where pain and suffering are often bound up with sexuality, we are now enabled, by artists who endorse this baroque historiography and the entanglement that characterises it, to scratch away the dust of a disembodied religiosity and gain access again to a religious life that is much closer to bodily experience.[23]

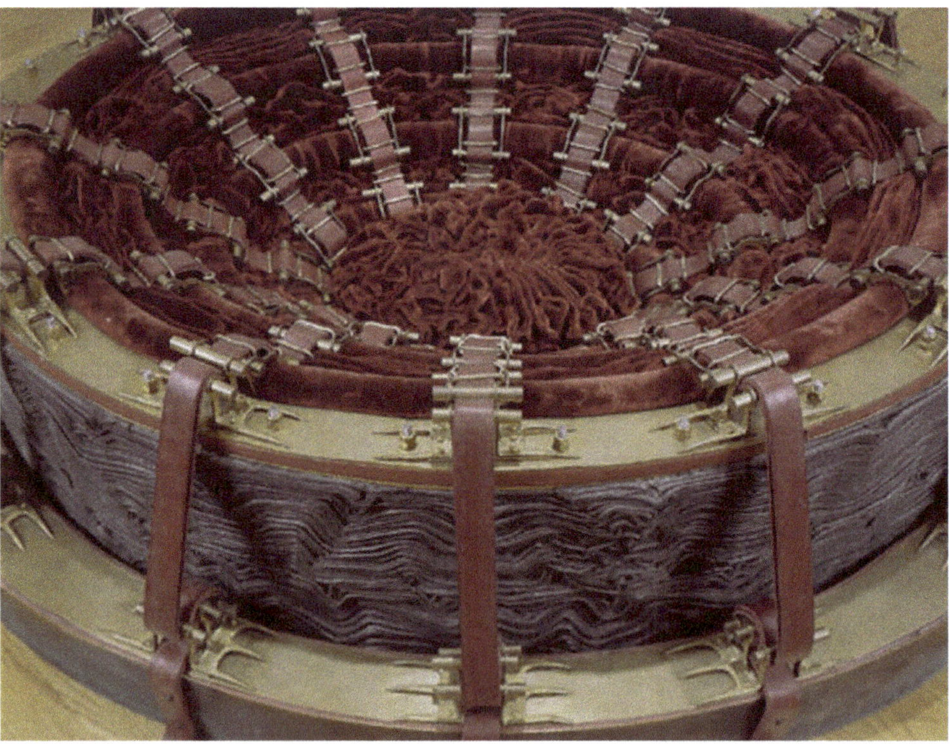

Cathy de Monchaux, *Red*, 1999, © Cathy de Monchaux

In this light, another work from the *Votive* exhibition, *Red,* by Cathy de Monchaux, challenges boundaries of the sacred and profane by adopting mixed messages: heraldic motifs reminiscent of imperially religious crosses and crests, and simultaneously, gynaecological-like instruments of fetish. *Red* collapses institutional order into private blossomings of flesh. The sculpture is obsessively created. With all the components cut by hand, the detailed clasps, buckles and leather belts tie down, and yet follow the formation of a concentrically descending vulva-like velvet interior. Like Ian Breakwell's *The Sermon,* there is a strongly public face to this work that nods to ecclesiastical and, in this case, royal protocol. Desires of the flesh are here enfolded, literally and metaphorically, onto the strictures of the law. But what is extraordinarily successful in this work is the manner in which these conflicting elements never overpower each other but are held together as palpable transgression. De Monchaux's *Red* becomes a powerful sign of the fertile body, the physically disciplined and restrained body and, yes, the sexually engorged body, but the enriched body as signifier of religious life in bodily experience.

Bynum Walker's caution against binary thinking is also helpful in discussing Serrano's work. If it were Christ's piss (like the dirty bath water of would-be saints), would the abject transfer to the realm of the sacred? What would we do with a phial of Christ's piss, other than venerate it? Moreover, does Serrano's photograph of Christ in piss, together with such uplifting and sublime aesthetics, redeem piss from being an ensign of the body's abject nature? In this shift from piss to a photograph of piss I have in mind Rosalind Krauss' argument, in referencing André Bazin's 'The Ontology of the Photographic Image', that photographs, by virtue of their process, are indexically linked to the objects they portray in ways that exceed representation: 'The photographic image is the object itself.' In this way, the photograph, together with its aesthetic qualities, might redeem the abject substance.[24] The act of pissing on the Koran in war lacks the devotional and aestheticising intentions of both Serrano and Kovats. The meaning of the image *Piss Christ* is much more complex than the meaning of either pissing on Christ or pissing on a crucifix, just as the meaning of the sculpture *Virgin in a Condom* is more multifaceted than the significance of comparing the Virgin Mary with an erection. Can we view these works from a position that is beyond the conventional binary of the pure and impure? If we consider the incarnational possibility that Christianity affords, to become as Christ, then Serrano's piss and Christ's piss — Serrano's body and Christ's body — may become as one. In the words of Damian Casey: 'God's place is with the abject every bit as much as it is on the high altar of the cathedral.'[25] In this light, *Piss Christ* could be seen as 'an attempt to retrieve the meaning of the incarnation'.[26] Casey contends that it is Serrano's 'exploration of the relation between the abject and the sacred that makes *Piss Christ* not only good art, but good religious art, bordering on the iconic'.[27]

When Bynum Walker cautions a straight forward assumption of binary thinking in medieval source material, she offers us a challenge to re-examine works such as *Piss Christ* and *Virgin in a Condom* from perspectives that are not preoccupied with the body as primarily sexual in function, or abject secretions. While both artworks are highly polemical and confrontational — this *is* piss and this *is* a condom — both artists deny a singularly blasphemous intent, alluding instead to both devotional and political intention. Both images have historical precedents where body fluids and the body's imagery are not clearly divided between the sacred and the abject. I contend that such historical perspectives inform a richer interpretation of *Piss Christ* and *Virgin in a Condom*. Seen from this perspective, these images signify the possibility of divine revelation through the body.

Conclusion

We cannot rely on a purely conventional understanding of blasphemy in understanding blasphemy in artistic contexts. Intentions matter to our reading of acts of blasphemy and change our perspective on whether they are acceptable. The context of the museum does more than reserve a space for artists to critique outside the realms of worship, but enables the possibility of artists operating across the parameters of critique and devotion. In this sense, the choice to curate *Votive: Sacred and ecstatic bodies* in museums offered the possibility to interpret Ian Breakwell's *Deep Faith* and Cathy de Monchaux's *Red* (and the other art works discussed above) *as* 'religious' works that operate outside conformist religious structures. In this respect museums and galleries have a role in providing a space for the expression of alternative, and sometimes unconventional, religious expression; offering artists, within certain restrictions, the possibility to articulate what they want. The polemical nature of the abject and sacred common to many of the artworks discussed in this chapter is not new. Contemporary binaries regarding bodily fluids, suffering and flesh are often bound up with sexuality, creating a sense of the religious that is disembodied. It is in a reappraisal of our perceptions of binary imagery (misunderstood by essentialist religious paradigms) that a solution emerges. Bynum Walker's research into medieval perceptions of the abject body as less sexual and more to do with fertility and decay indicate that the time at which something is viewed changes our understanding of whether blasphemy has occurred. It may be, that from the perspective of contemporary religious authority, these images are blasphemous, however, historical readings of the body in religious art make us question whether we must view works such as *Piss Christ* and *Virgin in a Condom* in this fashion. These works operate within a framework that is more complex than a conventional reading of blasphemy allows. They may also be interpreted as devotional, religious expressions.

Endnotes

[1] While the work of these artists provoked the greatest outcry, such juxtapositions of the sacred and profane are also characteristic of the work of Ian Breakwell and Cathy de Monchaux discussed later in this chapter in the context of the exhibition *Votive: Sacred and ecstatic bodies.*

[2] The exhibition *Votive: Sacred and ecstatic bodies* toured two venues in New Zealand, the Adam Art Gallery of Victoria University, Wellington, and the Dunedin Public Art Gallery, finishing in 2002. The project was collaboratively curated by Mark Jackson as writer/curator and myself as artist/curator and I acknowledge Mark Jackson's assistance in thinking through many of the issues in this chapter as well as Mel Hight, postgraduate candidate at AUT University. *Votive* responded to controversy surrounding Tania Kovat's exhibit *Virgin in a Condom* at the Museum of New Zealand Te Papa Tongarewa in 1998. *Votive* included works by: Ian Breakwell and Cathy de Monchaux (Britain); Pierre and Gilles (France); Megan Jenkinson and myself (New Zealand). In choosing the works for *Votive*, we attempted to encourage thinking beyond the binary of 'right wing fundamentalism' versus 'freedom of speech' and an environment respectful of differences of opinion.

[3] Kyla McFarlane, 2002, 'Incisions and Excesses', in *Votive: Sacred and Ecstatic Bodies,* Wellington and Dunedin: Adam Art Gallery and Dunedin Public Art Gallery, pp. 10-19, at p. 10

[4] McFarlane, ibid., note 2.

[5] 'Piss Christ exhibition 97.4', The Arts Law Centre of Australia, http://www.artslaw.com.au/reference/piss974/ (Viewed 27 April 2004.)

[6] Ibid.

[7] McFarlane, op. cit., note 2.

[8] 'Anger over Virgin in a condom art' 1998, *Dispatch Online,* http://www.dispatch.co.za/1998/03/11/foreign/condom.htm. (Viewed 20 December 2005.)

[9] Damien Casey, 2000, 'Sacrifice, *Piss Christ,* and liberal excess', p. 2, http://dlibrary.acu.edu.au/staffhome/dacasey/Serrano.html. (Viewed 20 December 2005.)

[10] Stephen Davies, 1991, 'Dickie's Institutional Theory of the Definition of Art', in *Definitions of Art,* Ithaca, N.Y. Cornell University Press, pp. 78-114, at pp. 83-84.

[11] McFarlane, op. cit., note 2, p. 13.

[12] Curated by Bruce Fergusson and Sarah Olsen.

[13] McFarlane, op. cit., note 2.

[14] Julia Kristeva, 1982, *Powers of Horror: An Essay on Abjection*, Columbia: Columbia University Press, p. 94.

[15] Ibid., p. 109.

[16] Anthony Julius, 2002, *Transgressions: The Offences of Art,* London: Thames and Hudson, p. 139.

[17] Ibid.

[18] Carolyn Bynum Walker, 1992, *Fragmentation and Redemption: Essays on Gender and the Human Body in Medieval Religion,* New York: Zone Books, p. 162.

[19] Ibid., p. 163.

[20] Ibid.

[21] Ibid., p. 162.

[22] Steinberg, Leo 1996, *The Sexuality of Christ in Renaissance Art and in Modern Oblivion,* Chicago: The University of Chicago Press, pp. 318-324.

[23] Mieke Bal, 1999, *Quoting Caravaggio: Contemporary Art, Preposterous History,* Chicago: The University of Chicago Press, p. 38, cited by McFarlane, op. cit., note 2.

[24] Rosalind Krauss, 1986, *The Originality of the Avant-Garde and Other Modernist Myths*, Cambridge, Mass: MIT Press, p. 203.

[25] Casey, op. cit., p. 3.

[26] Ibid., p. 6.

[27] Ibid., p. 2.

11

Negotiating the sacred body in Iranian cinema(s): National, physical and cinematic embodiment in Majid Majidi's *Baran* (2002)

Michelle Langford

Any religious utterance, act or gesture, stands in the shadow of — more or less, but never totally avoidable — perversion, parody and kitsch, of blasphemy and idolatry.[1]

Where have all the bodies gone? Modesty in Iranian cinema

In the post-revolutionary period, Iranian cinema has been subject to strict Islamic censorship regulations that dictate what can and cannot be show on screen, particularly in terms of the representation of women and romantic relationships between men and women. The rules relating to the representation of women mirror, in a highly exaggerated way, the codes of modesty relating to women in society more generally. Censorship functions to ensure that both onscreen bodies and the bodies of viewers in the audience remain modest. These bodies must be protected from un-Islamic, profane, blasphemous or sacrilegious utterances, acts and gestures: primarily those related to sex and un-Islamic behaviour. This is achieved in life primarily through the veiling of female bodies, and on screen by a 'screening' of such acts and suggestions of sexuality that might cause one to become impure or '*haram*'. The codes of modesty that prevail in society are greatly enhanced in the cinema, as all viewers are considered to be unrelated to the actors and characters who appear on screen. Modesty is maintained primarily by ensuring that onscreen women are appropriately veiled and clothed in loose-fitting clothing, and that physical contact between male and female bodies is avoided. Stories involving either emotional love or the suggestion of physical love between members of the opposite sex are generally avoided primarily due to the risk of violating the sanctity of pure, modest and Islamic bodies.[2] Film form, that is, the technical and stylistic devices for creating meaning in cinema, according to Hamid Naficy has also undergone a radical process of Islamicisation, which obliges filmmakers to uphold the principles of Islam.[3] In a religious context, where idolatry and imitating the creative act of

God is considered to be highly sacrilegious, it is a wonder that the creative audio-visual medium of film has been adopted so readily as an instrument for consolidating the revolution and educating the population about proper Islamic morals and behaviour. Indeed, despite his constant critique of cinema during his years in exile, Ayatollah Khomeini is said to have seen the potential of the film medium for promoting revolutionary (primarily Islamic) values.[4] Just as Western cinema and the popular and decadent pre-revolutionary cinema known as 'Film Farsi' were seen as an evil force that had corrupted the minds and bodies of the population during the Phalavi regime, in the post-revolutionary period, cinema was considered an appropriate vehicle for the purification of spectator's and by association the nation's mind, body and soul. With the enmeshing of state and religion brought about with the establishment of the theocratic government in 1979 and the establishment of Shari'a law, both individual and nation must necessarily reflect Islamic values.

Majidi Majidi's *Baran* (2001) is an extraordinary film which successfully depicts an adolescent man discovering his burgeoning sexuality, and falling in love with a beautiful young Afghan woman named Baran. Through the use of very clever and subtle cinematic devices, Majidi generates a deep sense of emotion and intimacy without ever showing any physical contact between the two, and without ever violating either the character's or the viewer's modesty. Additionally, by couching this love story in the broader context of the socio-economic condition of Afghan refugees in Iran, Majidi produces yet another level of discursive meaning where an ideal model of Islamic love and charity toward others may be perceived, effectively embodying a highly idealised conception of the nation. But, through its complex visceral engagement of the spectator's sensorium, *Baran* is a film that also explores the very limits of the sacred Iranian body on both the level of the national and individual citizenry. In this chapter, I wish to argue that through the simultaneous idealised embodiment of Iranian national Islamic values and the faltering, frail and very physical adolescent body of the central male character, Majidi is effectively negotiating the limits of the sacred body in Iranian cinema(s). I wish finally to demonstrate how film — which itself may be considered a body of sorts — may reach out figuratively to touch and move the bodies in the audience in ways that exceed simple observance of censorship regulations and generate vital connections between the viewers and the bodies on screen. In doing so, the film bears witness to the shadows that haunt any sacred utterance.

Embodying the nation

We see just such a reflection of individual and nation in the narrative trajectory of *Baran*. On one level, Majidi's film functions as an exemplary model of selfless devotion and modesty, particularly through its characterisation of the central male character Lateef, an adolescent gofer working on a building site on the outskirts of Tehran. The film traces his growing attachment to a young Afghan woman named Baran, who has come to the building site disguised as a young man named Rahmat in order to support her family following an accident that has rendered her father physically unable to work. Once Lateef discovers that Baran is really a woman, he is clearly struck by love's arrow and goes out of his way to please her and swoons in her presence. Eventually, however, Baran is forced to flee the building site as an illegal Afghan worker and Lateef goes in search of her. When he discovers the poor conditions in which she lives, and the harsh working conditions she endures, hauling large rocks from a rushing stream, he resolves to help her and her family by giving them all of his savings. Things do not go to plan, however, for Baran's father, Najaf, gives the money to his friend, Soltan, who needs it to return urgently to Afghanistan. Surprisingly, Lateef is not embittered by this situation, for he recognises that this man is just as desperate as Baran and her family. This is the first example of the self-sacrificing behaviour exhibited by Lateef throughout the film, putting collective needs above his own personal desires.

Lateef's behaviour also functions powerfully as an illustration of the Islamic principle of welcoming Muslim refugees and displaced peoples. During the Soviet occupation of Afghanistan (1979–89), Iran opened its borders to Afghan refugees who were classified by the newly formed Iranian government as *Mohajerin*, or 'involuntary religious migrants'.[5] This principle, which is enshrined in the Quran was, according to Aldeeb Abu-Sahlieh, adopted in the second Islamic Declaration of Human Rights in 1981:

> The homeland of Islam (dar-al-Islam) is one. It is a homeland for every Muslim, whose movement within [its domain] cannot be restricted by any geographical impediments nor political boundaries. Every Muslim country must receive any Muslims who emigrate thereto, or who enter it, as a brother welcomes his brother: 'Those who entered the city and the faith before them love those who flee unto them for refuge, and find it in their breasts no need for that which had been given them, but *prefer the fugitives above themselves though poverty become their lot*. And who is saved from his own avarice – such are they who are successful'… [Quran, 59:9][6]

Lateef's first act of self-sacrifice, of preferring the fugitives above himself despite the certainty that this will increase his own poverty, tends to cast him as an ideal figure of the Islamic nation as the Quranic principles are powerfully *embodied* in him. This embodiment of Islamic values is further emphasised in his second self-sacrificing act, which becomes for Lateef an act of effacing his own individual identity.

Throughout the film, Majidi places emphasis on the themes of identity and identification in a number of ways that provide commentary on Iranian civil society and the shifting policies toward Afghan refugees in that society. The first instance occurs during the first few minutes of the film in a scene where Lateef goes to a supermarket to purchase food for the construction workers. Lateef has had to leave his identity card in order to secure credit at the store. The shopkeeper points out that the account is long overdue and demands payment. At risk is Lateef's identity card, and we recognise that he risks the security of his personal identity for the good of the collective (the labourers). Later, as Lateef is checking into a hotel, we see a man denied a bed for the night because he does not have an identification card. Additionally, on two occasions, the illegal Afghan workers (who do not have work permits) are forced to flee the building site when a government inspector comes to check for illegal workers. It becomes clear, when the foreman of the site is asked to sign a document stating that no illegal Afghan workers are employed on the site, that these Afghans are no longer treated as *mohajerin* who 'were issued with identification cards known as "blue cards", and granted indefinite permission to stay in Iran legally'.[7] This detail of the film closely reflects Iran's changing policies toward Afghan refugees, who, after 1993, were no longer categorised as *mohajerin*, but simply as *panahandegan* (refugees), a term which 'was considered to have a pejorative nuance, even connoting impoverishment'.[8] These *panahandegan* were issued only with temporary registration cards, which made access to work and other civil services such as health care and education extremely limited. Lateef's strong sense of ideal Islamic devotion to the 'fugitives' is clearly being contrasted here with a view of the state's pragmatic approach to the refugee question.[9] By extension, this would appear to suggest that, while the government of the Islamic Republic of Iran is constitutionally bound to abide by the principles of Islamic law, this may not necessarily be the case in practice, given the explicit removal of sacred significance from the Afghan refugees, which seems to ignore the passage from the Quran cited above. Majidi certainly provides an ideal role model in his film, however, by revealing a considerable gap between this ideal behaviour and the practices of the state, he has presented us with an allegorical figure aimed at representing the opposite of that which he would appear to represent. Lateef's behaviour is revealed to be explicitly and unrealistically ideal. The presentation of the ideal individual is used to highlight the flaws of the state.

Throughout the film, Lateef continues to practice such sacred beliefs toward his fugitive neighbours. This is brought to a climax with a highly symbolic and self-effacing gesture. Having already given away his entire savings, Lateef decides to sell his identity card in order to provide Baran and her family with the money they need to return to Afghanistan. In aesthetic terms, Majidi sets up this scene as though Lateef is making a dangerous journey into the underworld, further emphasising the austere and self-sacrificial nature of his gesture. As Lateef makes his way through the busy bazaar making enquiries, suddenly, two mysterious men begin to chase him through the narrow alleyways of the bazaar. But, after successfully giving them the slip, another man approaches him and urges Lateef to follow. He leads Lateef to a dark, cluttered old basement, which further emphasises the theme of his descent into the corrupt underbelly of Tehran. Here, another man purchases his identification card. A close-up of the card signals the symbolic intensity of this moment, as the man removes Lateef's photo, and metaphorically erases his identity with a quick flick of his grubby finger. This act of selling his identity card is a powerful gesture in which Lateef shows his preference for the fugitives above himself, even though this will certainly ensure his own poverty. Lateef is the very embodiment of the ideal national subject envisaged for the post-revolutionary Iranian cinema by Khomeini, yet ironically his perfection reveals the cracks and contradictions, the shadow of the very nation-state he is supposed to embody.

Lateef's developing model behaviour effectively serves as a critique of, rather than as an example of, state practice. Furthermore, by choosing to relinquish his identification/identity he is effectively rendered a non-citizen, like the Afghan refugees, and therefore it is questionable whether he even stands for the state after all, but rather becomes one of the many displaced people of the region.

From embodied nation to embodied desire

If Majidi presents Lateef as embodying the ideal, self-effacing values of Islam through his devotion to a series of Afghan refugees on a socio-political level, and, as I have shown it is possible to read this as signifying the opposite of what it appears to, then we need to investigate the various levels at which embodied desire is simultaneously effaced and achieved through the use of cinematic devices and a very complex deployment of the sound track.

Despite the necessary effacement of the physical, sexualised body in Iranian cinema according to the mandates of censorship, throughout *Baran*, Majidi manages powerfully to suggest the sexual awakening of a young adolescent man, taking him through stages of confused outbursts of anger in the all-male environment of the building site, to the discovery of his own capacity for love of a woman. By staging this inner journey on a building site — ostensibly a male dominated arena — in which a woman (Baran/Rahmat) intervenes, Majidi is effectively attempting to argue for the necessity of interaction between men and women in order for appropriate subject formation to take place and respect for one another to be achieved. Ironically, however, the woman arrives disguised as a man. Certainly, throughout the film Baran is literally figured as a domesticating, ordering and beautifying influence upon this rather ramshackle and chaotic space. Michael Fischer has suggested that Baran functions metaphorically as a cooling influence on Lateef's hot-blooded adolescent temper,[10] although, I would argue, not without first firing him up. Thus, the film skirts the very edges of the sacred by alerting us to the pleasures of the flesh.

Adolescent awakenings

Even before the introduction of Baran/Rahmat to the film, we are provided with a glimpse of Lateef's burgeoning but floundering interest in the opposite sex. On his way back to the building site after shopping for bread, his attention is drawn by the sound of a woman giggling suggestively. We see him looking wistfully for a few seconds before the object of his gaze is revealed to be a young couple in a park playfully throwing a hat to one another. Such a playful but mediated tryst serves frequently in Iranian cinema as a coded substitute for a more intimate exchange, which is forbidden from the screen. The shot-reverse-shot structure of this brief scene leaves the viewer with no doubt that Lateef also longs for such female companionship as he chews distractedly on a piece of Afghan bread. Where the hat serves as a playful indirect signifier of forbidden physical contact — a reminder that the couple are not permitted to hold hands in public — the fleshy bread may be read as a cryptic clue or allegorical hieroglyph of Lateef's burgeoning desire to connect with another body. In fact, the bread is charged with such allegorical meaning from the very beginning of the film, when the viewer becomes attuned to the inherently fleshy qualities of raw dough. This is initially achieved through the evocative introduction of the soundtrack even before the first image has lit the screen. For a few seconds we hear some slapping sounds, not unlike the sound of a hand gently rubbing and slapping flesh. This is accompanied by breathing sounds, which are pushed to the very front of the soundscape, giving the cinema viewer the rather tactile sensation that someone is breathing in our ear. As with the momentary visual withholding of the source of the giggling woman, the few seconds during which vision is withheld allows the viewer's mind to wander, to invest these sounds with our own imaginations, to speculate on the kinds of images that may accompany them. In this sense, the black screen functions as a kind of veil,[11] highlighting that something has been hidden from view, and signalling that we must engage both our minds and senses in order to delve into the deepest layers of meaning presented by the film. Following this aural 'tease', Majidi provides an answer to the sound puzzle, revealing the source of the sounds to be a baker kneading dough, rolling it out and slapping it onto the hot stone to be cooked. Even though this image manages to dispel the more titillating, and potentially sacrilegious suggestions provided by the sounds, Majidi has managed to attune the viewer to the particularly fleshy qualities of the dough, and predisposed us to read sensuality into Lateef's consumption of it in the scene described above.[12]

Lateef's awakening adolescent desire is further emphasised moments later when he pauses to admire himself in a highly reflective glass door, fixing his hair, smiling and humming to himself, imagining perhaps that a girl might find him attractive. However, this moment of what may be described as narcissistic scopophilia — where he already perceives himself to be more man than he really is — is interrupted (metaphorically shattered) when a man pushes open the door from the inside, pauses to look at him suspiciously, thus bringing Lateef's self-reverie to an abrupt halt. His self-image is not yet fully formed as he balances on the cusp between adolescence and adulthood.

These are just the first of many clues that hint at Lateef's sexual awakening. On the building site, we witness other signs of his faltering and often misplaced attempts to assert his burgeoning masculinity. This fire that is burning inside him seems to function at times — such as those discussed above — as a calm, warming sensation, but at other times will flare out of control and provoke violent outbursts. Lateef frequently fights with his co-workers over highly insignificant matters, particularly once the young Rahmat (Baran disguised as a young man) comes to work on the building site. These outbursts become more frequent, particularly after Rahmat is given his job in the kitchen preparing meals and tea and Lateef must join the ranks of the labourers. Gradually, his outbursts become more focussed on Rahmat, showing ironically that he is learning to direct his adolescent rage. This rage, however, is suddenly turned to desire in a key moment when Lateef discovers that Rahmat is really a woman.

This scene is important for the way it is structured cinematically, for it is designed to generate a powerfully affective experience for the spectator as well as revealing the emotions that are being stirred up deep within Lateef's being. It also cleverly negotiates the censorship rules regarding the portrayal of women in Iranian cinema. The scene opens with a shot of Lateef going to fetch a heavy bag of cement. As he moves toward the camera, struggling to carry the heavy bag in his arms, wind blows a wave of white smoke across the screen, which irritates Lateef's eyes, causing a momentary loss of vision. The sound of the wind generates a highly mystical effect, appearing as a kind of energy that draws Lateef toward the kitchen area where Rahmat/Baran works. The soundtrack is then further layered with the distant sound of thunder, rain, and the faint sound of a woman humming. As Lateef blinks, a reverse shot of a curtain blowing in the wind briefly reveals the distant silhouette of a woman. Cut back to Lateef, still blinking he throws the bag of cement to the ground and rubs his eyes. The sound of wind continues to intensify, and having regained his vision, Lateef peers intensely toward the blowing curtain, the camera zooming toward him to indicate the sharpening of his vision. This movement is answered in the next reverse shot of the curtain, which now blows in slow motion, teasingly rising and lowering, providing another brief shot of the silhouette glimpsed earlier, but the curtain refuses to yield for more than a second or two. The movement and placement of the camera suggests a point of view shot, however when Lateef enters from screen right, we realise that Majidi has in fact placed us not *with*

Lateef, but beside him, therefore implicating us within the scene. The following shot, however, does not yet reveal to us a clearer view of the scene behind the curtain, we see Lateef seeing, his eyes widening, fixing his gaze upon the scene before him. Finally, Majidi provides us with a shot of Baran brushing her long black tresses, humming to herself wistfully as she does so. She is framed and 'veiled' by a frosted window that barely separates either Lateef or the viewer from her modesty with backlighting providing a further distancing effect to protect the modesty of all. In this highly affective scene produced by sound, framing, camera movement and movement within the frame, not only are we encouraged to feel the passion that Lateef feels, but to experience images and sounds viscerally.

Don't tell the mullahs!

Throughout *Baran,* Majidi effectively uses images and sounds to engage the viewer in what Vivian Sobchack refers to as a 'cinesthetic' mode of embodied spectatorship.[13] In her article, 'What my fingers knew', Sobchack argues that to experience a film is not simply a matter of 'seeing it'. Rather, our body functions as 'a 'third' term that both exceeds and yet is within representation'.[14] That is, although our bodies are ostensibly located outside and separate from the representations that appear on screen, through the cinema's engagement of our multiple senses, our bodies are necessarily also inscribed into or take part in the representation itself. In addition, she writes: 'All the bodies in the film experience — those on-screen and off-screen (and possibly that of the screen itself) — are potentially subversive bodies. They have the capacity to function both figuratively and literally.'[15] In coining the term 'cinesthesia', Sobchack draws on two psychoneurological conditions: synaesthesia and coenaesthesia. Synesthesia is an extreme, but rare condition in which the stimulation of one sense provokes a perception in another sense. Sobchack explains: 'Synaesthetes regularly, vividly, automatically, and consciously perceive sound as colour, or shapes as having a taste'.[16] A less extreme form of this 'cross-modal transfer' takes place in figural language. According to George Lakoff and Mark Johnson, because metaphors originate in concrete, sensate experience, 'metaphor is experiential and visceral'.[17] I would argue that the highly metaphorical film language used in *Baran*, combined with the clever use of off-screen sound, helps to engage the viewer in just this kind of cross-modal transfer. Not only does bread metaphorically evoke flesh, it does so largely because we have already heard/felt the potentially erotic fleshiness of the dough well before our sense of sight is brought into play. Similarly, in the scene in which Lateef discovers Baran's true identity, the enhanced sound of wind serves simultaneously as a metaphor for the swell of emotion being experienced by Lateef, and may cause a cross-modal sensation in the viewer of being touched by such a breeze.

The dominant role played by sound in producing these cross-modal sensory affects in *Baran* also evokes the second bodily condition discussed by Sobchack. According to Sobchack, coenaesthesia is a common, yet under-recognised perceptual experience in which 'our equally available senses have the capacity to become variously heightened and diminished'.[18] This capacity is more evident in children where the hierarchical socialisation of the senses has not yet fully taken place, but given the right stimuli, this may also occur in adults. Cinema has the most wonderful capacity to do this, and certainly, as I have already shown, through his complex use of sound[19] in *Baran*, Majidi certainly attempts to retrain his viewers' sensorium to privilege sound over or in addition to vision. This adds a highly affective and potentially erotic or subversive level of meaning to the film that plays off and against the pure, selfless devotion on a collective level, and the personal love for a woman on an individual level.

It is my contention that a figurative and literal exchange between potentially erotic bodies takes place in *Baran*. As in the scene discussed above, Majidi deploys complex cinematic techniques (sound, editing, camera and character placement) and stimulates our sensory organs (through evocative sounds and images) in order to weave the viewer into the very texture of the film. In doing so, he effectively allows the viewer to experience that which cannot be literally represented on screen. Our bodies effectively fill the gap imposed by censorship between the characters' bodies. In doing so, Majidi exposes the viewer to the possibility of what I would like to call 'sacrilegious affects', that is, a felt violation of the sacred modesty of the Iranian cinema screen. The cinema's potential for cross-modal transfer enables the superficial modesty of the on screen representation to be undermined by a transgressive potential in the aesthetic realm, capable of activating the forbidden (*haram*) sensations of the flesh.

Throughout the film, the sounds of wind, rain, thunder, running water, the fluttering of fabric and bird's wings, human breath, footsteps, voices, laughter and birds singing are all used to heighten the embodied sensory perceptions of the viewers and attune them to what must remain unrepresented, relegated to the space beyond the frame. Even a close-up of Lateef's finger wiping mud from a coin he finds in the street works to heighten our sense of touch. By the end of the film, our senses and emotions have become so heightened that we are prepared for the emotionally (and sexually) charged scene that closes the film. In this scene, Baran and her family are preparing to leave for Afghanistan and Lateef has come to their village to help. As Baran crosses the grey, muddy pathway she trips and the contents of her wicker bag spill out onto the ground. This functions as a moment of metaphorical explosion, betraying perhaps the feelings she has kept hidden throughout the film. We see among a variety of other fruits and vegetables, several bright red tomatoes, and some dried figs. Lateef rushes to Baran's aid and Majidi cuts to a close-up filmed in slow motion of Baran and Lateef picking up the spilled items. As their hands slowly and gracefully enter the frame a moment of tactile pleasure may be experienced by the viewer. Although, according to the rules of modesty, the characters do not physically touch, the framing of the image enables their images to overlap as they each reach for a ripe red tomato. They therefore 'touch' virtually in this brief and silent parting exchange, which is heightened by the contrast between the grey earth and the redness of the tomatoes, which provide a melodramatic sign of their passion. Here, the modest, restrained emotions depicted on screen overflow into the space between the viewer and the screen, into the dark space of the cinema where we may even 'steal' a publicly forbidden tactile moment. The almost-direct looks of the protagonists toward the camera that directly following this scene invite us to share in this intimate moment, further charging this affective relationship between the screen and the viewer. While, as I have shown, *Baran* adheres very strictly to Islamic censorship regulations, this relationship between screen and spectator set up by the film teeters on the precipice between the sacred and the sacrilegious, effectively pushing the limits of Islamic censorship that prevents intimacy between men and women from being depicted on screen. The modest bodies on screen are *shadowed* by the bodies of the spectators seated in the dark space of the cinema. But hush! Please don't tell the mullahs, because Iranian filmmakers have enough trouble with censorship as it is!

Endnotes

[1] Hent de Vries, 1999, *Philosophy and the Turn to Religion*, Baltimore: Johns Hopkins University Press, p. 11.

[2] More recently, however, numerous films have dealt with the subject of romantic love, including the present film under discussion. Some of these films, which also fall into the genre of the 'spiritual film', use romantic love as a means for discovering divine love. Many take traditional Persian Sufi poetry as their model, pivoting around an ambiguous presentation of earthly and divine love. A recent example of such a film is *God is Near* (*Khoda Nazdik Ast*, Ali Vazirian, 2007).

[3] Hamid Naficy, 2002, 'Islamicizing Film Culture in Iran: A Post-Khatami Update' in Richard Tapper (ed.) *The New Iranian Cinema: Politics, Representation and Identity*, London & New York: I.B. Tauris, pp. 26-65.

[4] This point is mentioned by numerous commentators including Richard Tapper in his introduction to *The New Iranian Cinema*, pp. 5-6; and Hamid Dabashi, 2001, *Close Up Iranian Cinema Past, Present and Future*, London: Verso, p. 32.

[5] Mohammad Jalal Abbasi-Shavazi, Diana Glazebrook et al., 2005, 'Return to Afghanistan? A Study of Afghans Living in Tehran' Afghanistan Research Evaluation Unit, Faculty of Social Sciences, University of Tehran, p. 12.

[6] Sami A. Aldeeb Abu-Sahlieh, 1996, 'The Islamic Conception of Migration' *The International Migration Review*, vol. 30, no. 1, pp. 37-57. p. 53. Emphasis added.

[7] Abbasi-Shavazi et. al., op. cit., p. 12.

[8] Ibid., p. 13.

[9] It should also be noted that the manager of the building site also treats the Afghans as *mohajerin*, paying them before the Iranian workers, much to the chagrin of those workers.

[10] Michael M. J. Fisher, 2004, *Mute Dreams, Blind Owls, and Dispersed Knowledges: Persian Poesis in the Transnational Circuitry*, Durham & London: Duke University Press. The metaphorical significance of Baran's name is twofold. It is at once the name of the river running through Karbul in Afghanistan and means 'rain' in Persian.

[11] Indeed, the blackness of the screen reminds me of the chador, the Islamic veil which is commonly used by devout Muslim women in Iran, and are required to be worn in all sacred spaces such as mosques and courtrooms. The chador is predominantly black, although a range of floral variants are often seen.

[12] Later in the film, Majidi employs a process of metaphorical slippage, which functions to confirm the allegorical (rather than statically symbolic) nature of the aural and visual imagery. The complex soundscape of the building site recalls the opening sounds, and a number of times we see Baran and other characters mixing cement by hand, recalling the tactile process of making bread by mixing flour and water. Thus both bread and cement may substitute for forbidden physical contact between men and women.

[13] Vivian Sobchack, 2000, 'What My Fingers Knew: The Cinesthetic Subject, or Vision in the Flesh' *Senses of Cinema,* vol. 5. http://www.sensesofcinema.com/contents/00/5/fingers.html. (Viewed 6 July 2004.)

[14] Ibid.

[15] Ibid.

[16] Ibid.

[17] Lakoff and Johnson quoted in Sobchack, ibid.

[18] Sobchack, op. cit.

[19] There are numerous other examples in the film, which I do not have space to discuss here.

12

Silence as a way of knowing in Yolngu Indigenous Australian storytelling

Caroline Josephs

I am, in this chapter, approaching three aspects of silence as a way of knowing — in relation to Yolngu story and storytelling — through one particular Yolngu story which I *cannot* tell. What I can tell — is *why* I cannot tell the story, and how pursuing the question of whether I could tell the story, and in what way, led me on a long intriguing journey.

The three aspects I want to deal with, in relation to one Yolngu story, are:

1. *protocol*s of being silent around storytelling — or *not* telling;

2. *inside/outside knowledge*, and touching into the silence surrounding, and in women's business; and

3. *embodiment* as a silent way of knowing when dancing country.

The way of storytelling

My approach is a step towards Yolngu ways of being and telling as far as may be possible for a non-Indigenous non-Yolngu storyteller and researcher, and to make the bridging necessary for a similar audience as myself. Yolngu epistemology is part of what I am terming *sacred epistemology* — a mystical tradition which includes phenomena such as revelation and epiphany, and of being present to the seen, the known, and at the same time, to Mystery, the Unknown, the 'between', the 'ship' of relating. In this process, being becomes Being, for Yolngu. It is also primarily an experiential approach to knowing, a felt sense in the body, and can not in my view, be met through analytic conceptual frames of reference. According to Greg Dening,[1] story is the only way such a sacred world may be represented. Current experiences are sung and told as contemporary expressions of the Dreaming, the moving from the *Wangga* to the present. Past and present thus become fused and ensure a future of deep intimacy with all beings.

My way of presentation is to work towards exemplifying such approaches — through personal story (never separate from Yolngu 'history' or Dreamtime story) and traditional storytelling, in ways that represent relationship with country, and with all beings, including kin with others of clan and tribe. I weave these storytellings with explanation in the non-Yolngu tradition to make the connections clearer for we who are non-Indigenous readers. Knowing, for Yolngu, is always being approached as an interior *experience* for the individual, albeit in the context of the tribe's cultural knowledge — it is as a consequence always done within silence. Outside or exterior experiences will always be parallelling interior internal experiences in symbolic ways, in feeling states and in states of mind. Storytelling is always intending to link each Yolngu to their own country, to plants, to animals, to all the Dreamings, and to each other, in particular kinship interrelationships which are articulated not only through storytelling, but are constantly reinforced through an elaborate and refined 'opera' of mark-making, music-making, protocols of relating presented in everyday life and ceremony both. (If you are my mother-in-law for example, there are certain kinds of body language to be presented in your company, and only certain kinds of humour may be displayed with certain family members). So, I am presenting a methodology pointing towards Yolngu ways of knowing at the same time as telling the stories.

The people, the place, the story

Yolngu people are Indigenous Australians living on their land which is in north-east Arnhemland, of Australia. Australian Aboriginal people have been on their land continuously for perhaps 40,000 or more years. (Yolngu language is probably around 5000 years old). Yolngu came into first contact with white people in the 1920s with a few anthropologists who travelled by boat to the remote area, in the 1930s with the establishment of a mission school, and with the impact of the multi-national bauxite miners, in the 1960s.

As a necessary precursor I am telling of the journey that led me to this Yolngu story. The story, commonly called in Arnhemland, The Wagilag Sisters Story, is a story of the Rainbow Serpent. Yolngu personal stories are bound together with ancestral stories. Narrative (or 'story') is inextricably woven with country, and body to country, and all beings to each other and to country through the laws of kinship.

In 1979 I met Wandjuk Marika, an Elder, important Law man, master *yidaki*[2] player, artist, from north-east Arnhemland — at a conference in Darwin where I was talking of the project I was running at the time across Australia. I was offering a presentation on 'The Curriculum Development Centre's Multi-Arts Project' in terms of the rainbow, with its many colours and strands. After, Wandjuk came up to me, shook my hand, and thanked me for the story of the Rainbow.

We sat in the garden for several hours (I don't recall how long — clock time ceased) as he told me stories of his life and, in the course of this, gave my children Aboriginal names. (It wasn't till decades later I learned the significance of the names and the relationships which they implied). Wandjuk told me three stories from his country, a thousand miles to the east in Arnhemland, including one of the Rainbow Serpent. Wandjuk was, what some anthropologists call, a 'bridge person' for his people, keen to describe his culture.

More than 20 years later, I was living in the bush in solitude on the south coast of New South Wales. It was an unprecedented year for pythons. I had never seen so many in the 25 years I had been visiting the place. Three snakes came to visit.

The first — huge — made its way up the *Angophera* (a native Australian tree) outside my window, and made its way through a hole and into the ceiling. It was to spend the winter there, no doubt attracted by the possums who inhabited the ceiling space during the day, too.

Another python, about six feet long, twined itself into the door jam and prevented my exit from the top storey to the outside deck, and downstairs to the bathroom. I stamped and 'danced' on the floor inside the door, 'Go away! Go away! This is not your place!' I told my not-welcome visitor. Strange echoes resounded — of the Wagilag Sisters. Much later I realised the parallels. In one part of the story, the sisters are singing and dancing to keep the snake from the door of their hut. Aah!

The third snake manifested when I arrived from Sydney to set up the house for a visit by Uncle Max[3] and a group of people. Uncle Max was to lead us up Gulaga, the sacred mountain of the Yuin people on the south coast, visible from the back cliff behind my home — known to the Yuin as 'pregnant woman with her feet in the sea'. (One of the sisters is pregnant in the Wagilag Sisters Story). I opened up the house and went on to the front deck. There on the threshold was a complete python skin — a gift — a word of poetry — evoking a shedding of skin, transformation.

Snake stories invaded my dreams. Snake stories arrived in different guises.

I recalled the Rainbow Serpent story Wandjuk had told me so many years before. I went down to the garage and found my 1979 journals and re-read the words I had written of my meeting with Wandjuk.

The snake visitations also led to a long conversation with an Aboriginal woman (not a Yolngu), at the end of which she said she thought I could tell the story and use my good judgment about what to tell.[4]

That was before I visited country of the story. I wasn't sure. It was early days. I read a number of versions of the story, and everything I could lay my hands on about Yolngu country and culture.

This story of the rainbow serpent is a *living* story I cannot tell. I am obliged to be silent on it. I only learned of the protocols surrounding this 'big' story while delving into the question of whether I could as a non-Yolngu researcher and storyteller tell the story. In the process of living with the question, I talked with many people. Why, I wondered, was it that I could not tell the story? After two years of talking with many *Balanda* (or non-Yolngu) people who had lived with Yolngu and worked closely with them, I found out about what may be called, 'protocols', in relation to the story.

Protocols

First, the story emerges out of the country of Arnhemland — the story track (or songline) moves from south-east to north. It intersects with another big creation story of another moiety. (Each story, as well as every person, every creature and every thing in Yolngu culture, belongs to one of two complementary moieties, either *Yirridja* or *Dhuwa*). The story is associated with three major ceremonies for both men and women. (Sometimes ceremonies are held separately, e.g., around menstruation and in former times, childbirth. Some major ceremonies are held for all.) To tell it out of country makes no sense, as the story, like the serpent, follows the route of Yolngu Ancestors as they travelled through specific country, which includes for example, the waterhole of Mirramina, in central Arnhemland.

Custodians of the storytellings are elders from five major clans. The place of the country where a storytelling is held will determine which part of the story will be told. It would never be told in what we as 'whitefellas' would assume to be its complete form, or any form we might find in a written 'text'.

The tellings would be carefully negotiated among the clans for a ceremony, ensuring that all clans would be agreeable — this is part of a bringing together and making of relationships of community, through preparation and negotiating processes. The parts of the story and the ways in which it would be told would depend not only on these factors, but the purpose for telling (for initiation, for funeral or another ritual or event), the people present, their ages, gender, and kinship with others, with the country, who the teller is, the relationship with Dreamings in the story. In addition, kinship (or relationship with all, and with other beings and humans) is mapped by the land — *gurrutu*. It interweaves and overlays everything.

The story in its oral forms — which traditionally it always is, perhaps accompanied by singing, dancing, mark-making on bodies — in a kind of multi-strand 'opera' of many senses. It is fluid and changing, dynamic, just like the Ancestors, moving through country, changing form many times — transformations that create country and are created out of country. The same story would never be told on two occasions. It changes. The important elements will however, be present.

I was told by Sophie Creighton, an anthropologist who has worked with Yolngu, that there are important distinctions also between the right to *hear* a story, the right to *tell* a story, and the *bestowal* of a story.[5]

Peter Sutton, a South Australian linguist writes: 'Ancestral Beings *are Stories* and their Sacred Dwelling Places *are* Story Places.'[6] When I first saw this brief inscription on some artefacts in the Museum of Australia in Canberra, I stopped dead in my tracks! Something happened in my body. I did not know what it was right then. The sentence would resonate in me for a long time.

What I finally discovered after some time was that my notion of someone telling a story, was not what it was about — the Ancestors (who are Beings, not necessarily only *human* beings) are the stories — and each is intimately dwelling as Place (in country). The tellers *become* the Ancestors, those who body forth *in* dance *as* Ancestors.

This turns our ordinary notions upside down — and inside out — which brings me to 'inside' and 'outside' knowledge among the Yolngu. I take this up later.

Here is, however, the version of the story which is an acceptable form; a public or outside version. It has been carefully worded by Yolngu. Each word is full of significance, layers of meaning, though it is framed in ways that avoid much detail of other now unable-to-be-public versions. This version I came to designate, a 'fixed version' to distinguish it from 'living versions'.

The story covers the territory of a number of clans, in particular the waterhole named Mirarrmina on the Upper Woolen River in Central Arnhemland. The waterhole is the home of 'Wititj' the Olive Python (sometimes also known as the 'Rainbow Serpent'), one of the most powerful of ancestral beings.[7] Accounts of the story vary with context and narrative, but the following details (the text tells us) occur in most versions.[8]

The Wagilag Sisters Story — A fixed version

Two sisters, the older of whom has a child, the younger is pregnant, are fleeing their home in the south-east. They are being followed by clansmen. The Sisters reach Ngilipidji, or the Stone Country of the Wagilag clan, from where they get their name. As they continue on their travels they encounter animals, plants and country on which they confer names, in essence bringing them into being. They decide to camp in the rich and fertile country surrounding the waterhole at Mirarrmina.

According to some versions of the narrative, one of the Sisters pollutes the waterhole, which arouses Wititj from his sleep. The younger Sister gives birth, further inciting the Snake. Unsuspecting, the Sisters make camp, build a bark hut, and try to cook the food they have caught, but things begin to go wrong — the animals and vegetables come to life and leap into the waterhole. Wititj emerges from the waterhole and creates a storm cloud with lightning and thunder to wash the Sisters into the well. The land is flooded as the first monsoon pours down its rains.

Frightened, the Sisters perform dances and sing sacred songs to deter the Python.

Finally the Sisters drop in exhaustion, and Wititj is able to enter the hut and swallow them, their children and their dog.

Shortly afterwards, the great Wititj develops a terrible stomach ache. He rises into the sky above the flooded landscape, and his groans attract the attention of other great Snakes from surrounding clan estates, who also rise up into the sky. They talk to each other and discover they have different names. When asked what ails him, Wititj lies about what he has eaten, realising that he has probably eaten beings of the same moiety. Finally, the pain becomes so great that he falls to earth and vomits the Sisters. (He retains the children, who belong to the opposite moiety, the Yirritja). When the Sisters are brought to life again by the bites of the stinging caterpillars, Wititj beats them with clapsticks (*malirri*), and swallows them again.

The Sisters' clansmen had followed them and were asleep by the triangular impression made in the ground by the Python's fall. The sisters come to them in a dream and reveal the secrets of the sacred dances and songs they had composed in their efforts to stop the rain.

This is the version of the story I was told by a number of expert informants[9] that I could tell and write.

'Outside' and 'inside' knowing

Almost two years after the big snake year in my south coast home I was invited to Arnhemland as part of a Music Forum (to include a small group of around 25 *Balanda* (non-Yolngu) anthropologists, ethnomusicologists, and an assortment of others like myself, an educator, with groups of Yolngu dancers and singers presenting and speaking) — to be followed by Garma, a festival — the occasion of Yolngu sharing their knowledge more widely with *Balanda* as public or 'outside' knowledge.

Howard Morphy, a much respected anthropologist who has worked with Yolngu for many years, says: 'The delicate and complex relationship between inside and outside [knowledge] provides the context for understanding the release of knowledge to Balanda.'[10] 'Outside' knowledge for Yolngu (according to Morphy) is analogous to 'inside' knowledge which is secret and sacred. There are layers to this knowledge — indicated by the kinds of words that are used in the storytellings for example. There will be other differences of course too. The public versions will use different words, not so-called 'power' words. Mandawuy told us, for example, of 30 words for the turtle, all with subtle variations and meanings for Yolngu.

Early in my explorations around the Wagilag Sisters story, I spoke with Nigel Lendon, who had curated the large exhibition of paintings representing 60 years of bark paintings of the story. This was held in the Australian National Gallery in 1998. As I spoke with him of the story, he stopped me suddenly. 'You know', he said, 'If I had used the word you have just used as the name of the snake in Arnhem Land, it would have meant death!' He told me of being stalked while in country. Curators had spent seven years negotiating the release of the story in a suitable form to be published in the exhibition catalogue. I felt distinctly uncomfortable at this news.

Later, I recounted this conversation to Howard Morphy. What did he think? In his understated way, he said: 'I think that is a *little* exaggerated'. However, Alan Fidock, with whom I had worked in Canberra over many years, and who had lived and worked with Yolngu for 13 years in Milingimby, agreed that I could not utter this name, a 'power word'.

What to be silent about, and what to speak? I knew I would have to move slowly and with sensitivity. Speaking could have certain very serious consequences. I did not wish to offend. I was getting conflicting messages. And women anthropologists had different ideas again about what could and could not be spoken![11]

Much later I was to learn from Howard Morphy:

Power names are called publicly at important stages of ceremonies the whole time, e.g. the thirty words for turtle are not used in mundane contexts. And the word you refer to as not being able to use — are used only in restricted private contexts. However very few words fit into this category. Most powerful names are known but treated as special. The silence or the interval between their sounding marks their significance and creates a sense of awe in their presence as well as the aesthetic power of their performance.[12]

Later, at the Music Forum at the Yothu Yindi studio on the Bay in Arnhemland, I asked Mandawuy a question about colour and body painting. He spoke in language to others, and eventually came back with an answer. What was the consultation I wondered? Perhaps, how to explain in terms appropriate to my level of understanding? I learned that one principle is to show respect, always ask if unsure, but on the other hand, only ask a question once. Later I found when I became closer to Gulumbu, I would ask her questions and she would simply turn slightly away, as though she hadn't heard, and then I would know not to pursue this line of questioning.

Gregory Bateson says: 'Secrecy can be used as a marker to tell us that we are approaching holy ground...'[13] Bateson's proposition is that secrecy (or the non utterance of certain things) was essential in the epistemological process. He says there is a 'necessity for the sacred':

> This is a very important and significant matter, that non-communication of certain sorts is needed if we are to maintain the 'sacred'. Communication is undesirable, not because of fear, but because communication would somehow alter the nature of the ideas.[14]

'*Communication* of certain things alters the nature of the ideas.' Silence, or 'non-communication' is *required* for the 'sacred', Bateson maintains.

Howard Morphy tells us more, specifically in relation to silence as a way of knowing in relation to Yolngu knowledge:

> And in many respects the layering of knowledge can be thought of as a pedagogical [or learning process] technique, though it is one that emphasises the *variability in understanding* that exists at a given moment among different members of the society. The layering is as important as the secrecy.[15] [my emphasis]

According to Morphy, it is not only the nature of the ideas, but the nature of the *process* for learning which renders silence significant. Both layering and silence have pedagogical intent, *are part of the learning process*. 'Inside' and 'outside' knowledge are seen to be different in Yolngu terms. Outside knowledge is freely available. (There are 'inside' and 'outside' versions of stories). 'Inside' knowledge is available only to certain people at certain stages, in certain circumstances. It is revealed in phases, with pauses, with silence between, as Morphy has indicated — a necessary part of a sacred epistemology or way of knowing.

Morphy indicates that the concepts of 'inside' and 'outside' are more than the English concept of 'secret'. 'Inside' for Yolngu is used, he says, in two complementary senses. The first is 'inside' in the sense of truth or *generative power*. The other is 'inside' in the sense of *exclusive* or *secret*. In the first, women and men are equally included. In the second, women are excluded from certain contexts and certain knowledge.[16] The Wagilag Sisters Story seems to hold both kinds of knowledge. This explained its being associated with both men's and women's business.

What Morphy has not articulated is that Yolngu women also hold certain knowledge secret from the men — certain women's business knowledge.[17] Rita Gross (1977) makes a strong case that men's and women's rituals, symbols and knowledges are always equal and complementary, without gendered hierarchy, 'co-equal and co-necessary'.[18] She refutes any sacred/profane dichotomy of male/female in Aboriginal religion and argues instead that the 'correct interpretation is to see women as embodiments and manifestations of a different kind of sacrality than that associated with males'. She notes that 'women's experience is inaccessible to males in the absence of articulate females'. Women's experience has not been fully articulated from within Aboriginal cultures.[19] I would argue that this is part of an 'unspoken story', a story *silenced or silent*, another story that has not been told; another aspect of 'silence'. This is the unknowable *by* one gender, *of* the other. Rita Gross goes further. She looks deeply into the Wagilag Sisters Story to conclude that 'women's unique experiences are potent metaphors in men's religious lives'.

Another important point to be remembered is that while 'outside' or public or children's versions may be simpler in form, they reflect, or are analogous with, the 'inside' knowledge, though this may not be immediately evident.

Helen Verran, a philosopher now working at Charles Darwin University, says:

> Yolngu knowledge is the intrusion of the Dreaming into the secular. The Dreaming is brought into the here and now by the doing of particular things at particular times by particular people...*Knowledge can only ever be a performance of the Dreaming, a bringing to life in the here and now of the elements of the other domain.* [20] [my emphasis]

'Dreamtime' in Yolngu is called *Wangarr*, and each language group will have a different term which is only approximated by the English term, 'Dreamtime'. Knowing in Yolngu is not about words, or descriptions, or abstract concepts. It is more related to being and actioning. I will return to Helen Verran's notion of 'performance' indirectly, through the dancing, a little later.

I could, (I was assured by Alan Fidock, Djon Mundine, Nigel Lendon, Sophie Creighton), write of the story and tell the story which had been carefully negotiated and published.

Revelation and epiphany are ways of knowing in Yolngu culture.[21] Such 'events' happen in silence. What is revelation? It is the known being connected to the Unknowable in such a way as to open up to all possibility.

In Yolngu culture, *Bir'yun* is a shimmering effect (seen in finely cross-hatched paintings) may occur through an experience of what may be termed 'epiphany' or 'revelation'. *Bir'yun* projects a brightness that emanates from the *Wangarr* Ancestral past which manifests in the present through storytelling, singing, art-making, dancing — or from the Ancestral Beings themselves. The brightness of *bir'yun* endows the painting with 'Ancestral power'.

This process probably has to be present in the painter in order to evoke it in the viewers. This may echo the state that has to be present in the storyteller for the effect to transmit to the audience during a storytelling. The process is similarly evoked in other forms of expression and sacred art in Yolngu (dancing, singing), where Morphy reports that there is a progressing from dark to dull, to light and brilliant, analogous to the transformation that arises in the process. It is present in the music which builds to a final shout, for example, as well as in the dances which sometimes build to a frenzy of dramatic and solo performances (especially as I noted, with the male dancers). I make the parallel of *bir'yun* with storytelling and my own experiences later in country.

Raymattja Marika-Mununggirity, Yolngu linguist from Yirrkala, has written of the relationship between the 'mythic' ancestors and the life that is currently lived by Yolngu:

> Knowledge is living, and it comes from a real world, it has real life, real events and real happenings. That's what happens with the old ancestral stories, we still relive that past history, we still sing it, dance and still bring it and fit it into the present. That's what makes the present world a meaningful world to live in.[22]

Past and present exist together, ensuring a future conserving the Ancestral states of Being, and are given meaning and significance through re-enactment.

Revelation transforms, transmits, opens up being into Being, opens up into all possibility. Where creatures can jump out of a fire, and run and jump into a waterhole, as in the Wagilag Sisters Story, transformation has occurred. Ancestral Beings can transform in such a way — where an experience is charged — as well as in a myriad other ways, and Yolngu re-enacting Ancestral Beings re-embody that transformation. In *re-storing* the behaviours of the Ancestral Beings, Yolngu *re-story* their own being creating Being, maintaining connection with Ancestors.

Howard Morphy, in writing of the nature of Yolngu knowledge, talks of the revelatory nature of Yolngu knowledge and its relationship with secrecy. He uses the word 'transmission' in this context. Transmission of knowledge assumes a direct experiencing, a taking in, a knowing through embodying or 'immediate presencing'[23] of that knowing.

Morphy points out that the phasing and structuring of knowledge through secrecy and through revelatory knowing — establishes a rhythm, that allows slow digestion or absorption, to occur (in the way that snakes digest their food). There are thresholds at each turning, structured by secrecy. Secrecy can 'mark division between inside and outside knowledge'.

Within such a story as the Wagilag Sisters, the potential exists for many layers of meaning in different contexts. As Nigel Lendon has pointed out —

there is no one meaning for the story — meanings shift in relation to context, juxtapositionings, and a particular moment in time:

> The search for a singular 'deep' authentic meaning is doomed to failure. Thus the greater interest for developing a knowledge of these works [paintings of the Wagilag Sisters Story] is in the potential for elements to carry multiple meanings, in different contexts, conjunctions and historical moments.[24]

In Yolngu culture, all is dynamic in relation to the Story or Story versions. Contiguous elements and multivalent significances are part of the storytelling.

I had come to understand that I could not *tell* the Wagilag Sisters Story in any way I chose. I held no authority to tell. *Not* telling underscores the importance of some secrets, the mysteries that cannot be spoken.

In Yolngu society, I cannot assume a *right* to know. I must wait, listen, until invited into various aspects of the assembling of understanding through action, relationship in the environment in concert with others, with creatures, through listening, through ritual, ceremony, through the body, through dance, through the remarks people casually offer, and in all the details of everyday life.

Story is therefore *history performed*. And, as Ancestors enact transformation, so contemporary Yolngu re-create or re-enact the transformations as they tell the stories, sing the songs, do the paintings on bodies, and dance the dances of the Ancestors. Storytelling is in this way transformative for those who participate. In Yolngu terms, a storyteller can produce a storytelling, but it is Reality that is presented, *not* just a story.

Let me tell you of one experience that I had at Garma.

First, the landscape.

We are on a vast bush site, a stringbark forest on top of the escarpment. Between the trees, the deep red earth appears. If you walk a few hundred yards to the edge of the escarpment you can see the sea in the distance. There are five hundred *Balanda* and five hundred Indigenous people (many from vast distances across the north of Australia) camped in tents dotted in among the trees. A large space opens up among the trees, covered by beach sand — the shape of a long triangle and almost as long as a football field — where the *bunggul* takes place, late each afternoon. The *bunggul* is the ceremonial singing, dancing, storytelling that happens each year of *Garma*. The 'boss man' of the ceremonies and the storyteller for Garma *bunggul* is Galarrwuy Yunipingu.

For much of *Garma* I have spent time sitting on the ground with the women in the Women's shelter, learning how to make string, making friends with the women, telling our stories to each other, and gradually getting to know Gulumbu, with whom I share an instant and easy rapport.

And so, to the story…

Silent embodying, dancing as re-enacting story

Franca Tamisari writes:

> Dancing establishes relationship between people, country and ancestors as well as between the participants in a ceremony… In Yolngu dances 'the body speaks — directly and in its totality' of our being-in-the-world and being-with-others.[25]

Let me remind you of a part of the Wagilag Sisters story:

> Frightened, the Sisters *perform dances and sing sacred songs* to deter the Python. Finally the Sisters drop in exhaustion, and Wititj is able to enter the hut and swallow them, their children and their dog.

> The Sisters come to [their clansmen] in a dream and reveal the secrets of the sacred dances and songs they had composed in their efforts to stop the rain.[26] [my emphasis]

It is the Sunday after *Garma* has finished, and most of the *Balanda* have gone. My companions from the Music Forum have gone to a motel, but I choose to stay on at the campsite, not wanting to sleep inside if I can be in the bush. I have tried to get an earlier flight out, unsuccessfully. I have heard today there is to be a ceremony, but I don't take too much notice, as I imagine it will be held deep in the bush, away from the eyes of myself, or other *Balanda*.

A handful of *Balanda* are still there at Gulkula, the *Garma* site, and about 300 Yolngu — gradually drifting into the *bunggul*[27] space.

It is hot in the sun. I have been collecting tea in large tin cans for the women, for Galarrwuy, for the women in the weaving shelter, back and forth in the heat to the kitchen, finding cups and sugar and milk to bring for them. It seems appropriate to tell Galarrwuy as I bring him tea, 'Gulumbu says I am *yeppa* (sister)'. He has shown us the elaborate head-dresses and armbands that will be for the boys, woven with coloured feathers. 'These must be special', I say. 'Special', he acknowledges, as he gently puts them back into a bag. Increasingly, it is emerging, that the ceremony will take place here in the *bunggul* space, for two boys from two clans, one of them Galarrwuy's son.

I go to join the women, as Gulumbu has invited me to do, sitting in the women's shelter near where she is tending the fire. She leaves me in the care of her daughter, Dhambit. Gulumbu, I realise only later, is Galarrwuy's sister. Kin establishes obligations, responsibilities, roles, everything. I observe that she has a leading role to play in the unfolding event.

The groups for singing and dancing have assembled on either side of the ceremonial space where the evening's *bunggul* for each day of *Garma* have, it seems, been gradually building to this climax.

In shelters[28] on opposite sides of the performance space where the figures of *Ganbulapula* [29] and a great funeral log stand, sit the groups of the two related clans. To the accompaniment of *yidaki* and clapsticks, they sing, each clan alternating, and the men and women of each clan also take turns to move into the performing space to dance in the sequence occasioned by the ceremony.

Eventually, I am told, the two boys from the two clans will emerge from the bush at one side, accompanied by the older men of both clans, to be ushered into the space for the climax of the initiation ceremony and circumcision. They are being prepared, painted up, in Yirrkala, the Yolngu town some distance away.

I stand near Gulumbu, tired now of sitting still in one place with the women in the shelter for most of the day, as the singing and dancing go on, and preparations around the *bunggul* continue. A great turtle is being roasted in the ground. (Gulumbu calls to me to come and look). It will later be fed to the clan elders at the end of the ceremony.

Gulumbu is tending the fire that is to be used for the 'smoking' of the relatives,[30] and for boiling the 'treatment' for the boys, following the ceremony. I get up, stiff, and beginning to feel my body mightily in need of movement after four or five hours of sitting still. I have been saying to myself to just observe, not ask questions on this special day, to be grateful to be present (which I certainly am) and wait. I cannot sit still any longer. My body won't allow it. I get up and walk across to Gulumbu at the fire. Standing opposite her as she stirs the 'treatment' over the fire, I begin to move my body a little as I see the women doing in the central sandy space.

I am itching to be dancing, restless from being still for so long.

Maarr, which manifests itself in the footprints left behind by ancestral beings in the landscape features, names, objects, designs, songs and dances — is not only ancestral power, it also refers to people's *innermost feelings of love and care, silent wishes* 'which make things happen', concealed desires which are not expressed but which nonetheless are felt and met.[31] [my emphasis]

I have always loved to dance almost more than anything else, and it is always hard for me to be on the periphery of any dancing, painful to be looking in, unable to participate. I am unsure of the codes here. I have been sitting in the shelter observing, cautious of moving or of asking questions, conscious that I am privileged to just be here watching, conscious too, of Gulumbu's having made my entry possible.

'Can you teach me the dance?' I ask Gulumbu. I do know this important principle of being in Yolngu country. Always ask. Be respectful. I have also been cautioned by a Balanda who has worked with Indigenous people for years: 'Don't ask more than once'. I can never know if what I am asking is crossing an unknown boundary. I am risking something, transgressing the boundary of being still, being quiet, just observing. It is risky business. But I trust this woman, her presence, her warmth. I have put on the armband she has made me. I am wearing the string with possum fur inserted into it she has given me.

Gulumbu looks up from her work of stirring the pot with the stringybark in it for the boys, straightens up from her task, then turns and gestures to the far side of the ground, 'You go right around the outside to that other side. Keep right behind, and do the dancing there'.

With her blessing on the enterprise giving me permission and courage, I walk carefully around the outer rim of all the people and the activity in the middle of the sandy performance space, trying not to run in my impatience to be dancing — to where the group of women are seated in another shelter, as they rest in between each segment of dancing. A tremor in my body. I am moving at last — always for me, a favoured state.

When the women of this clan get up again to dance, I kick off my shoes and begin to mimic them, staying well back in the background from all the people.

I have positioned myself where I feel myself to be solitary, inconspicuous, unobserved. There are only Yolngu here, but their attention is focused on what is happening in front of me, in the *bunggul*. I am well behind them all. I am enclosed in concentration, focused on being present to just the dancing. I have the dancing group of women firmly in my sights through a kind of soft focus vision, imitating as closely as possible their every movement — allowing my body to dance the movements, being there, simultaneously as it is happening. It is something I have learned to do — to let go and mirror the movements, be the moving bodies there, with my body-mind, here.

So it is startling for me to hear what next takes place in the sequence of events.

I have been dancing for just a few short moments alone, but in unison with the group a little distance away in the performance space. The lead dancer turns her head, continuing to dance as she does so, and calls over her shoulder to me, 'Come into the canoe with us!'

At the sound of her invitation, and without a nano-second's hesitation I leap into the performance space (it feels in many ways a great 'leap'), keeping my body and mind open to picking up the steps and the rhythms as they are done, moving with them. I am alert, but relaxed, excited, keeping my peripheral vision open, breathing into my belly and letting the body know, forgetting any thinking about this strange and daunting thing I may find myself doing, if the focus stumbles. It is my body which is the dancing, the knowing.

The reality of Yolngu performance, and especially dancing, is thus one of *epiphany and transformation in which relationships with place and people are established, lived-in and embodied by the dancers.*[32] [my emphasis]

I am aware of the other Yolngu women dancers, though I am focusing on the lead dancer. I am in line with the women. The lead dancer is in front of the other dancers, closer to the singers, and seems to emit the dance calls and to direct the dancers.

I am kicking up the dust with my feet touching the earth and sending dust rising as each foot turns in and up slightly to the inside with each step. (This is different from the men's 'hitting' the earth with their feet). The dust itself reminds me of a liminality of body meeting the country.

As the meaning of footprints can be said to reside in between, that is in the social, political links and emotional bonds they fashion between places and ancestral events as well as people and country, the meaning of dancing is between the steps, between the participants of a ceremony, the inter-subjective space of desire and compassion, love and competition, that one enters through dancing.[33]

My hands follow the dancers' movements. I bend slightly forward as they do, and turn as they do, re-enacting and re-embodying the journey of the Ancestors, re-storing it to the present, *re-storying* it in the present.

I am dressed all in black (with long white hair); they are in colourful dresses, their dark skin glistening in the sun. This country, this story, these people, this dancing, myself *Balanda,* here with Yolngu, now, all related, storied, in the dance.

My hands gesture the different aspects of being in the canoe. Just dancing, just following, being with the whole group of women, allowing my body to keep in tune with the lead dancer who gives signals for changes in the movements. I can just do it by focusing my attention and at the same time opening to the body and the vision of being with what the women are doing.

With a sharp shout the sequence is finished and we all retire to sit down and the women laugh and chat among themselves in language, a language I wish deeply to understand.

Corporeal connection is enacted and elaborated in the cosmology of Yolngu people in Northeast Arnhemland through images of *bodily transformations, journeys and traces*...the body as the 'hinge' between self and the world underlies the idea of ancestral power and the experiential character of Yolngu knowledge.[34] [my emphasis]

In the dance, the *body* provides a silent hinge between self, world, ancestral powers — through embodiment of ancestral power and ways of doing things. I was, though I could not reflect on it at the time, stepping directly into this embodying by being in the dance with the Yolngu women. No matter that I did not comprehend. I was enacting the story that was the story coming in the dance. I was in the canoe[35] with the women, travelling with them, in the in-between space and time between their culture and mine, between Ancestral Past and contemporary time at *Gulkula* and between that time and the writing now. Something of a liminal silent gap quality invoked this transforming — unplanned, unforeseen, startling.

My footsteps had taken me to Darwin and the meeting with Wandjuk so long ago, to *Garma*, and to meeting Gulumbu, Derrkngu, Rarriwuy, Wityana, Mandawuy, Raymattja, and other Yolngu people, and into the dancing. All of these events were connected it seemed to me, in tracings, in footsteps on the country, connected through a kind of silence, the in-between and ultimately in the embodiment that occurs as dancing the country.

I had traversed three kinds of silence to reach this place: the protocols of storytelling for Yolngu, the understanding of the parallelling of inside and outside knowing, and a culmination of stepping into and dwelling as ancestral spirit with the Yolngu women. All three kinds of silent knowing had coalesced and actualised in the dancing, and in the embodying of the stories in the land and of the land that had birthed them.

I left *Garma* with the dust of that place, Gulkula, on my feet.

'We are here now; we are the voice of the serpent,' say the Wagilag Sisters.

'Now I give you my ceremonies', says the Snake, with their voice. [36]

Endnotes

[1] At a conference on 'Writing the Sacred', The Australian National University, October 2002.

[2] Commonly called in the southern areas of Australia, 'didgeridoo' — a long hollow log instrument with a deep wind sound.

[3] *Dulumunmun, Yuin* Elder of the South Coast of New South Wales.

[4] From Tranby Aboriginal College in Sydney.

[5] I could find no written source for this information.

[6] P. Sutton, 1988, *Dreamings, The Art of Aboriginal Australia*, New York: Viking/Penguin, p. 19 (my emphasis). Sutton is writing of Cape York, but the same idea applies for Arnhemland.

[7] W. Caruana, and N. Lendon, 1997, *The Painters of the Wagilag Sisters Story 1937-1997*, Canberra: National Gallery of Australia, p. 9.

[8] Ibid., p. 9.

[9] Nigel Lendon, Djon Mundine, Alan Fidock, Allan Marrett, Sophie Creighton — experts on different aspects of Aboriginal and Yolngu culture.

[10] H. Morphy, 1991, *Ancestral Connections: Art and an Aboriginal System of Knowledge*, Chicago & London: University of Chicago Press, p. 98.

[11] Two Canberra-based women anthropologists told me that as the story was in the public domain I could tell it. (They had not however, worked specifically with Yolngu, but with other Indigenous Aborigines.)

[12] Personal email, May 2006.

[13] G. Bateson, and C. M. Bateson, 1987, *Angels Fear: Towards an Epistemology of the Sacred*, New York: Macmillan, p. 97.

[14] Ibid., p. 97.

[15] Morphy, 1991, op. cit., p. 77.

[16] Ibid., p. 96.

[17] Gulumbu Yunipingu, personal communication, August 2004.

[18] Rita Gross, 1977, 'Menstruation and Childbirth as Ritual and Religious Experience in the Religion of the Australian Aborigines', *Supplement Journal of the American Academy of Religion*, vol. 45, no. 4, pp. 1147-1181, p. 1147, 1150.

[19] There are exceptions, e.g., Deborah Bird Rose and Dianne Bell's work in Central Australia, Fiona Magowan and Franca Tamisari in Arnhem Land, Catherine Berndt.

[20] H. Verran, 2002, 'Discussion of the Philosophical Issues for Sciences and Scientists engaging with Indigenous Knowledge', Unpublished paper from talk, *Garma* (my emphasis).

[21] H. Morphy, 1989, 'From Dull to Brilliant: the Aesthetics of Spiritual Power among the Yolngu', *Man*, (N.S.), vol. 24, p. 28.

[22] R. Marika-Mununggiritj, 1991, 'How can *Balanda* learn about the Aboriginal World?' *Batchelor Journal of Aboriginal Education*, July, no.6, pp. 17-23, p. 24.

[23] Dr Tony Swain (Sydney University), expert in both Indigenous and Chinese religions and art, maintains that there is no 'transcendent' in Aboriginal religions.

[24] Caruana and Lendon, op. cit.

[25] Franca Tamisari, 2000, 'Dancing the Land, the Land Dances through us', *Writings on Dance*, no. 20, p. 31.

[26] The Wagilag Sisters Story, version in Caruana and Lendon, op. cit., p. 9.

[27] From *bon* and *bun'kumu* kneecap or knee; the knees of the performer moving up and down in the dance stepping are said to be talking (*bonwanga*). Tamisari, op. cit., p. 35.

[28] These are wood and bark-covered areas with sand on the floor.

[29] Ancestral figure associated with re-configuring of knowledge.

[30] Or cleansing.

[31] Tamisari, op. cit., p. 39.

[32] Ibid., p. 33.

[33] Ibid.

[34] Ibid., p. 3.

[35] The canoe is part of the Djang'kau Sisters story, not the Wagilag Sisters, but it has an in-between, liminal quality which seemed part of my experience at the time.

[36] The Wagilag Sisters Story, version Lenore, Mirelle, *Balanda* poet who lived in the Northern Territory for a time with Indigenous people. She was unable to locate the sources she used for her more extensive poem when I phoned her in Adelaide.

Bibliography

Abbasi-Shavazi, Mohammad Jalal, Diana Glazebrook et al. 2005, *Return to Afghanistan? A Study of Afghans Living in Tehran*, Afghanistan Research Evaluation Unit, Faculty of Social Sciences, University of Tehran.

Abu-Sahlieh, Sami A Aldeeb 1996, 'The Islamic Conception of Migration', *The International Migration Review* vol. 30, no. 1, pp. 37-57.

Ahern, Judith 1998, 'Andres Serrano talks with Judith Ahern', *Photofile*, no. 53, April, pp. 8-13.

Alleine, Joseph 1993, *Alarm to Unconverted Sinners etc*, London: Nevil Simmons.

Almond, Philip C. 1994, *Heaven and Hell in Enlightenment England*, Cambridge: Cambridge University Press.

Anon. 1706, *Roving husband reclaim'd*, London.

Arendt, Hannah 1973, *The Origins of Totalitarianism*, New York: Harcourt Brace & Company.

Ashley, K.M. 1990, *Victor Turner and the Construction of Cultural Criticism*, Bloomington: Indiana University Press.

D'Avenant, Sir William 1695, *Macbeth a tragedy: With all the alterations, amendments, additions and new songs*, London.

—— 1670, The Tempest, or the enchanted Island, London.

Avery, Emmett L. (ed.) 1960, *The London Stage 1660-1800*, vol. 2, Carbondale, IL: Southern Illinois Press.

Augustine, *The City of God*, Philip Levine (trans.) 1966, London: Heinemann.

Bader, Rudolf 1984, 'Indian Tin Drum', *The International Fiction Review*, vol. 11, no. 2, pp. 75-83.

Baggley, John 1987, *Doors of Perception: Icons and their Spiritual Significance*, London: Mowbray.

Bakhtin, Mikhail 1984, *Rabelais and his World*, Bloomington: Indiana University Press.

— 1981, *The Dialogic Imagination: Four Essays by M. M. Bakhtin*, Caryl Emerson and Michael Holquist (eds), Austin: University of Texas Press.

Ball, John Clement 1998, 'Pessoptimism: Satire and the Menippean Grotesque in Rushdie's *Midnight's Children*', *English Studies in Canada*, vol. 24, no. 1, pp. 61-81.

Barthes, Roland 1957, *Mythologies*, Paris: Seuil.

Bateson, G. and C.M. Bateson 1987, *Angels Fear: Towards an Epistemology of the Sacred*, New York: Macmillan.

Becker, Howard 1982, *Art Worlds*, University of California Press: Berkeley.

Bedford, Arthur 1706, *The evil and danger of stage-plays*, Bristol.

Beer, Robert 1999, *The Encyclopedia of Tibetan Symbols and Motifs*, London: Serindia Publications.

Berger, Peter 1967, *The Sacred Canopy: The Social Reality of Religion*, Garden City, N.Y.: Doubleday.

Boucher, Denise 1989, *Les fées ont soif*, Montréal: l'Hexagone.

Branigan, T. 2004, 'Tale of Rape at the temple sparks riot at theatre', *The Guardian*, 20 December. http://arts.guardian.co.uk/news/story/x0,,1377285,00.html (Viewed 11 June 2008.)

Brent Plate, S. 2006, *Blasphemy, Art that Offends*, London: Black Dog Publishing.

Bulgakov, Mikhail 1996, *The Master and Margarita*, New York: Random House.

Burckhardt, Titus 1967, *Sacred Art in East and West: Its principles and methods*, London: Perennial Books.

Bureau of Education 1965 (1920), *Selections from Educational Records, Part I* (1781-1839), H. Sharp (ed.), Delhi: National Archives of India. http://www.columbia.edu/itc/mealac/pritchett/00generallinks/macaulay/txt_minute_education_1835.html (Viewed 11 June 2008)

Burridge, Richard 1702, *A scourge for the play-houses: or the character of the English-stage*, London.

Bynum Walker, Carolyn 1992, *Fragmentation and Redemption: Essays on Gender and the Human Body in Medieval Religion*, New York: Zone Books.

Cabantous, Alain 2002, *Blasphemy: Impious speech in the West from the seventeenth to the nineteenth century*, Eric Rauth (trans.), New York: Columbia University Press.

Caputo, John 1993, *Demythologizing Heidegger*, Bloomington, Indianapolis: Indiana University Press.

Caputo, Rolando 1989, 'Forbidden Christ', *Cinema Papers*, vol. 71.

Carrier, Micheline 1978, 'Forum des lecteurs', *Le Devoir*, 28 December.

Carrington, Michael 2003, 'Officers, Gentlemen and Thieves: the looting of monasteries during the 1903/4 Younghusband Mission to Tibet', *Modern Asian Studies*, vol. 37, no. 1, pp. 81-109.

Caruana, W. and N. Lendon 1997, *The Painters of the Wagilag Sisters Story 1937-1997*, Canberra: National Gallery of Australia.

Casey, Damien 2000, 'Sacrifice, *Piss Christ,* and liberal excess'. http://dlibrary.acu.edu.au/staffhome/dacasey/Serrano.html (Viewed 11 June 2008.)

Casey Singer, Jane 2000, 'Pratapaditya Pal: Champion of the Himalayas', *Cloudband Magazine,* 21 July. http://www.cloudband.com/magazine/ (Viewed December 2003.)

Caslon Analytics 2007, 'Blasphemy'. http://www.caslon.com.au/ blasphemyprofile2.htm (Viewed 11 June 2008.)

—— 2007, 'Lead us not into temptation'. http://www.caslon.com.au/ blasphemyprofile4.htm#brian (Viewed 11 June 2008.)

Champion, Justin 1992, *The pillars of priestcraft shaken: The Church of England and its enemies, 1660-1730,* Cambridge: Cambridge University Press.

Christie, Ian and David Thompson 2003, *Scorsese on Scorsese,* London: Faber.

Clark, Sandra (ed.) 1997, *Shakespeare Made Fit*, London: Dent.

Clifford, James 1988, *The Predicament of Culture: Twentieth-Century Ethnography, Literature and Art,* Cambridge (MA): Harvard University Press.

Cobbett, W., T. B. Howell et. al. (eds) 1819, *A Complete Collection of State Trials,* London.

Collier, Jeremy 1698, *A short view,* London.

Congreve, William 1698, *Amendments of Mr. Collier's False and Imperfect Citations,* London.

Cordner, Michael 2000, 'Playwright versus priest: profanity and the wit of Restoration comedy', in Deborah Payne Fisk (ed.), *The Cambridge Companion to English Restoration Theatre,* Cambridge: Cambridge University Press.

Cowell, Alan 2004, 'Rape, religion and artistic freedom', *International Herald Tribune*, 29 December. http://www.iht.com/articles/2004/12/28/ features/bhatti.php (Viewed 11 June 2008.)

Critchley, S. 1992, *The Ethics of Deconstruction: Derrida and Levinas*, Oxford and Cambridge: Blackwell.

Crockett, Bryan 1995, *The Play of Paradox: Stage and Sermon in Renaissance England*, Philadelphia, PA: University of Pennsylvania Press.

Curtis T.C. and W.A. Speck 1976, 'The Societies for the Reformation of Manners: a case study in the theory and practice of moral reform', *Literature and History*, vol. 3, no. 1, pp. 45-64.

Dabashi, Hamid 2001, *Close Up Iranian Cinema Past, Present and Future,* London: Verso.

Danto, Arthur 1989, 'Critical Reflections', *Artforum International*, vol. 28, (September), pp. 132-133.

Davies, Stephen 1991, *Definitions of Art*, Ithaca, N.Y.: Cornell University Press.

Defoe, Daniel August 8, 1706, *A Review*, vol. 3, no. 95.

—— May 3, 1705, *A Review*, vol. 2, no. 26.

—— 1704, *The storm: or a collection of the most remarkable casualties and disasters which happen'd in the late dreadful tempest both by sea and land,* London.

Delumeau, Jean 1990, *Sin and Fear: The Emergence of a Western Guilt Culture, 13th-18th Centuries.* Eric Nicholson (trans.), New York: St. Martin's Press.

Derrida, J. 1992, 'Force of Law: The Mystical Foundation of Authority', in D. Cornell, M. Rosenfeld, D. G. Carlso (eds), *Deconstruction and the Possibility of Justice,* M. Quaintance (trans.), New York and London: Routledge.

—— 1988, 'Signature, Event, Context', in G. Graff (ed.), *Limited Inc*, S. Weber and J. Mehlman (trans.), Evanston, Illinois: Northwestern University Press.

Doniger W. and B. Smith 1991, *The Laws of Manu,* London: Penguin Classics, Penguin Books.

Douglas, Mary 1966, *Purity and Danger,* London: Routledge and Kegan Paul.

Dromgoole, Dominic 2004, 'Theatres role is to challenge religion', *The Guardian,* December 20. http://arts.guardian.co.uk/features/story/0,,1377489, 00.html (Viewed 11 June 2008.)

Dryden, John 1690, *Amphitryon: or the two Sosia's,* London.

Dubin, Steven C. 1992, *Arresting Images: Impolitic Art and Uncivil Actions,* New York: Routledge.

Duffett, Thomas 1675, *The Mock-Tempest: or the enchanted castle,* London.

Dumont, Micheline 1995, *Les Religieuses sont-elles féministes?,* Montreal: Bellarmin.

Dunton, John 1693, *The Athenian Mercury,* vol. 12, no. 7, November 14.

——1692, *The Athenian Mercury,* vol. 8, no. 25, November 22.

—— 1692, *The Athenian Mercury,* vol. 6, no. 17, March 22.

Dymkowski, Christine (ed.) 2000, *The Tempest,* Cambridge: Cambridge University Press.

Edwards, John 1705, *The preacher discourse shewing what are the particular offices and employments of those of that character in the Church,* (part 1), London.

Elliott, G.R. 1958, *Dramatic providence in Macbeth: A study of Shakespeare's tragic theme of humanity and grace,* Princeton, NJ: Princeton University Press.

Erdoes, Richard and Alfonso Ortiz 1998, *American Indian Trickster Tales,* London: Penguin.

Faure, Bernard 1998, 'The Buddhist Icon and the Modern Gaze', *Critical Inquiry,* vol. 24, no. 3, pp. 768-813.

Feinberg, Joel 1985, *The Moral Limits of the Criminal Law: Volume 2, Offense to Others,* New York: Oxford University Press.

Fingesten, Peter 1951, 'Toward a New Definition of Religious Art', *College Art Journal,* vol. 10, no. 2, pp. 131-146.

Fischer Michael M.J. and Mehdi Abedi 1990, *Debating Muslims: Cultural dialogues in postmodernity and tradition,* Madison, Wis: University of Wisconsin Press.

Fisher, Anthony and Hayden Ramsey 2000, 'Of Art and Blasphemy', *Ethical Theory and Moral Practice,* vol. 3, pp. 137-167.

Fisher, Michael M.J. 2004, *Mute Dreams, Blind Owls, and Dispersed Knowledges: Persian Poesis in the Transnational Circuitry,* Durham & London: Duke University Press.

Flynn, Maureen 1998, 'Taming Anger's daughters: New treatment for emotional problems in Renaissance Spain', *Renaissance Quarterly,* vol. 51, no. 3, pp. 864-886.

—— 1995, 'Blasphemy and the Play of Anger in sixteenth century Spain', *Past and Present,* vol. 149, pp. 29-56.

Foote, G.W. 1886, *Prisoner for Blasphemy,* London: Progressive Publishing. http://www.docstoc.com/docs/396832/Prisoner-For-Blasphemy (Viewed 11 June 2008.)

Foucault, Michel 1977, 'What is an Author', in D. F. Bouchard (ed.), *Language, Counter Memory, Practice: Selected Essays and Interviews by Michel Foucault,* D. F. Bouchard and S. Simon (trans.), Ithaca, N.Y.: Cornell University Press.

Freedberg, David, Oleg Grabar et. al. 1994, 'The Object of Art History', *The Art Bulletin,* vol. 76, no. 3, pp. 394-410.

Friedman, Lawrence S. 1997, *The Cinema of Martin Scorsese,* Oxford: Roundhouse.

Galavaris, George 1981, *The Icon in the Life of the Church,* Leiden: E. J. Brill.

Gaskell, Ivan 2003, 'Being True to Artists', *Journal of Aesthetics and Criticism,* vol. 61, no. 1, pp. 53-60.

Gilbert, Creighton 1998, 'What did the Renaissance patron buy?', *Renaissance Quarterly*, vol. 51, no. 2. http://www.questia.com/googleScholar.qst? docId=5001355899 (Viewed 11 June 2008.)

Gilchrist, Kate 1997, 'Does Blasphemy Exist?' Arts Law Centre of Australia. http://www.artslaw.com.au/Publications/Articles/97Blasphemy.asp (Viewed 11 June 2008.)

Goodman, Nelson 1968, *Languages of Art,* Indianapolis: The Bobbs-Merrill Co. Inc.

Greenblatt, Stephen 1990, 'Resonance and Wonder', in Ivan Karp and Steven Lavine (eds), *Exhibiting Cultures: The poetics and politics of museum display*, Washington D.C.: Smithsonian Institute.

Gross, Rita 1977, 'Menstruation and Childbirth as Ritual and Religious Experience in the Religion of the Australian Aborigines', *Supplement Journal of the American Academy of Religion*, vol XLV, no. 4, pp. 1147-81.

Gupta, Chandra Bhan 1954, *The Indian Theatre*, New Delhi: Munshiram Manoharlal Publishers.

Hardt, M. and A. Negri 2001, *Empire,* Harvard: Harvard University Press.

Harris, Clare 1999, *In the Image of Tibet: Tibetan painting after 1959,* London: Reaktion Books.

Heins, Marjorie 1993, *Sex, Sin, and Blasphemy: A guide to America's censorship wars*, New York: The New Press.

Herd, E. W. 1989, 'Tin Drum and Snake-Charmer's Flute: Salman Rushdie's Debt to Günter Grass', *New Comparison*, vol. 6, pp. 205-18.

Hoffman, F. 1989, 'More on Blasphemy', *Sophia,* vol. 28, no. 2, pp. 26-35.

Hume, Robert D. 1999, 'Jeremy Collier and the Future of the London Theatre in 1698', *Studies in Philology*, vol. 96, no. 4, pp. 480-511.

Hunter, Michael 1992, '"Aikenhead the Atheist": the Context and Consequences of Articulate Irreligion in the Late Seventeenth Century', in Michael Hunter and David Wootton (eds), *Atheism from the Reformation to the Enlightenment*, Oxford: Clarendon. Press.

Huntington, John C and Bangdel Dina 2003, *The Circle of Bliss: Buddhist Meditation Art*, Chicago: Serindia.

Hussain, Ijaz 2006, 'Who is more civilised: Iran or the West?', *Daily Times, Pakistan*, 4 January. http://www.dailytimes.com.pk/default.asp? page=2006%5C01%5C04%5Cstory_4-1-2006_pg3_5 (Viewed 11 June 2008.)

Huston, Nancy 1981, 'Blasphemy in "Nouvelle France" Yesterday and Today', *Maledicta,* vol. 5, no. 2, pp. 163-169.

Hyde, Lewis 1998, *Trickster Makes this World*, New York: North Point Press.

Ivanov, Gjorgie 2004, Re(calling) the future, *Eurozine.* http://www.eurozine.com/articles/2004-03-25-ivanov-en.html (Viewed 11 June 2008.)

Jackson, David and Jackson, Janice 1988, *Tibetan Thangka Painting: Methods and Materials*, Ithaca: Snow Lion Publications.

Jones, Peter 1990, 'Respecting Beliefs and Rebuking Rushdie', *British Journal of Political Science,* vol. 20, no. 4, pp. 415-437.

Julius, Anthony 2002, *Transgressions: The Offences of Art,* London: Thames and Hudson.

Kant, Sri Krishna 1997, Convocation address, Sri Sathya Sai Institute of Higher Education. http://www.sssu.edu.in/pdf/CG_Address1997.pdf (Viewed 11 June 2008.)

Keysen, L. 1992, *Martin Scorsese*, New York: Twayn.

King, Shelley, David Edgar et. al. 2004, 'We must defend freedom of expression', *The Guardian,* 23 December. http://arts.guardian.co.uk/news/story/0,,1378818,00.html (Viewed 11 June 2008.)

Kirby, Terry 2004, 'Violence and vandalism close theatre', *The Independent,* 21 December. http://www.independent.co.uk/arts/theatre/news/article25779.ece (Viewed 11 June 2008.)

Kircher, Athanasius (ed.), 1677, *China Illustrata*, Amstelodami: apud Jacobum á Meurs.

Kirup, James 1976, 'The Love that Dares to Speak its Name'. http://gaytoday.badpuppy.com/garchive/events/070502ev.htm (Viewed 11 June 2008.)

Krauss, Rosalind 1986, *The Originality of the Avant-Garde and Other Modernist Myths*, Cambridge, Mass: MIT Press.

Kristeva, Julia 1985, 'Stabat Mater', *Poetics Today,* vol. 6, no. 1-2, pp. 133-152.

—— 1982, *Powers of Horror: An essay on Abjection*, Columbia: Columbia University Press.

Krutch, Wood 1924, *Comedy and Conscience after the Restoration,* New York: Columbia University Press.

Kuspit, Donald 2004, *The End of Art*, New York: Cambridge University Press.

Larochelle, Renée 1995, '"Théâtre. Les fées ont soif". Au fil des Événements, Université Laval', 12 October. http://www.scom.ulaval.ca/Au.fil.des. evenements/1995/45/011.html (Viewed 26 August 2008.)

Lawton, David 1993, *Blasphemy*, Philadelphia: University of Pennsylvania Press.

Levinas, Emannuel 1989, 'Ethics as First Philosophy', in S. Hand (ed.), *The Levinas Reader*, S. Hand (trans.), Oxford and Cambridge: Blackwell.

Levy, L. 1993, *Blasphemy: Verbal offense against the sacred, from Moses to Salman Rushdie*, New York: Knopf.

Lewy, Günter 2000 (1964), *Nazi Germany and the Catholic Church*, New York: Da Capo Press.

Lindberger, Örjan 1956, *The Transformations of Amphitryon*, Stockholm: Almqvist and Wiksell.

Lipstadt, Deborah 1993, *Denying the Holocaust*, New York: Free Press.

Loetz, Francisca 2002, *Mit Gott handeln: von den Zürcher Gotteslästerern der Frühen Neuzeit zu einer Kulturgeschichte des Religiösen*, Göttingen.

Love, Harold 1980, 'Who were the Restoration Audience?', *The Yearbook of English Studies*, vol. 10, no. 1, pp. 21-44.

Ludden, David 2006, *Making India Hindu*, Oxford: Oxford University Press.

Malraux, Andre 1974, *The Voices of Silence*, St Albans: Paladin.

Marasinghe, E.W. 1989, *The Sanskrit Theatre and Stagecraft*, Delhi: Sri Satguru Publications (India Book Centre).

Marcuse, H. 1978, *The Aesthetic Dimension*, Boston: Beacon Press.

Marika-Mununggiritj, R. 1991, 'How can *Balanda* Learn about the Aboriginal World?', *Batchelor Journal of Aboriginal Education*, July, no. 6, pp. 17-23.

Marsh, Joss 1998, *Word Crimes*, Chicago & London: University of Chicago Press.

Martin, Jean-Hubert 2003, 'The World's Altars and the Contemporary Art Museum' *Museum International* , vol. 55, no. 2, pp. 38-45.

McFarlane, Kyla 2002, 'Incisions and Excesses', in *Votive: Sacred and Ecstatic Bodies,* Wellington and Dunedin: Adam art Gallery and Dunedin Public Art Gallery.

Merivale, Patricia 1990, 'Saleem Fathered by Oskar: Intertextual Strategies in 'Midnight's Children' and 'The Tin Drum', *Ariel: A Review of International English Literature,* vol. 21, no. 3, pp. 5-21.

Morgan, David 2005, *The Sacred Gaze: Religious visual culture in theory and practice*, Berkeley: University of California Press.

Morphy, H. 1991, *Ancestral Connections: Art and an Aboriginal System of Knowledge*, Chicago and London: University of Chicago Press.

——1989, 'From Dull to Brilliant: the Aesthetics of Spiritual Power among the Yolngu', *Man* (N.S.), vol. 24, no. 1, pp. 21-40.

Mortensen, Reid 1994, 'Blasphemy in a secular state: A Pardonable sin?', *UNSW Law Journal*, vol. 17, no. 2, pp. 409-431.

Naficy, Hamid 2002, 'Islamicizing Film Culture in Iran: A Post-Khatami Update' in Richard Tapper (ed.), *The New Iranian Cinema: Politics, Representation and Identity*, London & New York: I.B. Tauris.

Nandi, Bhatia 1963, *Acts of Authority/Acts of Resistance: Theatre and Politics in Colonial and Postcolonial India*, Michigan: University of Michigan Press.

Nash, D.S. 2004, 'Secularization's failure as a master narrative; Reconnecting Religion with Social and Cultural History', *Cultural and Social History*, vol. 1, no. 2, pp. 302-325.

—— 1999, *Blasphemy in Modern Britain 1789 to the Present*, Aldershot: Ashgate.

Nietzsche, Friedrich Wilhelm 2003 (1886), *Beyond Good and Evil: Prelude to a philosophy of the future*, London: Penguin.

Norton, Rictor 2002, 'Mea Culpa', *Gay and Lesbian Humanist*. http://www.pinktriangle.org.uk/glh/214/norton.html (Viewed 11 June 2008.)

Olivelle, P. (trans.) 1999, *Dharmasutras, the Law Codes of Ancient India*, Oxford: Oxford University Press.

Olson, David S. 2001, 'The New Religious Right Versus Media Wrongs: AFA Fights Temptation', *Journal of Film and Video*, vol. 53, part 2/3, pp. 3-22.

Pal, Pratapaditya 2003, *Himalayas An Aesthetic Adventure*, Art Institute of Chicago, Chicago.

Pelikan, Jaroslav 1990, *Igmago Dei: The Byzantine Apologia for Icons*, The A.W. Mellon Lectures in the Fine Arts, 1987, The National Gallery of Art, Washington, D.C.: Princeton University Press.

Perret, Roy W. 1987, 'Blasphemy', *Sophia*, vol 26, no. 2, pp. 4-14.

Peshkin, Alan 1992, 'Experience Subjectivity', Qualitative Interest Group, College of Education, University of Georgia, 1992 conference proceedings, Keynote Address. http://www.coe.uga.edu/quig/proceedings/ Quig92_Proceedings/peshkin.92.html

Phillips, Ruth B. 2004, 'Disappearing Acts: Exposure, Enclosure, and Iroquois Masks', in M.S. Phillips and G. Schochet (eds.), *Questions of Tradition*, Toronto: University of Toronto Press.

Pipes, Daniel 1990, *The Rushdie Affair*, New York: Birch Lane Press/Carol Publishing Group.

Popkin, Richard 2006, *Disputing Christianity: The 400-year-old Debate over Rabbi Isaac Ben Abraham Troki's Classic Argument*, Amherst, N.Y.: Humanity Books.

—— 1992, 'Jewish Anti-Christian Arguments as a Source of Irreligion from the Seventeenth to the Early Nineteenth Century', Michael Hunter and David Wootton (eds), *Atheism from the Reformation to the Enlightenment*, Oxford: Clarendon Press.

Price, David 1994, 'Salman Rushdie's Use and Abuse of History in Midnight's Children', *Ariel: A Review of International English Literature*, vol. 25, no. 2, pp. 91-107.

Pringle, Helen 2006, 'Are we capable of offending God? Taking blasphemy seriously', in Elizabeth Burns Coleman and Kevin White (eds), *Negotiating the Sacred: Blasphemy and Sacrilege in a Multicultural Society*, Canberra: ANU E Press.

Radhakrishnan, S. 1989 (1978), *Indian philosophy*, New Delhi: Oxford University Press.

Radin, Paul 1972, *The Trickster: A Study in American Indian Mythology*, New York: Schocken Books.

Reith, Gerda 1999, *The Age of Chance: Gambling in Western Culture*, London: Routledge.

Rhie, Marylin and Robert Thurman 1991, *Wisdom and Compassion: The Sacred Art of Tibet*, London: Thames and Hudson.

Riley, Jonathan 2005, 'J. S. Mill's Doctrine of Freedom of Expression', *Utilitas*, vol. 17, no. 2, pp. 147-79.

Robillard, Edmond 1978, 'Forum des lecteurs', *Le Devoir*, 18 December.

—— 1978, 'Opinions', *La Presse*, 15 December.

Rosenbaum, Jonathan 1988, 'Raging Messiah: The Last Temptation of Christ', *Sight and Sound*, vol. 57, no. 4, pp. 281-82.

Rosenfeld, Sybil 1960, *The theatre of the London fairs in the 18th century*, Cambridge: Cambridge University Press.

Rushdie, Salman 1980, *Midnight's Children*, New York: Knopf.

Said, Edward 1978, *Orientalism*, New York: Vintage Books.

Saint-Colomban, Bernard Larivière 1978, 'Arts et Spectacles – Lectures', *La Presse*, 15 December.

Santoro-Brienza, Liberato 2003, 'Art and Beauty in Antiquity and the Middle Ages', in Stephen Davies and Ananta Ch. Sukla (eds), *Art and Essence,* Westport, Conneticut: Praeger.

Sauer, E. 2003, *The Archaeology of Religious Hatred in the Roman and Early Medieval world,* Stroud: Tempus Books.

Schoeps, Hans Joachim 1965, *The Jewish-Christian Argument,* London: Faber, 1965.

Schroeder, T. 1970 (1919), *Constitutional Free Speech Defined and Defended in an Unfinished argument in a case of Blasphemy,* New York: De Capo Press.

Schwerhoff, Gerd 1998, 'Starke Worte: Blasphemie als theatralische Inszenierung von Männlichkeit an der Wende vom Mittelalter zur Frühen Neuzeit', in Martin Dinges (ed.), *Hausväter, Priest, Kastraten: Zur Konstruktion von Männlichkeit in Spätmittelalter und Früher Neuzeit,* Göttingen.

Sharma, Arvind (ed.) 2004, *Advaita Vedanta: An Introduction,* New Delhi: Motilal Benarsidas.

Sherlock, William 1692, *A practical discourse concerning a future judgement,* (2nd edn.), London.

Skorupski, John 1989, *John Stuart Mill,* London: Routledge.

Sobchack, Vivian 2000, 'What My Fingers Knew: The Cinesthetic Subject, or Vision in the Flesh' *Senses of Cinema,* vol. 5. http://www.sensesofcinema.com/contents/00/5/fingers.html (Viewed 28 August 2008.)

Soroush, Abdolkarim 2002, in Mahmoud Sadri and Ahmed Sadri (eds) *Reason, Freedom, and Democracy in Islam: Essential Writings of 'Abdolkarim Soroush,* London: Oxford University Press.

Spurr, John 1990, 'Virtue, Religion and Government: the Anglican Uses of Providence', in Tim Harris, Paul Seaward and Mark Goldie (eds), *The Politics of Religion in Restoration England,* Oxford: Blackwell.

Stallybrass, Peter and Allon White 1986, *The Politics and Poetics of Transgression,* Ithaca: Cornell University Press.

Steinberg, Leo 1996, *The Sexuality of Christ in Renaissance Art and in Modern Oblivion,* Chicago: The University of Chicago Press.

Stone, Karen 2003, *Image and Spirit: Finding meaning in visual art,* London: Darton, Longman and Todd.

Summers, Montague 1922, *Shakespeare adaptations: the tempest, the mock tempest, and king Lear,* London: J. Cape.

Sutton, P. 1988, *Dreamings, The Art of Aboriginal Australia*, Sydney: Viking/Penguin.

Talbot, William 1704, *A Sermon preach'd before the Lords spiritual and Temporal in Parliament assembled, in the Abbey-Church of Westminster, on Wednesday, January 19, 1703/4*, London.

Tamisari, F. 2000, 'Dancing the Land, the Land Dances Through Us', *Writings on Dance*, vol. 20, pp. 31-43.

Tarasov, Oleg 2003, *Icon and Devotion: Sacred spaces in Imperial Russia*, London: Reaktion Books.

Tertullian, 1966, *De Spectaculis*, T.R. Glover (trans.), London: Heinemann.

Thomas, K. 1971, *Religion and the Decline of Magic*, London: Weidenfeld and Nicholson.

Thompson, David and Ian Christie (eds) 1990, *Scorsese on Scorsese*, London: Faber and Faber.

Tillotson, John 1702, *Fifteen sermons on several subjects*, London.

Tillyard, E.M.W. 1974 (1943), *The Elizabethan World Picture*, Harmondsworth: Penguin.

Toren, Christina 1988, 'Making the present, revealing the past: The mutability and continuity of tradition as process', *Man* (n.s.), vol. 23, no. 4, pp. 696-711.

Tully, James (ed.) 1988, *Meaning and Context*, Princeton: Princeton University Press.

Tutchin 1704, *The Observator*, vol. 2, no. 77, December 29-January 1.

——1703, *The* Observator, vol. 2, no. 31, July 21-24.

Unsworth, Clive 1995, 'Blasphemy, Cultural Divergence and Legal Relativism', *Modern Law Review*, vol. 58, pp. 658-677.

Vanbrugh, John 1698, *A short vindication of the relapse and the provok'd wife, from immorality and prophaneness*, London.

Villa-Flores, Javier 2007, 'On Divine Persecution: Blasphemy and Gambling in New Spain', in Susan Schroeder and Stafford Poole (eds), *Religion and Society in Colonial Mexico*, New Mexico University Press: New Mexico.

de Vries, Hent 1999, *Philosophy and the Turn to Religion*, Baltimore: Johns Hopkins University Press.

Webster, Richard 1990, *A Brief History of Blasphemy: Liberalism, Censorship and 'The Satanic Verses'*, Southwold: The Orwell Press.

West, Cornel 2004, *Democracy Matters: Winning the Fight Against Imperialism*, New York: Penguin.

Wildmon, Donald with Randall Nulton 1989, *The Man the Networks Love to Hate*, Wilmore: Bristol Books.

Williams, Aubrey 1975, 'No Cloistered Virtue: Or, Playwright versus Priest in 1698', *Publications of the Modern Language Association*, vol. 90, no. 2, pp. 234-246.

Wilson, Bryan 1982, *Religion in Sociological Perspective*, Oxford: Oxford University Press.

Wolfe, George 2002, 'Inner Space as Sacred Space: The temple as a metaphor for the mystical experience', *Cross Currents*, vol. 52, no. 3, pp. 400-411.

Yarrow, R. 2001, *India Theatre, Theatre of Origin, Theatre of Freedom*, Richmond, Surrey UK: Routlegde Curzon.

Zipes, Jack (ed.) 1987, *The Complete Fairy Tales of the Brothers Grimm*, New York: Bantam.

Other sources

'1997: Gay paper guilty of blasphemy', *BBC On this day*. http://news.bbc.co.uk/onthisday/hi/dates/stories/july/11/newsid_2499000/2499721.stm (Viewed 11 June 2008.)

Anon. 1988, 'Anger over Virgin in a condom art', *Dispatch Online*. http://www.dispatch.co.za/1998/03/11/foreign/condom.htm (Viewed 11 June 2008.)

Anon. 2005, 'French Court Bans Christ Advert', BBC NEWS (online), March 11. http://news.bbc.co.uk/2/hi/europe/4337031.stm (Viewed 11 June 2008.)

Anon. 2005, 'Springer Protests pour in to BBC', *BBC News (Online)*, 6 January. http://news.bbc.co.uk/1/hi/entertainment/tv_and_radio/4152433.stm (Viewed 11 June 2008.)

Anon. 2008, 'Mandala of the Five Dhyani Buddahs', Summit Lighthouse. http://www.tsl.org/Masters/buddhas/dhyani/frintroduction.html (Viewed 11 June 2008.)

Burstyn v Wilson, 343, U.S. 495 (1952)

Ewan, E.A. 1961, 'A Study of the Works of Jeremy Collier', D.Phil thesis, Oxford University.

'HH the Sakya Trizin Visits North America', *The Snow Lion Newsletter*, http://www.snowlionpub.com/pages/N50_1.html (Viewed September 2006.)

Holy Bible, 1952 [1611], New York: The British and Foreign Bible Society.

Indian Penal Code (1860)

Interights and *Article Nineteen* 1995, *Blasphemy and Film Censorship*, submission to the European Court of Human Rights in respect of *Nigel Wingrove v the United Kingdom*. *Article 19/Interights*, London.

Isaacs, Tina Beth, 1979, 'Moral crime, moral reform, and the state in early eighteenth century England: a study of piety and politics', PhD thesis, University of Rochester, NY.

Journal of the House of Lords, vol. XVI, p. 175: opening of the ninth session of Parliament, 3 December 1697.

'Little Pebble', http://www.shoal.net.au/~mwoa/ (Viewed 11 June 2008.)

'Teachings of A.C. Bhaktivedanta Swami Prabhupada', Bhaktivedanta Book Trust. http://www.krishna.com/en/node/492 (Viewed 11 June, 2008.)

'The Stupa Information Page', http://www.stupa.org.nz/ (Viewed September 2006.)

'Tibetan Buddhist Teachings on The Mandala of the Five Dhyani Buddhas', http://www.tsl.org/Masters/buddhas/dhyani/index.html (Viewed September 2006.)

Verran, H. 2002, 'Discussion of the Philosophical Issues for Sciences and Scientists engaging with Indigenous Knowledge', Unpublished paper from talk, *Garma*.

'Visions of Ecstasy', *Student's British Board of Film Classification*. http://www.sbbfc.co.uk/case_study_visionsofe.asp (Viewed 11 June 2008.)

'William Kamm' http://users.bigpond.net.au/wanglese/pebble.htm (Viewed 11 June 2008.)

Index